MINQUA UNAMI OKEHOCKING

&

THE DOWN RIVER NATIONS

by

Anita L. Wills

Copyright © Anita L Wills
ISBN: 9798599434689

All rights reserved no reprints, quotations, or copies without express permission of the author. This work is creative nonfiction. This work is based on the lives and history of actual people. The historical events are told from the authors memory and perspective. Disclaimer: This is a creative Non-Fiction work which depicts actual events as truthfully as recollection permits and/or can be verified by research. The persons and events depicted are for the most part verified by historical documents. The opinions expressed are from my observations and analogy of the information herein and are mine alone.

Disclaimer: This is a creative Non-Fiction work which depicts actual events as truthfully as recollection permits and/or can be verified by research. The persons and events depicted are for the most part verified by historical documents. The opinions expressed are from my observations and analogy of the information herein and are mine alone.

DEDICATION

This has been a long journey and I am grateful to who stopped along the way to support me. To my mother and father who were our first inspiration and educators. To my cousins who were more like brothers and sisters and my Grandparents on both sides. To my Monacan Indian family especially Cousin Victoria Ferguson whose support and advice is invaluable. In the beginning it was Cousin Perry Pennington and I searching through records in and around Virginia. He inspired me to keep searching and I truly miss his wise counsel. Rest In Peace Cousin Perry Job well done.

To my children and grandchildren who are the reason that I began documenting our family history. My oldest grandson Kerry Baxter Jr., whose life was taken asked questions that I wanted him to have the answer to. Those who are still here deserve a history that is all-encompassing and not cut short because of the debate about Critical Race Theory (CRT). We are the Indigenous People of Turtle Island whose Ancestors settled this land over 20000 years ago. To my brother George Baxter Junior is has passed on for always encouraging me and cheering my success. To Dr. Anthony Baxter who critiques my work and encourages me to continue.

To Cousin Lionel Pinn whose research and writings about our Native Ancestors was another branch on the tree. To cousins Constance Cole and Patricia Harmon-Smith my Down River Cousins. Thanks to the Martin-Robinson family who have shared invaluable information and background on our Native lines. Another person who unselfishly shared information was James Nickens our Native Cousin who has passed on.

Thanks to the Monacan Indian Nation for preserving our history. Finally, to the ancestors, for the clues left behind for us to follow and for guiding and protecting me. We look 7 generations back and prepare 7 generations into the future.

TABLE OF CONTENTS

CHAPTER ONE
OUR LAND OUR STORY OUR HISTORY..........................9

CHAPTER TWO THE LAND OF OUR
ANCESTORS...45

CHAPTER THREE
THE DOWN RIVER
NATIONS...95

CHAPTER FOUR
SEPARATING THE PEOPLE FROM THE LAND................ 133

CHAPTER FIVE
THE NANZATTICO FIRST NATIONS PEOPLE
OF THE RAPPAHANOCK... .161

CHAPTER SIX
DIGGING UP OUR ROOTS.. 179

CHAPTER SEVEN
THE EASTERN SHORE PINN CONNECTION 193

INDEX ....…..….241

AUTHOR'S PAGE.. 263

Natural Bridge a Monacan Indian Historical Site in Amherst County Virginia. Cousin Victoria Ferguson a Member of the Monacan Indian Tribe was an Interpreter and re-enactor for many years.

Right to Left Author Anita Wills Brother George Baxter Jr. (Center) Brother Anthony Baxter (Left)

PREFACE

This is a book written to memorialize the lives and struggles of my ancestors. My mother Vivian Martin-Baxter is the one who piqued my curiosity with the oral history of our that she gave to me. She was so excited when I traveled and shared the documents that I found. I miss her and her enthusiasm when I joined the DAR something that she wanted to do but was too ill to travel. She told me we were Native and that about the Massacres and lynchings that occurred to move our ancestors from the land.

There are times I wake up and have an intuition about where to search and find information. I did not imagine there would be DNA in 1978 when my mother and I started our project. The DNA puts my maternal line in Spain over 14000 years ago. Our Paternal DNA is indigenous from what is now Columbia South America. But it is the Indigenous ties that were even more deliberately removed with name and racial redesignation. With the Trail of Tears and massacres and the Mission Schools. All of that did not happen in a vacuum. There are records and this book came from the records and oral history that were left.

We look forward 7 generations and back 7 generations. Preparing for one and learning from the other. Thank you, ancestors, for the clues you left behind for me to follow and for guiding and protecting me.

CHAPTER ONE

OUR LAND OUR STORY OUR HISTORY

"Whole Indian Nations have melted away like snowballs in the sun before the white man's advance. They leave scarcely a name of our people except those wrongly recorded by their destroyers." Dragging Canoe 1776"

Feel a need to interject here that as I have been researching and documenting my ancestral lines I do not run into much outward opposition. But there are the Gatekeepers there to protect the narrative that has allowed our people to be landless and disenfranchised in our own homeland. They are not the usual suspects some of them look like us but owe their allegiance to the powers that be. They show up and pretend to support but are backstabbing sale outs. If the shoe fits wear it! "For What Does It Profit A Man (or woman) to Gain the World and lose their soul…,"

We live in a Country that calls itself the greatest Country the World has ever seen. Yet no mention is made of how it was possible for them to reach that greatest. There is no mention of the Wars or the Colonialism and Neo Colonialism. They ignore the Empires that existed prior to Colonization here in the Americas in Africa Asia and the Middle East.

No mention that the wealth America claims was built on stolen native lands with stolen African labor. That is the basis of America where the same people who benefitted from free land and labor will call anyone who seeks equal distribution of the stolen land and wealth a Socialist. That is the very definition of Americus Vespucci sailed before Columbus and helped to outfit Columbus' third voyage. He outfitted his own voyage to look for the Indian subcontinent (which had eluded Columbus). He sailed in 1499, seven years after Columbus first landed in the West Indies. Vespucci made trips in 1499 and 1502, and a third in 1503. There was a race to find the "Indian" Continent between these two who were both funded by the "Holy" Roman Empire.

As Indigenous to this land, our heritage was hijacked by foreign invaders who forced upon our ancestors a foreign religion, a foreign language, and a foreign name. The invading Europeans violently forced their culture upon our ancestors, the original Natives, while also determined to annihilate them culture, spiritual life, language, and, in fact, their very existence. America was born on our land. We were here thousands of years before there was an America.

The original name of this continent is Camanchaca or Turtle Island, as well as other Native names. In that sense, the native peoples of this continent are not "American", but indigenous. America is a European construct, one not native to our land. American is not a race or ethnicity. It is a nationality, proving only where one was born and is not a racial designation. Settlers who come here and claim they are "American" denying their ancestral History and instead claim to be American A Country that was Colonized about 500 years ago.

Fighting the brutal, long-lasting effects of Settler Colonialism on Turtle Island is a struggle for the preserving of, and the honoring of, our culture, our history, and heritage. We are Indigenous to this land, our Homeland. Our cultural roots run deep, connecting us to the land, to our forefathers and foremothers. It is also a Tie to Creator here on our ancestral homeland.

Our Maternal Roots

My mother (Vivian Martin-Baxter), was raised on a farm, where everything was made from scratch including butter and buttermilk. She made ice cream from scratch using rock salt and mixed in fruit nuts or vanilla. A favorite was the strawberry ice cream with fresh strawberries that smelled and tasted so good.

Those were our wonder years especially when she would talk about the family history.

In the Winter Cousin Owen Jones would ride his sled by our house. He was our maternal cousin and lived in Erculdon which was a part of Coatesville. Owen Jones's mother Great Aunt Ida Ruth Jones was our maternal Grandmothers sister. We would hear the sleigh in the winter and mom would say, "There goes Cousin Owen!"

The inhabitants of what is now Pennsylvania Maryland Delaware and parts of Virginia were the Indigenous People of the Turtle Island. The traversed the entire continent of North and South America from the Northern Tip of Greenland to Argentina! According to Mom long before the Europeans came our Native ancestors inhabited the entirety of what they now call the Americas. They named it after an Italian Man Americus Vespucci whose voyage was paid for the Roman Catholic Church. They also funded Columbus voyage to their "New" World.

They were the Conestoga and Haudenosaunee (Iroquois) and Susquehanna who lived throughout the region and by the Waterways. Great-Great Grandmother Tamzin Paige Martin was Mohawk, and our Martin Johnson and Green lines were from the

"Under Haudenosaunee law, 'Gayanerkowa,' (the land) is held by the women of each clan. It is principally the women who are responsible for the land, who farm it, and who care for it for the future generations."

In what is now Delaware and Chester County Pennsylvania the indigenous inhabitants were the Okehocking who more than likely paid tribute to the Susquehanna. Unlike the Five Civilized Tribes which included the Cherokee, the Iroquois Territory included the Ohio Valley Pennsylvania Delaware New Jersey New York and extended to parts of Canada.

The Iroquois were negotiating with the so-called founding fathers, and it was Chief Jacob Brant who led the negotiations.

MINQUA UNAMI OKEHOCKING & THE DOWN RIVER NATIONS

The parents of Joseph Brant were Mohawks whose home was at Canajoharie on the Mohawk River in New York. Brant, however, was born on the banks of the Ohio River in 1742 while his parents were on a hunting excursion to that region, and was given the Indian name of Thayendanegea, meaning "he places two bets."

Our direct and allied families interconnected in what is now Lancaster County Pennsylvania. The County was built around Conestoga Town as Settlers crowded in and pushed Natives out. They were run into the hills then called the Welsh Mountain Tract. Although Green ancestors owned land there, they were not allowed to move around freely.

The Manokin who were listed with the surname of Davis in Maryland in 1704 and who were promised they could live in peace on the Okehocking Tract were now isolated and under siege. There was no peaceful transition because a peaceful transition allows for land to be passed from generation to generation and that has only been possible for settlers. Even the Amish who are isolated by choice were given land that they have passed on from generation to generation.

The Conestoga Tribal Village is now under the Conestoga Dam and like other sites unreachable by descendants. The village was a settlement at the southern end of the once vast range of the Susquehannock Nation or Conestoga Indian Nation, which once extended from the northern reaches of Maryland to the along the southern width of southern New York State and southern Catskills where a related people, the Six Nations of the Iroquois Confederacy held western settlement in check for 200 years.

The territory encompassed the entire drainage basin of the Susquehanna River which shares the tribe's root name and extended to the drainage divides of the flanking mountains both to the East to the Delaware nation and to the West to Shawnee lands. The town is the earliest established known surviving settlement of the tribe, and it is known that William Penn himself visited to negotiate with the tribal leaders.

The Counties cut off the boundaries of the land and any natives found on those lands were killed or run off. They came with their Bible and used Christianity as a basis to steal kill and destroy. The site is also one known to be among the last occupied of the Susquehannock town sites in Pennsylvania as they faded into obscurity.

Throughout the majority of the seventeenth century, the Susquehannock-Conestoga were a strong fierce Indian people who also came to be known locally as the Conestoga's (meaning "Buried Pole Place" or "town," much like "Can-ah Da" means "Buried Pole Place" or "town" in other Iroquois languages). Excavations revealed log-cabin like structures and cemeteries.

The village was occupied from the 1690's to about 1725 — well after the collapse of the Susquehannock nation in the 1670's, after which the village moved to different sites within a 414-acre tract. It was an important meeting place between various Native American tribes and Pennsylvania government officials, including William Penn. Of the early European Settlers of Conestoga, we find that thirty-eight of them were signers of the petition in 1728 to create the county of Lancaster, out of 188 signers from the entire county. German-Swiss, all signed it. The Court records in Chester County as to Conestoga township in those days show that both the English and the Swiss took part in public affairs.

This settlement differed from the Pequea settlement to the east. While the Pequea colony, at Willow Street, were all Swiss Mennonites, the settlement along the Conestoga consisted of a Scotch-Irish and English core, bordering on both sides of that river, surrounded by scores of German Swiss on all sides. [1]

Okehocking Preserve constitutes 155 acres of the 500-acre land grant from William Penn to the Okehocking band of the Lenai Lenape Indians, the first Native American land grant

---

[1] In 1763, the Paxton Boys raided a later Conestoga Town village.

in the American colonies. Due to the constant fear of being removed from their grounds, the Okehockings petitioned the Provincial Council for a secure tract of land where they would no longer be mistreated. They probably chose the Williston land because of a symbolic turtle-headed rock outcropping located within the Okehocking Tract.

The Okehocking Clan belonged to the Unami (known as the Down River People), one of the three Leni Lenape tribes. The Unami Tribe's symbol was the tortoise, who they believed represented mother earth and was a symbolic "intermediary between the visible and invisible worlds around them."

The Unami Tribe was part of the Algonquin Nation, better known as the Leni Lenape, the "Original People." Lenape was the Native name for the Delaware River. European settlers changed the river's name to Delaware; hence the Leni Lenape were labelled Delaware by the settlers. The scholarly consensus of the translation of Okehocking is "encircling land" - "okay" meaning Delaware encircled, "hocking" meaning land or earth. In October 1702 the Okehocking Clan (or band) accepted the grant of 500 acres of mostly rugged and undulating ground.

Unlike the tracts owned by the English Quaker farmers (Charles Whitaker, Francis Yarnall, Peter Thomas, and Thomas Massey) who lived nearby, this piece of land, except for the flood plain, was of little agricultural value. The land configured as a tilted square, located just north of present-day West Chester Pike, south of Goshen Road and bounded by Garrett Mill and Plumsock Roads.

The orientation of this piece of land was unusual since all other tracts in Williston Township were of rectangular shapes whose boundaries followed either an east-west or north-south axis, and paralleled township lines. Instead of following property lines in the usual manner, the Dorchester Road, laid out in 1710, ran directly through the center of the Okehocking lands, and divided the tract in half.

The increasing immigration of European settlers along the

lower regions of the Crum, Ridley, and Chester Creeks encroached upon the Leni Lenape lands, forcing the Indians to migrate inland and northward. The Okehocking Clan, consisting of no more than two dozen men, women, and children, relocated to the Williston Land and used it for their summer encampment from 1696 to the mid 1730's.

They wintered northward in their ancestral hunting grounds near the upper Schuylkill. By inhabiting two different locations yearly, they did not overuse any one area and thereby render it useless. In essence they created their own crop rotation system. The floodplain along Ridley Creek provided limited fertile ground for the raising of crops. Burning of the fields to rid brush and undergrowth provided open ground for planting of crops, especially maize (multi-colored Indian corn), their main staple. Since the clan was migratory, their crop harvest was scant.

In addition to crop growing, the women were the gatherers of fruit, seeds and nuts found in the nearby forests, and frogs and turtles from the streams. The men hunted game and fished. Although the land was known as Okehocking Indian Town, no archaeological digs have revealed any traces of an "Indian Village."

The clan lived in tent-like structures which enabled them to be more mobile, and by trading with the European settlers, the Okehocking learned to use metal instead of stone implements and utensils. They utilized a stone-tipped arrow shaft, and preferred hunting with a bow, because of its noiseless character which did not alert their prey.

The Natives who lived throughout Pennsylvania forests for centuries, did not understand the concept of land ownership and the creation of private property lines. These feelings were in direct contrast with the posture of the nearby Quaker farmers, who purchased land from the Colonial Governor, established perimeter borders, and controlled the right of access.

As the Okehocking continued to pursue game beyond the

confines of their land, the neighboring landowners became increasingly annoyed. In 1718 the Natives began the exodus from their summer home along the Ridley Creek. They removed initially to the Shamokin area (Swatara Creek), however they continued to return to their summer hunting grounds in Williston Township until 1735.

The Lenape settled in Oklahoma, where by 1900 they had become farmers and merchants. In 1738 the Yarnall brothers, Amos, and Mordecai, received proprietary patents for the vacated land.[2]

Anyone reading this would believe that this took place peacefully and Natives were not forced off their lands. Yet in the 1700's our ancestors were being pushed off their lands in Pennsylvania. The Quakers set up Poor Houses and Workhouses many of the Natives were sentenced to the poor house because they had no land. They were made homeless pushed off their lands and sent to the workhouses or "Poor" Houses.

The children were sent to Orphan Homes because the parents could not provide for them or were deceased. This is the story that we the Down River People do not have a chance to tell. Our Ancestors were run off the land even after William Penn ceded land they stole back to the Okehocking. They do not even want our ancestors on the land that is not fertile because we are a reminder that they were intruders.

Guns and laws were used to continue to remove our ancestors who eventually showed up as Servants or farmhands. The work was humiliating and back breaking but at least they were on the Ancestral Lands. Great Grandfather William Penn Martin was a overseer for King Ranch in Chester County and lived on the land where the Unami, Minqua, and Okehocking had a Village.

---

[2] Allegheny —Cartlidge (1730), Arch.Pa., I. 254, 1852. Alleeganeeing. — Cartlidge (1730), Arch. Pa., I., 261, 1852

To be among the Settlers they had to change their names and use "Christian" names. Can we go to Europe and demand that Europeans use Native or African or Muslim Names? They who have Colonized much of Africa, Turtle Island, Australia, India, and anywhere else they could land do not want to be Colonized. Go figure!

Our struggle is linked to the struggles of the ancestors. We are not separate from them we are them. My Indigenous Ancestors lived throughout the Americas and their struggle since the inception of Colonialism is my struggle. No matter what "ism" exists, Capitalism, Socialism, Communism or Racism our struggle is Spiritual.

The only Alpha and Omega in existence is Spirit because every being that is born will die regardless of what "System" they live under. Any System built on lies and deception can be easily exploited and the older I get the more I see similarities in the "isms" we all live under.

It is what happens in between that should matter and most humans yearn for that in-between. The ism's have been exploited by those whose lust for power and greed seeks to wipe us as a people out of history. By us I mean afro/indigenous who are only seen as products to exploit by those who practice isms. That is why some Americans are on their High Horse about Critical Race Theory (CRT) before even knowing what it is. Yet they want the statutes of Columbus planted throughout the America's as a reminder of the brutalization of Native People.

A Native American man in Montana has what may be the oldest DNA in America. After getting his DNA tested, Darrell "Dusty" Crawford learned that his ancestors were already in the Americas about 17,000 years ago, a Montana newspaper.[3]

This is not news to those of us who are Indigenous to these lands and know that it goes back further than that. But it

---

[3] Geggel, Laura; This Man's DNA Is the Oldest in North America; https://www.livescience.com/65437-oldest-dna-north-america.html; published May 08, 2019

seems not seem to matter unless a European "Discovers" new information. You can see that on Maps that Africa and Mexico are like a puzzle that was at one time connected. The Aborigine in Australia got there by land at least 80000 years ago.

In 1998 I was accepted into the Monacan Indian Nation a State Recognized Tribe in Amherst County Virginia. This was the culmination of almost 20 years of documenting my family History in America Europe and Africa. In 2018 our Tribe received Federal Recognition and we are in the process of putting together what was torn apart since Colonization.

Monacan Indian Tribe is Siouan made up of Natives who are mixtures of Saponi and Tutelo and other allied tribes. That is not our families only Native Connection as we are a mixture of Iroquois, Manokin, Wicomico, Susquehanna, Tutelo, Saponi, Monacan, Nanzattico, Cheraw, and other Nations forced together after Colonization.

The Evans, Redcross and Pinn ancestors are mentioned on the original rolls for Amherst County Virginia. From the time of Colonization onward our people were dispersed through racial reclassification, the Trail of Tears forced assimilation and outright massacres. Our Evans, Pinn, Jackson, Bowden and allied lines were forced into Pennsylvania from Fredericksburg Virginia, in 1853 because of their activities in freeing slaves.

Wicomico (Yeocomico) Indian Nation

Rawley Pinn my grandfather four times removed served in the Revolutionary War from Amherst County. He married Sarah Redcross-Evans and their son James Pinn, and his 2nd wife Jane (Jinsey) Cooper-Powell is my direct ancestor. After James was killed his children fled Amherst County and settled in Fredericksburg Virginia. Laws were passed allowing for the forced Indenture of Free Blacks and Mulattoes. This was the quasi-free status of Free Persons of Color (FPC) in Virginia.

Although Rawley and his tribe were Wicomico from Lancaster County Virginia he went into the interior of Virginia and may have been a Scout. That is where he met and married

Sarah Redcross Evans his future wife. Sarah descended from Jane (Bnu) Gipson a Cheraw Indian woman from North Carolina. He and Sarah owned farmland in Amherst County which he and his sons James and Turner Pinn farmed.

In 1783 a tax record for Amherst County Virginia lists Rawley Pinn as a white man and in 1785 he is listed as Mulatto. In 1785 he is listed as living with 8 other Mulattoes. My belief is that Rawley lived with his wife Sarah Redcross Evans and some of her family. There was an ongoing lawsuit at that time from some Evans family members who were suing for their freedom.

That lawsuit left a genealogical record that led from Jane Bnu Gibson (the Elder) to her descendants. They were Cheraw from North Carolina, and her children were Indentured to Goodrich Lightfoot who then enslaved them and future generations. The lawsuit stated that the descendants of Jane Gibson (the elder) were Natives and that the person who enslaved them was Gordon Lightfoot.

Goodrich Lightfoot is connected to the origins of the "free colored" Evans family of Granville County, who descend from Morris Evans and his wife Jane Gibson the younger. Some of Morris and Jane's descendants were illegally held as slaves by and later sold to other slave owners. The Evans descendants were able to obtain their freedom by proving they descended from a free Indian woman – Jane Gibson the elder who was the mother of Jane Gibson the younger.

Sherwood Lightfoot's estate was located on the banks of the Pamunkey River, directly across from the Pamunkey Indian reservation. In 1707, Col. John Lightfoot died, and his sons Goodrich and Sherwood Lightfoot inherited his large land holdings along the Pamunkey River which he originally purchased in 1686. [4]

Revolutionary War Soldiers

Rawley Pinn along with other Natives was in the Revolutionary War from Amherst County along with his brother

Robert, and nephews John, James, and Billy who marched from Indiantown Lancaster County. They joined with Marquis De Lafayette and marched to Yorktown the last and winning battle of the Revolutionary War.

The Yorktown Battle was fought after a defeat at the Battle of Camden South Carolina, by the British General Cornwallis. Fresh from his victory, he headed for Yorktown, where he was soundly defeated. In our family Camden and Yorktown are not just historical events. We commemorate them because our ancestors fought in both battles. Charles and Ambrose Lewis fought at Camden and Rawley Pinn, John Redcross, and Benjamin Evans fought at Yorktown.

The Unit was made up of Natives and Mulattoes who distinguished themselves on the battlefield. Rawley Pinn marched with his unit from Amherst County under the command of Major William Cabell Junior. Rawley was with Colonial Daniel Gaines' unit, as were John Redcross and Benjamin Evans. They were in the 2nd Virginia Calvary, and they left Amherst County on June 21, 1781. Halfway to Yorktown, they joined the unit of the Marquis De Lafayette. The units marched into history, by way of the Siege of Yorktown. Although the men of color received little public recognition.[5]

Once the war ended, they headed back to Amherst County and Rawley became a success farmer and Baptist Minister and was part of the Ana Baptist Movement. He founded Fairmount Baptist Church there in 1792 and it exist to this day. His grandson and my Great-Great Grandfather Reverend Robert A. Pinn were Baptist Ministers in the Ana Baptist (against Slavery) tradition.

Rawley received more land after his Revolutionary War

---

[5] Their names were listed in the Lynchburg News & Advance in 1884 (Amherst County, Virginia) and in a booklet published by the daughters of the American Revolution.

Service, but that land is no longer in the family. Settlers moved in squatted on the land and thanks to the racist laws it disappeared. There are rumors that my ancestor James Pinn was killed for the land he owned.

In the year 1869, just four years following the end of the Civil War, Rev. Robert Andrew Pinn became Pastor. Born in Virginia in 1817 he was registered as a "free Negro" in Fredericksburg in 1839. Rev. Pinn IV was a descendant of a Robert Pinn I, born about 1710, was Yeocomico (Wicomico) Aborigine the Eastern Shore of Virginia and Maryland. Their land was taken by European Settlers and became Maryland and Virginia.

We are the original people of these lands! These words came out of my mother's mouth from the time I was a child. Our ancestors lived throughout Canada, New York New Jersey, Delaware, The Ohio Valley, Maryland, Virginia, and North Carolina. Indigenous People have been on these lands thousands of years before Colonization. They created what are now roads and Highways that Europeans used to travel to the Interior. The paths led to the villages of the Minqua, Unami and Okehocking some of whom were fragments of the Susquehanna and Tributary tribes like the Conestoga.

In 1998 I was accepted into the Monacan Indian Nation a State Recognized Tribe in Amherst County Virginia. This was the culmination of almost 20 years of documenting my family History in America Europe and Africa. In 2018 our Tribe received Federal Recognition and we are in the process of putting together what was torn apart since Colonization. Our Tribe is Siouan made up of Native who are also mixtures of Saponi and Tutelo. That is not our only Native Connection as we are a mixture of Iroquois, Manokin, Wicomico, Susquehanna, and other Nations forced together after Colonization.

It was making the connection with my Indigenous Ancestors that was so difficult. Not that I did not know who they were but that we were denied the right by the State to claim that heritage. They lived throughout Colonial America and Canada after being pushed off their Ancestral lands.

There was a lot of effort spent in removing Turtle Island People from their land and Culture. The tactics of assimilation involved removing children to Mission Schools and separating males and females. It involved the intermixing of white men and native women which was the same tactic with white males and African Women during and after slavery.

There were laws against black and white marriages and a black male could be lynched. However, the children of miscegenation were predominately white men and Native or African women. Laws were passed that punished Native Men who were redesignated as Mulatto, Colored, or Negro from being with white women.

The laws written by and approved by white men did not apply to them. That was especially true of any atrocities including rape of African or Native women. The atrocities committed against Native Children in Mission Schools are just beginning to be discussed. Turtle Island is all the land and waterways occupied by Indigenous People from as far North as Greenland and as far South as Chile. Therefore, I ran into brick walls as the racial makeup of my ancestors changed at the whim of European Colonizers.

For instance, with my Virginia Lewis ancestors, I found that they were Nanzattico Indians. The entire tribe of adults were sent to Antigua as slaves in 1704. They were the original Rappahannock whose villages were in what is now King and Caroline County Virginia. Ambrose and Charles Lewis were identified as Mulatto boys in Court records from King George County. Their father "Indian" Charles was about 5 years old when his parents were sent to Antiqua as slaves.

Charles and Ambrose were Indentured as Seamen on the Rappahannock River and operated the Page Galley. That is where they were when the Revolutionary War started, and both signed on as Seamen. They remained on the Page Galley and then served on board the Dragon Ship a War Ship that was manned by Native and Mulatto Soldiers.

Charles and Ambrose Lewis left numerous records including a Pension Ambrose filed for himself and Charles after the Revolutionary War. He first filed in Virginia and then in the newly formed Government in Washington DC. Ambrose testified about his service in front of the Senate, and it is a part of the permanent record of the First Senate Meeting in Washington DC.

Charles Lewis was one of the Mulatto businessmen at Rockets' Landing after the Revolutionary War. In the final decades after the Revolutionary War the port was used to transport slaves and other commerce was moved along the James River. Wealthy landowners and merchants, including Charles Lewis, George Nicholson, and the Mayo family, established warehouses, taverns, and shops to capitalize on the opportunities brought by trans-Atlantic commerce. Charles settled in Henrico County and owned a lighthouse in Northumberland County.

Within three generations the Nanzattico were enslaved their children indentured and their grandchildren racially reclassified. With my Pinn lines they were also racially reclassified some as White while others became Mulatto. It was according to the Colonizers how best they could be used. Matoaka (Pocahontas) was taken to England and forced to bear a child by a European. That child became the white line of the Powhatan through Matoaka who also had a Native son and a husband who was Powhatan.

Our Pinn ancestors were in the Revolutionary War out of Amherst County and Lancaster County. It is believed that William Billy Pinn is the forefather of Sgt., Robert A. Pinn whose father William fled to Ohio from Virginia. William Pinn II may have been the son of William (Billy) Pinn who was in the Revolutionary War along with his father Robert brothers James and John. Robert's brother Rawley, who is my direct ancestor, served out of Amherst County Virginia.

Their Villages in Northumberland and Lancaster County Virginia and on the Eastern Shore of Maryland were divided and they were forced to join the Wicomico Parish Church in Northumberland County Virginia. The forming of States and Counties cut off much of Native Territory and made it easier for White Settlers to take control of their ancestral lands.

Descendants of Rawley and Robert Pinn fought in the Civil War out of Ohio and Pennsylvania. Great Uncle Corporal Walter Samuel Pinn, my Great Uncle fought in the 54th Massachusetts Company D. as did, Charles and Louis. If there is a tangled web met to deceive it is how things are written and understood in America's History.

For instance, there were Natives fighting with the United States Colored Troops during the Civil War. Some of those Natives were my ancestors and relatives. It may have been the genius of Frederick Douglass to call it the "Colored" Troops and not the Black or Negro Troops. Great-Great Grandfather, Robert Pinn, was one of the unsung heroes of the Underground Railroad.

Walter Samuel Pinn
Age at enlistment: 19
Enlistment date: 19 Mar 1863
Residence at enlistment: Lancaster County, PA
Profession at enlistment: barber (alt.: clerk)
Rank in: private
Rank out: Corporal
Company: D
Fate at Ft. Wagner: survived
Mustered-out date: 20 Aug 1865

He and his family were free blacks living in Virginia, until 1853, when they fled to Columbia (Lancaster County), Pennsylvania. He was a vocal Baptist Minister in Virginia and continued to Minister in Columbia (Pennsylvania), until he was forced to flee to Burlington New Jersey.

Robert Pinn IV was from a long line of Virginia's Free Colored Population. His grandfather, Rawley Pinn was a Revolutionary War Soldier, who fought at The Siege of Yorktown. His wife, Elizabeth Jackson-Pinn, was also a descendant of Free Persons of Color, and her grandfather, Charles Lewis was a Sailor and Soldier during the Revolutionary War.

Their son, and my Great Uncle, Walter Samuel Pinn, was a Corporal with the, 54th Massachusetts USCT, Company B. Also serving in the Unit were the sons of Frederick Douglass, Charles, and Louis. Walter Samuel Pinn was the brother of my Maternal Grandmother Leah' Ruth-Martin's Mother. While in training, Colonial Robert Shaw promoted him to Corporal. Walter Samuel's father, Reverend Robert A. Pinn, was a Minister in Virginia, and fled with his family, to Columbia Pennsylvania in 1853.

Prior to signing with the 54th Massachusetts, Walter Samuel was a Barber in Columbia, Pennsylvania, and lived a comfortable life. He wrote letters from the Battlefield to his parents and siblings, detailing his life on the Battlefield. Through his letters, he introduced his oldest sister Katherine to her husband, James McPherson. Their unit picked up a slave boy, named Samuel Ruth, in Savannah Georgia and left him with his parents, who lived in, Burlington New Jersey.

That slave boy, Samuel Ruth, married Walter Samuel's youngest sister, Maria Louisa Pinn. The couple settled in Erculdon Pennsylvania (a part of Coatesville) and are my Maternal Grandmother Leah Ruth-Martins' parents. After the Civil War, he returned to Virginia with his mother and younger siblings, where he died of consumption at the age of twenty-two. He did not marry, nor have any children, but his deeds speak volumes.

"I was born in the town of Massillon Stark County State of Ohio. Where I experienced all the disadvantages peculiar to my proscribed race. Being born to labor I was not permitted to enjoy the blessings of a common School education, it is hardly necessary to say that little can be expected of me, so far as correct composition is concerned.

In '61, when the whole of the Loyal North was aroused by reason of the cowardly assault upon Fort Sumter, I was very Eager to become a Soldier, to prove by my feeble efforts, the black man rights to untrammelled manhood. I was denied admission to the ranks of the loyalists, on account of my color not being of that kind which is considered a standard in this country." Sergeant Robert A. Pinn

Robert A. Pinn, attorney, and Civil War hero received the Congressional Medal of Honor from President Abraham Lincoln in 1865. Pinn was born free to William and Zilphia Broxton-Pinn, in Stark County, Ohio on March 1, 1843. His father William Pinn escaped Servitude and fled to Ohio at the age of eighteen. He worked on farms for several years before marrying Zilphia Broxton, a white resident of Stark County. Pinn and his nine siblings were born on the family farm in Stark County. He married Emily J. Manzilla, in 1867 and the couple had one child a daughter, Gracie Pinn-Brooks.

Pinn attempted to join the Union Army at the beginning of the Civil War but was blocked from enlisting because of his race. He joined the 19th Ohio Infantry in 1861 as a civilian worker, marched south with the regiment, and despite his non-military status, fought at the Battle of Shiloh in Tennessee in 1862. Afterwards he fought in several other engagements although not an enlisted soldier.

President Abraham Lincoln authorized the use of African American troops in combat after issuing the Emancipation Proclamation on January 1, 1863. Pinn then joined the 5th United States Colored Troop (USCT), Infantry Regiment in Massillon, Ohio, on September 5, 1863.

Sgt., Robert A. Pinn Massillon Ohio
Congressional Medal of Honor winner (Civil War).

Because of his combat experience, Pinn was promoted to Sergeant on October 18, 1863, just over a month after he joined the regiment. He was promoted to First Sergeant on September 1, 1864. Pinn received the Medal of Honor for his heroic action at The Battle of New Market Heights near Richmond on September 29, 1864. He took command of his company after all the officers had been killed or wounded. President Abraham Lincoln awarded him the Medal of Honor on April 2, 1865.

Sgt., Pinn mustered out of service at Carolina City, North Carolina, on September 20, 1865, and returned to Stark County, Ohio. He studied at Oberlin College from 1874 to 1877. He then taught school in Cairo, Illinois, and Newberry, South Carolina. He returned to Ohio and Oberlin where he completed his law studies, and was admitted to the Ohio Bar in 1879, becoming the first black lawyer in Massillon County.

Sergeant Pinn had a distinguished career as an attorney and a Pensions and Claims Agent for the U.S. Pension Bureau. He was active in the Republican Party where he served as a delegate to the 1891 Ohio convention that nominated William McKinley for Governor. Pinn was the first African American Commander of Hart Post 134 of the Grand Army of the Republic and remained active in the GAR, until his death on January 1, 1911.[i]

My family and I are Pinn Descendants through the Pinn/Evans Lines both of which are Natives from North Carolina and Virginia. Rawley Pinn was born about 1740 in Indiantown Virginia to Robert I and Margaret Winas-Pinn. Robert & Margaret were members of the Wicomico Parish Church in Northumberland County.

There are numerous records of him being fined in Hoggs Heads of Tobacco for missing Church or not paying tithes. By 1760 he was no longer mentioned, and Margaret was agreeing on indentures for her children. Rawley Pinn was Indentured as a Cooper as was his brother Robert while their sister was Indentured as a Housekeeper. The next mention of Rawley was him living with a Robert Pinn III (his nephew) near Yorktown (Virginia). After that he shows up in Amherst County married to Sarah Redcross-Evans.

Our Evans, Redcross and Pinn ancestors are mentioned on the original rolls for Amherst County Virginia. From the time of Colonization onward our people were dispersed first through racial reclassification, and some intermixed with White and/or with Free Blacks. Others left and headed for Canada or were marched to the interior on the Trail of Tears.

Our Pinn lines were forced into Pennsylvania from Fredericksburg Virginia, in 1853 because of their activities in freeing slaves. Great-Great Grandfather Reverend Robert A. Pinn was a Missionary Baptist Preacher who followed in the steps of his Grandfather Rawley Pinn. He and Elizabeth Jackson were married in 1838 in Fredericksburg Virginia.

She was the daughter of Samuel and Maria Lewis-Jackson; and her father was the son of James and Patty Bowden-Jackson; who were also married in Fredericksburg. While Patty

Bowden-Jackson was the daughter of Mary Bowden (and Unknown Male); Her husband James Jackson was the son of a servant woman to Charles Yates named Sylvia. Patty and James married after the death of Charles Yates in 1811 not having permission to marry until after his death.

James Jackson was identified as a Mulatto by Charles Yates who held his Indenture along with his brother William's in Fredericksburg Virginia. Maria Lewis is our direct ancestor through Charles and Hannah (?) Lewis. Charles and his brother Ambrose were descendants of the Nanzattico Indian Tribe whose adult members were sent to Antiqua as slaves.

Rawley Pinn my grandfather four times removed was in the Revolutionary War from Amherst County. Rawley's parents were Robert Pinn I and his wife Margaret Winas- Pinn. Their tribe the Wicomico was in Lancaster and Northumberland County Virginia. He married Sarah Redcross-Evans, and my direct ancestor is their son James Pinn, and his 2nd wife Jane (Jinsey) Cooper-Powell who also has native roots. After James was killed his children fled Amherst County and settled in Fredericksburg Virginia. Amherst County were forcing Natives and Mulattoes and putting them into forced Indentures.

Although Rawley was Wicomico from Lancaster County Virginia he left and settled in the interior of Virginia where he married Sarah Redcross Evans. She was a direct descendant of Jane Bnu-Gipson (the Elder). A Native woman whose children were racially reclassified and enslaved. Rawley and Sarah owned land in Amherst County which he and his sons James and Turner Pinn farmed.

Rawley along with other Natives was in the Revolutionary War from Amherst County along with his brother Robert, and nephews John, James, and Billy who marched from Indiantown Lancaster County. Rawley's unit joined with Marquis De Lafayette and marched to Yorktown from Amherst and fought in the last and winning battle of the Revolutionary War.

MINQUA UNAMI OKEHOCKING & THE DOWN RIVER NATIONS

The Yorktown Battle was fought after a defeat at the Battle of Camden South Carolina, by the British General Cornwallis. Fresh from his victory, he headed for Yorktown, where he was soundly defeated. In our family Camden and Yorktown are not just historical events. We commemorate them because our ancestors fought in both battles. Charles and Ambrose Lewis fought at Camden and Rawley Pinn, John Redcross, and Benjamin Evans fought at Yorktown (they are all descendants of the Native People of Virginia).

They were not only soldiers, but Natives, who distinguished themselves on the battlefield. Rawley Pinn marched with his unit from Amherst County under the command of Major William Cabell Junior. Rawley was with Colonial Daniel Gaines's unit, as were John Redcross and Benjamin Evans.

They were in the Second Virginia Calvary, which left Amherst County on June 21, 1781. Halfway to Yorktown, they joined the unit of the Marquis De Lafayette. The units marched into history, by way of the Siege of Yorktown. Although the men of Color received little public recognition.[6]

Once the war ended, they headed back to Amherst County and Rawley became a successful farmer and Baptist Minister and was part of the Ana Baptist movement. He founded Fairmount Baptist Church there in 1792 and it exist to this day. His grandson and my Great-Great Grandfather Robert A. Pinn were also a Baptist Minister in the Ana Baptist (against Slavery) tradition.

Rawley received more land after his Revolutionary War Service, but that land is no longer in the family. Settlers moved in squatted on the land and thanks to the racist laws it disappeared. There are even rumors that my direct ancestor James Pinn was killed for the land he owned.

---

[6] The names were listed in the Lynchburg News & Advance in 1884 (Amherst County, Virginia) and in a booklet published by the daughters of the American Revolution.

In the year 1869, just four years following the end of the Civil War, Rev. Robert Andrew Pinn became a pastor at Monumental Baptist Church in Philadelphia Pennsylvania. He was a Traveling Baptist Preacher and had left Amherst for Fredericksburg. He was registered as a "free Negro" in Fredericksburg in 1839 when your racial identify was determined by Europeans.

He was the first after Rev. William Jackson (his brother-in-law), to give stability and consistent leadership marked by relative longevity. During his years as pastor the church underwent a rebuilding project that would meet the needs of a growing congregation well into the 20th century.[7]

Anything Europeans want they pass a law for, and they pass laws against anything black and brown citizens want. We are seeing that now as they strive to overturn voting rights laws that are supposed to be guaranteed in the Constitution. Laws on the books may or may not apply those who commit crimes according to the Judges leaning the defendant.

In some of our Native and mixed raced lines the racial classification changed from Indian to Mulatto or Colored or Negro. There were also cases where they were classified from Indian to white. The racial re-classification was done at the behest of and to benefit Europeans.

Even now when many in power know the truth, they go to great lengths to deny or cover it up. In my case it is important to have a historical context in which our ancestors lived. Natives, Africans, and Europeans mixed in our family over hundreds of years, and through varying circumstances. My Native ancestors were on their own land when the Colonizers arrived and changed the trajectory of Turtle Island.

It is curious to me that speaking about Critical Race Theory (CRT) is an issue with some who are in denial about

---

[7] Heinegg, Paul; Free African Americans; Pinn, Robert A; . According to the website, www.freeafricanamericans.com

America's History. Truth is it is taught in Upper-Level College Courses in Law School. Makes no sense for the concern these days as Critical Race Theory (CRT) is all over social media including Tik Tok and Instagram. It is in more effective mediums than a textbook given that most of us have wide access to social media. So much for not in my school and the naysayers. The more educated Americans become the harder it is to fool the masses.

It is amazing how Europeans will speak of being in America for five generations as if that is a long time. Yet we who are Indigenous are treated like interlopers on own ancestral Homeland. There is no context or mention of the methods used to take the land. Their history does not honor the land and labour of Native and African slaves who were forced to build this country. Natives to this day face forced assimilation having children taken and adopted out or removed to Mission Schools and/or outright slaughtered. Native women are at the greatest risk of being raped and murdered to this day in America.

Africans faced rapes whippings slavery and death at the whims of the European Settlers who through Manifest Destiny seek to subjugate Indigenous People. Both are prevented by law from financial and land compensation, getting jobs education or even traveling freely. Not only did Europeans introduce racism and benefit from it they live in denial of its effects. Unfortunately, the ones who do not fit into this category are not in positions of power.

There is a lot of lip service and no concrete action as more and more Europeans move to America. The focus is blocking immigrants coming from Haiti, Mexico, South America and the Caribbean. There are more people coming from Countries of Europe and the Former Soviet Union Countries. Russia has launched an attack on the Ukraine and now Ukrainians are at the Southern Border seeking asylum. They are the only ones being allowed to enter through the Southern Border.

Not their fault but it is the United States Government that

refuses to see those fleeing from Haiti the Caribbean Mexico and South America as in need of a safe place. It is almost like they don't know or want to acknowledge that Utah New Mexico Texas Colorado California and Arizona were a part of Mexico for thousands of years.

As a person of mixed raced African European and Indigenous ancestry tracing my family history has been a daunting task. The Africans who were enslaved did not have names until slavery ended. Natives were stripped of their names and given European names. The documents with the racial classifications including census records led to brick walls until I stopped looking at the race.

When I started (in 1978) it was mainly a hobby of older white retired people. It became a passion with me once I teamed up with others in family like Cousin Perry Pennington and his wife Xanthia. Cousin Perry was a Pinn descendant who had done quite a bit of research on Pinn/Ruth lines. Besides my mother my aunts were extremely helpful especially Aunt Cora Aunt Ramona and Aunt Pearl.

Cousin Perry is now deceased, but I think of him every time I make a find and want to email or call. Cousin Ida Jones-Williams was also helpful with our Pinn/Ruth lines from Virginia. I am grateful to all my family who supported me throughout this journey. I miss my mom and those who have passed now but I remember the laughter and joy on their faces. I have pictures of them smiling and treasure each and everyone.

Our Coatesville Family

Our family was comprised of my dad mother and 6 siblings. There were four brothers who were older, me (Anita) and two younger sisters. Back in the 1950's dad worked in Lukens Steel Mill and mom stayed at home. He always had at least two jobs and at one point he was also our Constable. Dad was a linguist who wrote and spoke seven languages which almost got him arrested on Federal Charges of being a "Communist" Sympathizer.

My brother Nathan Baxter wrote a fitting Eulogy of who

our father was and I am including excerpts here:

"First, I want to say he was no Saint and had his shortcomings and character defects. But for a black man born in 1918, in Orangeburg South Carolina, to a family of 16 children he managed to survive and make ends meet. He was raised in Pennsylvania from the age of four. He was a genius and My father George Baxter Sr. Spoke twelve languages. Which were five more than my brothers and sisters knew about. Besides English, Italian, French, Russian, German, Spanish and Portuguese, he spoke Latin, Hebrew, Chinese, polish, And Austrian.

He was on the FBIs hit list from the 1940s years after his death in 1971. He realized it when he picked up our Party line in the 1950's and an FBI Agent was asking his neighbor about him. He studied agriculture and developed his own formula for pest control, and that became his way of making a living. His formula was so powerful that the exterminating company in reading Pennsylvania wanted to buy it.

Dad was able to go from county to county killing bugs. J.C.Erlichman was the exterminating company that wanted to buy his formula. They didn't care that he was exterminating black homes, but he was picking up white clients, as well as black and white businesses. I just want to bring attention to this man from Coatesville Pennsylvania."

Mom sniffed at J. Edgar Hoover coming after dad and said that he was "Colored" himself, but "They" (meaning whites) could have him. Being a linguist did not help my father get into a better position even when he was in World War II. As a Colored man he was sent to pick cotton in Texas something that his dad and my grandfather never wanted for his children. That is they fled South Carolina in 1920 and moved to Pennsylvania.

Mom always had a hobby or way to make pin money and liked to purchase things from the Sears Catalog. We have Amazon today but back in the day it was the Sears Catalog that we ordered from. She had an old singer sewing machine and made many of our outfits. She also enjoyed knitting, and crochet and made Baby Blankets booties hats and outfits from scratch.

The big kitchen table that we ate meals on would be turned into a staging area for whatever craft she was working on. It was in our Kitchen in Coatesville Pennsylvania that I learned our family's oral History. That is where I came to find out our family history is the history of America.

Our Maternal Grandparents Charles and Leah Ruth-Martin owned a farm in Honeybrook (Chester County Pennsylvania) which mom and her siblings were raised on. Much of what she knew of cooking crafting cleaning and baking came from being raised on that farm. She knew how to use Hops and make Beer how to churn butter from Cow's milk and how to mix herbs.

Grandpop Charles Frederick Martin was an only child who grew up playing with his cousins in the Welsh Mountains. He attended Quaker School in Williston where he was allowed to grow his hair long. Bayard Rustin attended the same School. His mother also attended that school as did his grandmother who raised him. We are related to the Rustin's through our Davis lines. Grandpop Martin attended the Quaker School at Williston until the 10th grade.

Great Grandfather William Penn Martin was an overseer for the King's Ranch in West Marlboro Township. He worked on the land that our Native ancestors had been on for thousands of years. He did not own the land he worked and the beef he raised was sent on a Cattle Drive to Texas once a year. This was in the early 1900's and yes there were Cowboys in Pennsylvania and Great Grandfather Martin was one of them.

They were not poor but had no ownership of the land they worked. Great Grandfather William Martin also worked for Maurice Darlington a prominent Quaker living in the area. When he passed, he had no land to pass to his only child and son or his wife. Great Grandmother Lydia Martin moved off the ranch and lived her remaining years with her sister in Coatesville.

Grandfather Charles Martin fared better having acquired property from his mother's sister Aunt Clara Green-Snowden. He was an only child and dotted on by his mother and father. When he farmed, Grandfather Martin's staple crop was corn which included White Lightening or Corn Liquor even after it was illegal. I am told it was the best in the County from some of the older people I spoke to. At one time Elliott Ness came to arrest Grandpop Martin and after their car broke down grandpop helped them fix it and they gave him a pass.

That is one of the stories going around about Grandpop Martin. He was also a Mechanic and had a car repair business and vehicles in the barn. Underneath the floorboard of the Barn was his stash of Corn Liquor and the cars were used to transport the liquor up to the Welsh Mountains.

Things changed for me when mom started telling us the family history. Carolyn who was two years younger had by then joined us in the kitchen. I started going in early to help mom prepare for dinner the biggest meal of the day. She was an excellent storyteller who kept us enthralled and entertained when we were little. This was especially true in the Winter months when we were stuck in the house for days on end.

By the time I was about 12 years old I knew who in the family was what whether they were Native White African or a mixture. My grandmother Leah Martin's paternal lines the Ruth's came to the area after the Civil War. Great Grandfather Samuel Ruth was a slave in Savannah Georgia and 13 years old when the Civil War broke out.

Great Grandfather Samuel Ruth was rescued during General Sherman's March to the Sea by the 54th Massachusetts, when he was 12 years old. His mother Great-Great Grandmother Leah Warner was born in Guinea West Africa. His father Robert Ruth was a white man from Germany and owned his mother. These lines are African and European which shows up in my

DNA Cousins who pop up on Family Tree DNA and Ancestry.

Mom who everyone called Vi (short for Vivian) told me about our ancestors who were free and in the Civil War out of Lancaster County . They were in the 41st United States Colored Troops and trained at Camp William Penn. They were Great-Great Grandfather Henry Green and Great-Great Grandfather Uriah Martin. Henry and Uriah's brothers Benjamin Green and William Penn Martin II were also in the Civil War.

Uriah and Henry are descendants of the Down River Nations in Maryland and Virginia. Uriah's father Great-Great-Great Grandfather Charles Martin and mother Sarah Johnson Martin were mixed raced Native/European. The Quakers intermixed with Natives who resided in what is now Williston in Chester County Pa and Ridley Park in Delaware County Pa.

I am back tracking on the Johnson lines which connected to in Pieces of the Quilt The Mosaic of an African American Family. He appears to be one of our Johnson's but may not be directly related. This is what has happened as we attempt to put together what was stolen from our family.

It is heart breaking to think of how children and families not only of Africans, but Natives were deliberately torn apart. At some point our Martin/Johnson lines intermixed with Quakers throughout the Delaware Valley. Sarah Johnson one of our Great-Great-Great Grandmothers was the daughter of a Native Woman and a mixed raced native/white Quaker man.

These intermarriages occurred early on in Maryland, Delaware, and Pennsylvania and indeed throughout Colonial America. It was one means of getting control of the land especially when it was a white man and Native woman. Quiet as it is kept many Native Tribes are Matrilineal not Patrilineal and women were the heads of tribes.

It is through Sarah Johnson's lines that we trace back to Thomas Garrett who is my third Cousin five times removed. Garrett was a Quaker and Abolitionist in Delaware. He is a cousin through my maternal ancestor Great-Great-Great

Grandmother Lydia Davis-Green who was the daughter of Joseph and Hannah Underwood Davis.

Thomas Garrett (b. Aug 21, 1789, Delaware County Pa; d. Jan 25, 1871, William De), was an American abolitionist and leader in the Underground Railroad movement before the American Civil War. For his fight against slavery, he was subject to threats, harassment, and assaults. A $10,000 bounty was established for his capture. This is one of our Native/Quaker lines with the intermixing of Quakers and the Okehocking who William Penn promised that they could remain on their ancestral land.

Pencader Hundreds Delaware is one of the Native Communities of my Davis, Green, Johnson, Martin, and interconnecting lines. Pencader Hundred lies within the area originally known as The Welsh Tract. This tract of 30,000 acres, granted by William Penn on October 15, 1701, to David Evans, William Davis, and William Willis, extended from Delaware into Cecil County, Maryland.

Our Native Davis Lines had villages in that region specifically at the Falls of Somerset County Maryland. In the Winter they moved inland to Delaware and Pennsylvania. Europeans also move from place to place and hold Town Homes but when Natives moved inland their land was taken by Settlers.

In Chester County Atglen was one of the places our Martin and Johnson Ancestors lived. Uriah Martin was born in Atglen Chester County Pennsylvania in 1838) to Charles and Sarah Johnson- Martin. Sarah and her siblings were baptized at the New Garden Meeting in Chester County, Colony aka Province of Pennsylvania

- March 4, 1681- The Pennsylvania Colony, aka Province of Pennsylvania, was founded.
- November 1682 - The first 3 Pennsylvania counties formed were Bucks, Chester, and Philadelphia Counties.
- December 7, 1787 – The State of Delaware was ratified as the first State.

- December 12, 1787 -The State of Pennsylvania was created as the 2nd state.

Chester County Bucks and Philadelphia were the three original Counties formed by William Penn in 1682. The other Pennsylvania Counties came from the original three. York County was created from parts of Lancaster County and the importance of the division is that Natives were still there, and their villages were divided. Chester and Bucks County were formed out of Philadelphia County. Native Villages and land were carved up with no regard to the people who welcomed them.

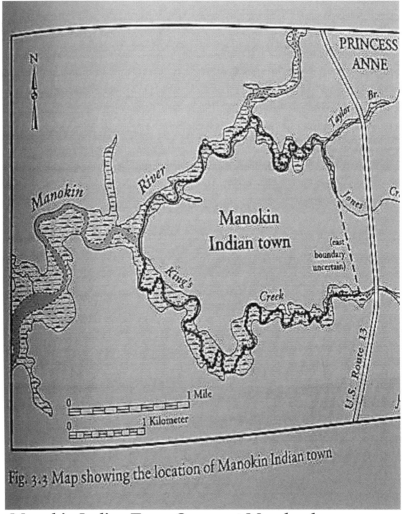

Fig. 3.3 Map showing the location of Manokin Indian town

Manokin Indian Town Somerset Maryland

Lydia Johnson Daughter of Charles Johnson and Mary his Wife was Born the 24th day of the 5th month 1790 about the 6th hour in Evening

William Johnson Son of Charles Johnson and Mary his Wife was Born the 6th day of the 3rd month 1792 About the 7th hour in the morning

Jethro Johnson Son of Charles Johnson and Mary his Wife was born 19th day of the 8th month 1794 about the 8th hour in the morning

Elizabeth Johnson Daughter of Charles Johnson & Mary his Wife, was born the 14th day of the 7th month 1797. About half after the 10th hour in the Evening

Benjamin Johnson Son of Charles Johnson & Mary his Wife was born the 28th day of the 2nd month 1800 About the 7th hour in the Evening

Deborah Leslie Johnson Daughter of Charles Johnson & Mary his Wife was Born the 30th day of the 6th month 1802

Mary Rice Johnson Daughter of Charles Johnson & Mary his Wife was born the 26th day of the 1st month 1804

Sarah Johnson daughter of Charles Johnson and Mary his wife was born the 14th of 12th month 1807.

Ann Johnson daughter of Charles and Mary Johnson born the 3d of 3 month 1811.

Charles Johnson son of Humphrey and Mary Johnson and father of the children above mentioned born the 20th of 7th month 1765

Great-Great-Great Grandmother Sarah Johnson-Martin Born in Chester County Pa

"Charles an Indian belonging to Captain Goodrich Lightfoot died October 9, 1722." [8]

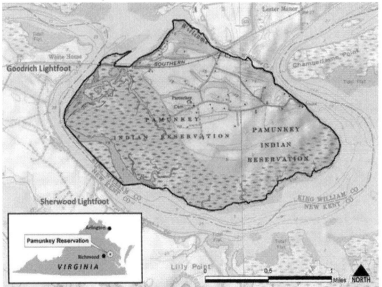

Goodrich Lightfoot removed children of Jane Bnu-Gibson (the elder) to his plantation in Virginia. They were to serve Indentures but instead were enslaved. It took several generations before they were heard in court. Lightfoot lived on properties that were about 1 mile apart and directly across from the Pamunkey Indian Reservation.[9]

---

[8] Source: The Vestry Book and Register of St. Peter's Parish of New Kent County, VA 1684-1786. Page 64

[9] Field Notes, Vol. 24 vol. 1, January 6, 2016; Virginia's Pamunkey Tribe Almost Gains Federal Recognition; http://archive.wetlandstudies.com/newsletters/2016/January/Pamunkey.html; October 16, 2022

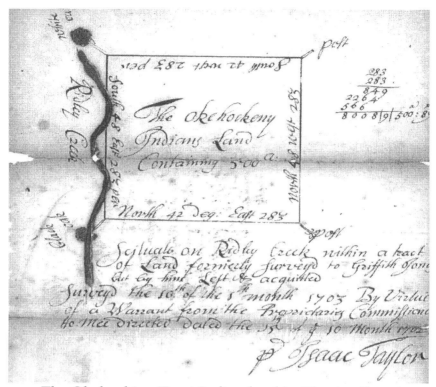

The Okehocking Tract-Indian land in Chester County Pennsylvania

Bear Mountain is the spiritual center of the Monacan community. The Bear Mountain Indian Mission School, ca. 1868, was originally built for church services and is listed on the National Register of Historic Places. Virginia's racial segregation laws excluded Monacan children from public schools. The school provided a seventh-grade education until 1964, when high school first became available to Monacan students. In 1968, an Episcopal mission was established on this site, which included a frame extension to the schoolhouse. A fire in 1930 left only the schoolhouse intact. The building now belongs to the Monacan Indian Nation.

CHAPTER TWO

THE LAND OF OUR ANCESTORS

"Only after the last tree has been cut down; Only after the Last River has been poisoned; only after the last fish has been caught; Only then will you find out that Money cannot be eaten!" Cree Indian Prophecy

Indigenous People lived throughout the region long before European Settlers divided up the land. They were the Susquehanna, Mohawk, and allied Native Nations of the Delaware Valley. Contrary to the narrative given by some historians they had a highly developed civilization with some living in villages made up of Longhouses while others lived in Tepees. One of the first actions of Settlers was to remove Natives from the Waterways which was the lifeblood of Villages.

In this accounting of the First People who occupied the regions defined by the Susquehanna and Delaware Rivers and the Atlantic Coast. We seek to honor our ancestors and keep their history and memories alive. Theirs is a history that lives on through us their descendants in our words deeds and spirit.

The Susquehannock Native Americans have had many aliases; the French called them the "Andaste." The Dutch and Swedes used the Delaware Indians' name for them, which was "Minqua," meaning stealthy or treacherous. Toward their decline, the Susquehannock tribe was also known as "Conestoga" to Natives and Europeans in Pennsylvania.

MINQUA UNAMI OKEHOCKING & THE DOWN RIVER NATIONS

The name they are best known for now, Susquehannock, is what Captain John Smith's Algonquian-speaking guides referred to them as. Subsequently, Smith recorded them as such, with slight variation on spelling. Originally Smith, as well as Father Andrew White, recorded them as "Sasquashahannockes."

An issue with the Narratives given by European Colonizers is their tendency to look for the history of Indigenous Nations from without mentioning that they were the catalyst to those conflicts. They were the ones who carried weapons and rumors from tribe to tribe. Not to say there was not conflict only that it was exacerbated by the divide and conquer warlike attitude of Europeans.

Europeans had no idea what life was like before Colonization and were not interested in finding out. If the Natives were warlike, they certainly would not have allowed the Pale face strangers to land on their shores. Their historian's write narratives that make the colonizers look like heroes. The fear of teaching the true history sends many into hysterics and to banning books. These days we have social media and the Internet and sooner or later the truth is going to be told.

Turtle Island was a land of pristine forests, clean running water, fresh air, and plenty of flora and fauna. There was plenty of fish and game fresh air and food that kept away infectious diseases. They lived in a Paradise that sustained them for thousands of years before Colonization. They and their descendants were pushed off the land by disease forced, marches, massacres, and laws favoring European Settlers.

Indigenous Nations have been subjected to a holocaust that has gone on for over 400 years. Here on our own homeland which was taken over by invaders welcomed to our shores. The Ancestors were surprised by the brutality that was visited upon them. Using the Doctrine of Discovery, the Catholic Church made edicts against Indigenous People.

Early on it was Church Wardens who made laws allowing confiscation of Indigenous Lands. The Episcopalian and Anglican Churches continued the same policy of Indian Removal by Any Means Necessary. Using God and their Religion as an excuse to commit unimaginable atrocities. We should not forget that the Royal Families in Britain controlled the Churches. The Roman Catholic Church is run by the "Holy" Roman Empire. The churches function under the banner of Christianity to do very un-Christ like deeds.

The Church Wardens used their Laws to change the groups' identity from Indian to Mulatto, then Colored, then Negro, and finally black. In Virginia some of our Native ancestors were moved from their Villages into enclaves of Free Persons of Color. One such enclave was Fredericksburg, and another was Rockets Landing in Richmond.

When I looked for them in records they were identified as Free Persons of Color (FPC). In Pennsylvania there was an enclave in the Welsh Mountains who were Tri-Racial Isolates and referred to as Mulatto or Colored. The racial identity changed when the Natives intermixed with whites and Blacks who fled to the Welsh Mountains.

Pennsylvania had whites who were poor and convicts who fled into the Mountains. Some of the children were light enough to pass and we know of family that passed. It is understandable when faced with an onslaught of racism and economic deprivation. If the finger is pointed it should be at the laws that favored Europeans over Native and African People.

The racial reclassifications began with the colonial use of the name Indian, a reference to the people of India. Columbus was on a voyage to India and stumbled upon the Arawak in the Caribbean. The tribe had a name and identity, land, and freedom all of which was wiped out by the Colonizers.

In 2015 I travelled to Cuba and saw the graves of the Spanish who had Colonized the Island. The guide told us that Spain had reclaimed Columbus remains and that he too had been buried in the white Cemetery. They gave him more dignity in death then he and Spain ever gave the Arawak or enslaved Africans in life.

Their New World

Colonizers came under the banner of Christianity first the Catholics then the Anglican Church then the Episcopalian Church. Bearing their Bible and proclaiming they were doing Gods Will. Carrying guns and a willingness to kill steal and destroy in the name of their God. In the name of Jesus Christ a Beta Israel Jew from Ethiopia Europeans ravaged Australia America and Africa.

Who would not want to leave Europe where they were poor outcast peasants and come to America? It was billed as the "New World" as if it did not exist until Europeans arrived. Plenty of land stolen from Natives and cities built from Slave Labor. On arrival they became a White American Person no matter how poor they were in Europe. That false Narrative of European superiority continues to this day.

Christians often state that the Jews are Gods Chosen People once they recognize Christ as their saviour. The Inquisition which was particularly brutal to Moors and Jews was an edict from the Roman Catholic Church. The Jews are accused of killing Christ when it was the Romans. Every depiction of Christ shows the Romans Crucifying him, yet it is the Jews who are blamed.

In America Religion and/or Spiritual Practices was not a choice for Native People nor African People. It was a means of slavery and forced assimilation and was enforced by the Church Warden. It is interesting that they would use a term like Warden for a Church. It is the same terminology used for the Prison Systems which were originally run by Churches.

It was the Quakers who founded the Prison System in Pennsylvania. In America a European can create any Religion or deity he or she chooses with impunity. Not so for Native and African people, whose believes preceded European Christianity by thousands of years.

Europeans arriving in the New World met people who had rich and established cultures and languages. The Skraeling were probably a people we now call Thule, who were the ancestors of the Inuit in Greenland and Canada and the Inuit in Alaska. The Taino were a people spread across multiple chiefdoms around the Caribbean and Florida. Based on cultural and language similarities, they had separated from earlier populations from South American lands, now Guyana and Trinidad.

The Spanish brought no women with them in 1492 and raped the Taino women, resulting in the first generation of "Mestizo "mixed" (Mixed Ancestry) people. A similar situation happened in Virginia where the first to land were ship loads of men. Immediately upon arrival, European alleles began to flow, admixed into the Indigenous Population, and that process has continued to this day. European DNA is found today throughout the Americas, no matter how remote or isolated a tribe might appear to be.

Europeans use the excuse that Natives were not "Always" here as if that justifies the atrocities committed against them. We know Europeans were not always here nor were they always in Africa or any other place they Colonized. At least as indigenous people we know where our ancestors were for the last twenty thousand or so years.[10]

The European Creed of Manifest Destiny or more like "A

---

[10] Rutherford, Adam, A Brief History of Everyone Who Ever Lived: The Human Story Retold Through Our Genes; The Atlantic, https://www.theatlantic.com/science/archive/2017/10/a-brief-history-of-everyone-who-ever-lived/537942/, March 11, 2021

Lie Told Often Enough Becomes the Truth" a philosophy some White Nationalist live by. There is also a Crest or Motto that says, "Anything We Take by Blood is Ours to Keep" is a War Cry! This is the Motto that keeps us at War with other Countries, especially in Africa and the Middle East.

They do not seem to want Wars with Countries where there are European looking People! We have heard the stories others tell about our Ancestors and our history, but they do not speak our truth. We owe it to the ancestors to speak of their lives, struggles, and triumphs. It is in the tradition of African and Native People to speak our stories to each succeeding generation.

Hearing a Griot tell our history is in and of itself more intimate than the written word. It is thousands of -years-old and the oldest form of Communication. There are also drawings found in caves that are thousands of years old. Drawing is the earliest form of the written word and no different than Hieroglyphs. It goes back before written history and has outlasted some written documents.

Natives were often identified as black by whites as in the case of Levin Davis a Dark Skinned Native from Sussex County Delaware. The designation of Indian changed in the 1700's to Mulatto, Colored, Negro, or Black. There were some who if light enough were designated as white. Colorism and racism were instituted during Colonization. Native men were rounded up and separated from their families. Wearing a cross meant that they were Christian. A requirement for them to travel hunt or fish.

Our ancestors were redesignated colored in Pennsylvania as were we my mother and her mother and father. Over several generations they listed our races as Mulatto, Colored, Negro, and/or black. Mom spoke of her father Grandpop Martin, who was of mixed raced Native/African/White ancestry.

Grandpop Charles Martin attended Quaker School until he was twelve years old. In his school picture, he is wearing his long hair in a Ponytail. His parents were William and Lydia Green-Martin both of whom were of mixed raced heritage. Lydia was the daughter of Henry and Susanna Brown- Green (who was also a Green).

Lydia's father Henry Green lived in what is known as the Welsh Mountain Region of Lancaster County. Although they were called Squatters by the locals, the land belonged to them and was part of the 10000-acre Conestoga Tract promised to Natives by William Penn. They owned the land and then went back and got original Warrants and Patents from Penn's sons.

They worked to clear the land and paid for it only to have retaken. That is what happened with the Okehocking Tract and with the Conestoga Tract. None of that land has clear title, but it does not matter because Indigenous Peoples rights were stolen with their land. Some of the lands have been taken over by the State of Pennsylvania for Parks or by Eminent Domain.

The land grab began with the Colonial Government and continued with the Federal Government and trickled down to State Governments. It went from Native People to White Males and trickled down from there. The purpose of taking the land was to monetize it using deeds lease mortgages Land Grants and other forms of paper. Natives saw and continue to see the land as sacred and not to be sold. After all our ancestors have been here for thousands of years and their bones are buried throughout the Americas. Who would sale their ancestral lands. Certainly not Europeans who only monetize aboriginal land that they Colonize.

Great-Great Grandfather Henry Green was arrested for participation in the Christiana Resistance where he and other Free Blacks confronted a Slave Owner and White Militia at the home of William Parker. The date of the incident was 9/11/1851. The incident happened 250 years before 9/11/2001, when terrorist attacked the Twin Towers and other targets here in the United States.

MINQUA UNAMI OKEHOCKING & THE DOWN RIVER NATIONS

After the men were freed in a trial where they were represented by Thaddeus Stephenson, Henry Green and many of the other men surfaced again and fought in the United States Colored Troops during the Civil War. Henry Green who fought for the rights of Slaves to be Free in the Christiana Resistance and in the Civil War was hounded the rest of his life by Officials.

He was arrested at 67 years old for stealing and sent to jail. Even after serving in the Civil War, he was not given respect and was hunted by the local Law Enforcement. How ironic that people who came and stole the land imprisoned those whose land they stole.

The Greens lived on land that was part of the Conestoga Manor Grant which was 10000 acres. That was their land even before William Penn ceded it to them. Yet the settlers did not allow them to rest until they were moved off that land. They could not stomach those afro/indigenous people who were economically independent and living on their own land.

The Davis/Greens were Natives who traveled the Great Minqua Trail long before Colonization. The trail led from Philadelphia into the interior of Lancaster County Pennsylvania from Delaware. This was a trail they used for thousands of years to travel from Maryland into Sussex County Delaware and then into the Interior of Pennsylvania and points northeast and West. The descendants of the Minqua, Unami and Okehocking no longer have rights or access to their ancestral homeland.[11]

I speculate that after Conestoga Indians were massacred in Lancaster County in 1763, many of our Native ancestors left the area. Those who were part of the Iroquois Federation fought on the British side during the Revolutionary War and afterwards were forced into Canada. Some returned to work on their ancestral land for European Settlers.

After the Indian Massacre in 1763 by the Paxton Boys,

---

[11] Wills, Anita; Black Minqua, 2012, The Life and times of Henry Green, Morrisville: Lulu Publishing

Pennsylvania declared that there were no more Indians. The census records dropped the designation of Indian and noted Natives as Colored, Negro, Mulatto, or Black. The Welsh Mountain Greens also intermixed with Whites and the Children were labeled as Mulatto or Colored.

Also on Grandpop Martin's maternal side are the Greens whose lines traced from Sussex County Delaware and Somerset Maryland. When the Settlers changed borders, they had no regard for the Native People or their borders. In fact, they went out of their way to cut through villages.

I found Joseph and Hannah Davis in Sussex County when they married in 1811. They were the parents of our ancestors George and Lydia Davis-Green. with George Green about 1830, George and Lydia were the parents of our direct Ancestor Susanna Green, who was born about 1840. They are listed as Mulatto or Colored in the census. Several of the Graves and Church records from our Martin and Green Ancestors, were found in the Episcopalian Churches in Pennsylvania and Virginia.

In the Octorara Presbyterian Church in Pennsylvania there is a "Colored" Graveyard with the surname of Martin. At Saint Martin's Church in Concord (Delaware County Pennsylvania), is the name of our ancestor, Benjamin Green who joined the Church in 1838. He is listed as Colored in the Church Registry.

Lancaster County and the Meaning of Nine Points

Great-Great-Great Grandfather Benjamin Green left Bucks County and moved to Gap and Nine Points. I have been curious about the 9 points and wanted to know the significance to my ancestors. I believe that 9 points had to do with the directions and has spiritual significance to the Conestoga and my ancestors.

They moved back and forth along the Waterways over thousands of years until the settlers moved in. Great Grandmother Lydia Green-Martin was born at nine points in Lancaster County. The families were run out by whites who fired on them and stated that they ran them off from the Hollow another name for 9 points.

MINQUA UNAMI OKEHOCKING & THE DOWN RIVER NATIONS

The meaning of 9 in Native Beliefs

"Eight appears only as a multiple of four, "doubling" its action, while the last important number for American Indians is nine, which can be regarded as a multiple of three (the world vertical). Ceremonies of various tribes last nine days: Holyway and Blessing way of the Navajo, Wuwuchim, Marau and the Snake Dance of the Hopi, the mid-winter festival of the Iroquois, and "nine 'works' make the annual cycle of ritual, social and political life of the Tewa" (Gill and Sullivan 301).

It also consists of nine major ceremonies "corresponding to the nine universes of Creation" and "representing the universal laws of life" (Waters 238, 125). The Hopi believe "the nine most important prophecies, connected with the creation of the nine worlds: the three previous worlds on which we have lived, the present Fourth World, the future three worlds we have yet to experience, and the worlds of Taiowa, the Creator, and his nephew, Sotuknang" (Waters 334).

American Indian Beliefs often refers to numbers that do not only represent the system of world order and spatial-temporal relations (two – the creation itself; three and nine – the temporal structure; four, five and six – the spatial one; seven – both structures), but also remain important symbols and life as reference points for the people.[12]

Our families were deliberately separated by Colonization and the racism inherent in that system. It is like a jigsaw puzzle and maze finding and connecting the pieces. It is a task made more difficult because the Government itself supported slavery and the removal of Natives and African People. The search to reconnect the pieces has taken me all over the world to Europe, Africa, Melanesia, Canada and back to where we started on Turtle Island (now America).

At 67 years old Henry Green a Landowner, participant in

---

[12] Brinton, D.G. Myths of the Americas: Symbolism and Mythology of the Indians of the Americas. New York: Multimedia Publishing Corp, 1976.

the Christiana Resistance and Civil War Veteran was being harassed and arrested. They hounded him until the day he died because of his race and status as a landowner.

The Trail of Tears was not the only removal of Native People it was the final solution. Before that atrocity there were continued pushes to remove Natives People from their Ancestral Lands. They were sent as far away as Africa and close as the Caribbean as slaves.

Iroqouis Federation Leaders

The Iroquois Federation's leaders Queen Aliquippa, Chief Jacob Brant, and Molly Brant Johnson are related in that we are from the same tribe. They are connected on my maternal grandfather's lines and like many Native People we were separated during strife. The lines start with the Mohawks being assimilated into Christianity prior to the Revolutionary War. Children were taken after massacres and sent to mission schools.

In the case of Jacob Brant, he attended a Methodist Seminary while his sister Molly (my direct ancestors) was a servant to Sir William Johnson and bore 7 children by him. This was the same scenario that took place with Matoaka (Pocahontas). In America White males are above the law and can do no wrong. This is part of their so-called manifest destiny. Of course, Johnson was an older married white man but faced no repercussions for his actions.

They had villages in the Ohio Valley, New York, New Jersey, Delaware, Maryland, Pennsylvania, and Canada. It was a vast Territory that required setting up and tearing down Villages. Our Johnson Martin lines connected in New York and New Jersey. The forced removals caused a rift in the oral traditions, and it did not help that once Natives were Christened their Native names were changed.

The History of Canada

Canadian History covers the period from the arrival of the Paleo-Indians thousands of years ago to the present day. Prior to European Colonization, the lands encompassing present-day Canada was inhabited for millennia by Indigenous People, with distinct trade networks, spiritual beliefs, and styles of social organization. War.[13]

The now British Colony was divided into two provinces in 1791. The Indigenous tribes were still there on their ancestral land as Europeans carved up the Continent. In 1867, (after the American Civil War), the Province of Canada was joined with two other British colonies forming a self-governing entity.

From the late 15th century, the French Colonization of the Americas and expeditions explored, colonized, and fought over various places within North America in what constitutes present-day Canada. The colony was claimed in 1534 with permanent settlements beginning in 1608. France ceded all its North American Possessions to the United Kingdom in 1763 after the Treaty of Paris (1763) at the end of the 7 years'
"Canada" was adopted as the legal name of the new country and the word was conferred as the country's title. One of the tribes inhabiting Canada were the Mohawk who moved between what is now Canada and America.

More Iroquois Connections

From the Mohawk we are of the line of George Ohyeatea Martin, born on 26 Dec 1767 in Canajoharie Castle, Mohawk Valley. He died on 08 Feb 1853 in Salt Springs, Grand River Brant, and is buried at Mohawk Chapel. When he was 30, He married Catherine Rolleston, daughter of James Rolleston and Sarah (Wife of James Rolleston), in 1798 in Georgia, New Jersey, USA. The Nanfan Treaty shows the territory that the Mohawk controlled throughout the region.

---

[13] Department of State Office of Historian; Treaty of Paris, 1763; The Treaty of Paris of 1763 ended the French and Indian War/Seven Years' War between Great Britain and France, as well as their respective allies. In the terms of the treaty, France gave up all its territories in mainland North America, effectively ending any foreign military threat to the British colonies there; https://history.state.gov/milestones; September 30,2022

George Ohyeatea Martin and Catherine Rolleston had the following children:
- Joseph Martin was born on 27 Sep 1792 in Upper Canada. He died on 26 May 1865.
- Margaret Martin was born on 23 Apr 1791. She died on 24 Oct 1870.
- Mary Martin was born on 24 Feb 1803. She died before 1852.
- Peter Martin was born on 21 Feb 1796. He died after 1861.
- George Martin was born on 01 Mar 1794. He died after 1822.
- Helen Martin was born on 17 Feb 1798 in Canada. She died on 27 Mar 1866 in South Walsingham, Ontario, Canada. She married Sakayergwaraton John Smoke Johnson (our ancestor) in 1815.
- Chief Jacob Martin was born on 11 Jul 1801 in Onandaga, Ontario Canada. He died in 1858 in Ontario Canada.
- Peter Martin was born about 1802.
- George Martin (known in Mohawk as Shononhsé:se', meaning "he is of the long house" or "the house is too long for him"), Mohawk chief and interpreter; b. 23 Dec. 1767 in Canajoharie (near Little Falls, N.Y.); d. 8 Feb. 1853 in Salt Springs, near Brantford, Upper Canada.

Little is known about George Martin's youth. In the early 1780s he married Catherine Rollston, who was alleged to be of Dutch ancestry and had been captured by the Mohawks when she was 13. She was brought to the Indian settlements on the Mohawk River, adopted by the prominent Mohawk family of Teyonnhehkewea, and given the name Wan-o-wen-re-teh (which means "throwing over the head"). The Martins had one daughter, Helen, who later married John "Smoke" Johnson*, and one or more sons.

Martin had participated, according to an obituary, in the American Revolutionary War, after which he and his wife moved with the Six Nations to the Grand River (Ont.). There, on a high bluff overlooking the river, they built a house, their lands becoming known as the "Martin Settlement."

It was here, since Martin was an interpreter, that the British government's presents to the Six Nations, for their continued loyalty, were distributed granddaughter Evelyn Helen Charlotte Johnson suggests that George had a fierce temper and that he had some influence within the community.

Unlike his contemporary Joseph Brant [Thayendanegea*], was not involved as a major spokesman in dealings with other Indian peoples or with the government, nor did he participate as a negotiator or signatory in any of the land surrenders involving the Six Nations. As an interpreter, he mediated between the Six Nations and government officials in various disputes.

Martin served as "Confidential Interpreter" to William Claus*, the deputy superintendent general of Indian affairs from 1799 until the latter's death in 1826. During the War of 1812, and likely earlier, he was an interpreter for the Indian Department, in whose service, Joseph Brant Clench later certified, he was "noted for zeal, bravery and general good conduct."

Although he once conveyed a message from the Seneca chief Red Jacket [Shakóye:wa:tha] in New York State calling on some of the Six Nations in Upper Canada not to fight as allies of the British, he remained firmly loyal. At the urging of Joseph Willcocks*, he helped to persuade the Six Nations to send warriors to Amherstburg, Upper Canada, to take up arms with Major-General Isaac Brock* in the late summer of 1812.

Martin was present, as an interpreter, for two British victories at least, Beaver Dams (Thorold), Upper Canada, in June 1813 [see William Johnson Kerr*] and Fort Niagara (near Youngstown, N.Y.) in December. In early January 1814, along with John Brant [Tekarihogen*], Henry Tekarihogen*, and others…,"

Although it is uncertain when he became a chief, he assumed new responsibility when he was appointed a war chief by a council held on 22 Feb. 1815. At the same time, he was given the task of ensuring that non-Indians did not trespass upon the Six Nations' lands. He immediately acted upon this duty, reporting in a letter to Claus that very day that Augustus Jones* and Kanonraron (Aaron Hill) - both "snaking and mean Fellows" - were attempting, along with Henry Tekarihogen, to get the Six Nations' chiefs to surrender their right to some salt-springs on the reserve.

Martin continued to keep Claus informed of conditions on the Grand River in succeeding years. In September 1816 he wrote that his people were experiencing "very bad" times. Corn most all dead some families have nothing at all to eat this winter."

There was, however, in his view, little chance of "your friends" moving from the Grand unless the British government provided them with "better Country somewhere." Alluding to reports he could not substantiate, he believed it was only "those people that was not a friend of the Government" who were intending to move, possibly to the "Wabash" in the Ohio country or to western Upper Canada.

By the early 1840s Martin, then about 80 years of age, appears to have retired to his home. Since his friend William Claus was long dead and because resident superintendents were being appointed to work directly with the Six Nations, Martin's influence waned and his place as an interpreter was taken over by his son-in-law, John "Smoke" Johnson.

He had been involved with other Six Nations Indians in supporting the government during the rebellion of 1837-38 in Upper Canada. He took no part, however, in the negotiations for the surrender in 1841 of the Six Nations' land on the Grand River, which was to be managed on their behalf by the crown [see Tekarihogen], or in other important matters affecting the Indians during the 1840s.

Martin, who was raised as a warrior in the Mohawk valley

and experienced war as an ally of the British crown, was a man shaped by the 18th century, not the 19th. At his death in 1853, he was described by the Toronto Globe as "the last of the old warriors residing on the Grand River, that have taken part in the two great struggles between England and the United States."

He left to his successors, John "Smoke" Johnson and his son George Henry Martin Johnson*, a legacy of loyalty to the crown in time of war and cooperation as an interpreter in peacetime, sometimes over considerable opposition.[ii]

This line of our Martin and Page ancestors came into Pennsylvania from New Jersey. Charles Martin my Great-Great-Great Grandfather married Sarah Johnson. When he was 30, George Martin his father married Catherine Rolleston, daughter of James Rolleston and Sarah (James Rolleston).

Sarah is described as Mulatto by her son and my Great-Great Grandfather Uriah Martin. She died about 1840 and Charles remarried a woman named Elizabeth from Delaware who was described as Mulatto. They had a daughter and son named James and lived in Lancaster in 1860 according to the census.
Connecting to Virginia Native Ancestors

Mom remembered that Grandmother Martin spoke of going to Philadelphia to visit her Maternal Grandfather and his last name was Pinn. He was a Pastor in Philadelphia and was The Reverend Robert A. Pinn. He was the father of her mother Maria Louisa Pinn-Ruth. This was an afro/indigenous line that came out of Virginia and intermarried with the Great Granddaughter of Charles Lewis.

The Pinn line originated as Wicomico Indians at Indiantown now located in Lancaster County Virginia. Originally, they were on the Eastern Shore of what is now Lancaster and Northumberland in Virginia and Wicomico County Maryland. They are yet another line of Native Ancestors whose racial category was changed to Mulatto. They were a tributary tribe to the Powhatan in that region and their village encompassed the Eastern Shore of Virginia and Maryland.

Mulattoes in Fredericksburg Virginia

It would take years and my first book to realize that Fredericksburg is where our Virginia lines converged. Fredericksburg was where Free Persons of Color could live own property marry and make a living during slavery. It was a quasi-free existence in a country founded on White Male Privilege. In Henning's Statutes at Large is the blueprint for racial classification of Natives, Africans, Free Blacks, Mulattos, Negroes, and Coloreds.

The Mulattoes existed not from Natives but from Whites intermixing with Africans and Natives. The Natives racial identity was also used as a means of resolving the Indian problem. It was a way to block any claims to land or rights that existed prior to Colonization. The Natives were required to convert to Christianity, attend Mission Schools, and accept the changing of their racial status to either White, Colored, Negro, or Mulatto.

Paper Genocide effectively wiped-out Native Identity and autonomy. By the time they understood the motives of Europeans, their rights, identity, and land had been stolen. Their Villages and Lands were taken over by squatters and their sacred sites turned into attractions for the Amusement of Europeans. Armed Settlers surrounded them there to protect the Interest of the Colonizers.

Turtle Island

Our ancestors have been here for thousands of years and Turtle Island was in Pristine Condition vastly different from what it is now. Native spiritual beliefs encompass the earth the sky plants and animals and human beings. We do not need to co-op religious text rewrite them and make us Gods. We see ourselves as a part of the sacred no more and no less. In the Seneca language, the turtle is called Hah-nu-nah, while the name for an everyday turtle is ha-no-wa.

Does that mean we worship a Turtle? Creator imbues Animals with human qualities because they too are a part of the sacred. They were not put on the earth to be subjugated or used by humans. The core of the creation story relates to a time when the planet was covered in water. Different animals all tried to swim to the bottom of the ocean to bring back dirt to create land, but they all failed.

A muskrat was the last animal to attempt the task. The muskrat swam deep and remained under water for a long time. Eventually the muskrat resurfaced with some wet soil in its paws. Sadly, the swim took the muskrat's life, but Nana bush (a supernatural being who has the power to create life) took the soil and placed it on the back of a turtle. With this act, land began to form, and the land became Turtle Island.

Some Surnames and History

In Pennsylvania the Green, Davis, Stewart, Boots, Harris, Nocho, Henson, Awl, Parker, Watson, Woodburn, Stewart, Coleman, and Martin Ancestors lived on the Welsh Mountains. It was the winter refuge for the Down River Nations in what is now Somerset County Maryland. It was also a stop on the Underground Railroad which to this day has not been acknowledged.

These surnames were given to our ancestors by European Settlers after they were Christened. Some of our ancestors intermarried with the Quakers and others with then Dutch in Lancaster County. Some also intermarried with Mennonites. Some Welsh Mountain Surnames

One of the families that lived on the Mountain was the Awl intermarried with our Green lines. Jacob Awl married Nancy Green the daughter of Charles Green. They are a Native line I am continually researching, and they are propertied to be Seneca. They may have come to Conestoga with Queen Aliquippa who camped there in the 1700's while meeting with William Penn. Or they may have been there and helped her set up Camp.

The Awl Family intermarried with the Greens on the Mountain. Jacob Awl Married Nancy Green and they were the Parents of Nathaniel Awl;

Nathaniel Awl

Mt. Hope cemetery
Elizabeth Juliet Awl
28 Apr 1913 – 22 Jun 1913
Mathew Awl
1844 – 24 Oct 1912
Anna Aul
1916 – 28 Mar 1936
Helen Rice Awl
9 Oct 1900 – 17 Jun 1935
Jacob Awl
1845 – 1 Nov 1912
Elizabeth Juliet All
28 Apr 1913 – 22 Jun 1913
Mathew All
1844 – 24 Oct 1912
Anna Aul
1916 – 28 Mar 1936
Helen Rice Awl
9 Oct 1900 – 17 Jun 1935
Jacob Awl
1845 – 1 Nov 1912 (Father to Nathan)
Malin A Awl
5 Jul 1916 – 16 May 1951

Nathaniel Matthew Awl (15 October 1900 - 9 September 1994) is buried in the Mellinger Mennonite Cemetery. He was the son of Jacob Matthew Awl (??? - 1 November 1912) who is buried at the Mt. Hope Cemetery and Nancy Green (30 March 1867 - 8 January 1931). Nancy was the daughter of Charles & Harriet DeWitt Green. She remarried after Jacob's death to Oscar Jay. Nancy is buried in the Mt. Hope Cemetery. Nathaniel's obituary was published in the Intelligencer Journal on 10 September 1994.
Burial Notices for Nathaniel Awls' Wives
1 - Helen Rice Awl (9 October 9, 1900 - 17 January 1935). She was the daughter of Albert Rice & Jennie Lloyd. She is buried at the Mt. Hope Cemetery (Free Will). Her obituary was published in the Intelligencer Journal issue of 18 January 1935. She had a

daughter Eleanor.

2 - Annie Turner Awl - She died at the age of fifty-five and was the daughter of Philip & Annie Turner and was born in Greenville, SC. She had a daughter Eunice Jones. Obituary was published in the Lancaster New Era on 13 February 1954.

3 - Delores Floyd Awl died in 1987 at the age of 61. She was born in Reidsville, NC and was the daughter of Mr. & Mrs. Frank Floyd. She is buried in the Mellinger Mennonite Cemetery.

Nathaniel's Sister Rev. Mrs. Margaret M. Halliger - died at the age of 68. She operated a boarding house and was a member of Holiness & Trinity Church. She had a daughter named Joyce Gray. Obituary in Lancaster New Era dated 7 July 1977. She was a widow. Nathaniel was arrested according to the Intelligencer Journal dated 29 June 1935 for maintaining a disorderly house and violating state liquor laws (moonshine). It was during Prohibition.

America the Melting Pot

America the "Melting" Pot is anything but or else those like me of mixed raced heritage would not have to fight for our place at the table. The race mixing was not a design of Native or Africans but Europeans. It was a part of their Colonization methods used not only in America but Australia the Caribbean Asia and Africa. That was one of the methods used to gain land, labor and thus power. There is a regional difference between Tri-Racial Isolates and Melungeon, but both are mixed raced groups of people.

The Melungeon are descendants of people of mixed ethnic ancestry. Before the end of the eighteenth century, they were discovered living in limited areas of what is now the Southeastern United States. Notably in the Appalachian Mountain Range near the point where Tennessee, Virginia, and North Carolina converge.

Some of our Virginia ancestors took to the Mountains and are now considered Melungeon. Many of the whites who are passing come from Tri-Racial-Isolate and Melungeon

Communities. In other words, some of the whites aligned with the racist groups in the South and North are related. They are our DNA Cousins on Family tree DNA and on Ancestry usually with no profile picture.

Our families racial mix of Native, European, and African is unique to America and the result of the racist laws of Colonizers. The census in America historically defined people by skin color to be some degree of African or some degree of white, from zero to one hundred percent. Our families were not allowed to forge our own identity because the Powers that Be felt threatened. America is now divided but the entire country was built on Manifest Destiny and the lie of White Supremacy.

The Cultural experience of being African American is invaluable despite the bigotry and racism meant to separate us. When I advocate it is the media who label me African American while I am afro/indigenous as well as European. Our experience in America was not one of White Privilege but of afro/indigenous oppression against me our ancestor's family and descendants. Both have suffered equally from the acts of people who themselves have no identity. People who have an Identity do not need to co-opt others land and History.

The Black Church gave us tools to survive the onslaught against our existence as anything but slaves. Kudos to the uniquely African American Churches in our Community. That is one institution they could not block us from participating in and we made it our own. We were able to be free of prying eyes and organize through songs and other methods.

Our Native ancestors were not even given the opportunity to be in a place free from pressure to assimilate. They were carted off to Mission Schools run by the Catholic Church and other Religious Institutions against the wishes of the Community and Families. Some were fostered out or adopted to white families never to be returned. The rest were redesignated as Colored, Mulatto, or Negro a form of paper genocide.

The Catholic and Anglican Churches called Natives

Savages and Heathens who were beneath White Europeans. The Christian Church goes back to Christ in the Middle East over two thousand with the line of Christ coming out of Ethiopia into Egypt. That is his mother's line that left Egypt and crossed the sea into Israel. It has been atrocity on atrocity since the crucifixion of Christ.

We sing about Go Down Moses Way Down in Egypt Land…, while not addressing head on the racism in our own land. By that statement I mean most of the African American Churches do not address racism head on. We know about Doctor King and the Nation of Islam and other Congregations. But if most of the African American Churches stood up, we would be Free by Now!

The Racial Caste System

Whatever the eyeballs of Europeans saw and was written down became our racial identity. There were some folks able to pass and most left the community lest they be outed. Our maternal lines in Pennsylvania are listed as Colored Mulatto Negro or Black yet there were some who passed.

You could be all or some of those things within a lifetime. Like our Grandparents who were born Mulatto and died as Black people. This took place in Pennsylvania not South Carolina or Mississippi. On some of our Grandfather Charles Martin's documents he is listed as white.

The following article highlights the pit falls of racial designations:

"The method of representing race as fractions is a vestige of the time before miscegenation was outlawed. Because huge pockets of the globe profited by subjugating the 'colored' races, they had to ensure a distinction between the white and the rest to hold on to authority.

This led to the genesis of ubiquitous laws that banned any relationships across the arbitrary racial divide. Now, just putting up laws, did not completely stop the creation of multi-raced individuals. The men who over saw the making of the laws themselves had Mulattoes in their families. In fact, sexual abuse in the plantation was rampant with even eminent leaders like Thomas Jefferson culpable.

Not to mention, the select few who had the courage to see beyond their day and age. Across the oceans, the colonizers abused their respective enslaved women resulting in a burgeoning biracial population."[14]

There was no one way used to bring the colored populations under control during Colonization. In some instances, White Settlers intermixed and had children with the Natives, but that process was too slow. We know that African women bore children by their white slave owners like Thomas Jefferson. Although it was a White Patriarchal Society the child held the status of the mother. When the mother was a slave or servant so was the child.

The Bowden's of Popes Creek

My direct ancestor Mary Bowden (b. 02 Feb 1720) was the daughter of William and Mary Hilliard-Monroe Junior, the uncle of President James Monroe. Mary Bowden's mother Mary Hilliard- Monroe and Father William Monroe Junior entered into a marriage that was voided by the courts at Montross Virginia. It did not matter because the laws of the Colonizers did not protect black and brown people.

When they were mentioned, it was as property belonging to the slave master with a dollar value. Their lives and labor belonged to the white man who saw himself as Gods Chosen. He would watch the slaves in the field and complain about how hard his life was. Mary Bowden's Daughter Patty was given as a gift to years of age. She was under a 30-year indenture and had several children born during her service. Patty Mary Bowden's daughter had a brother Dominic Tapscott who is purported to be the

---

[14] Agarwal, Shourya There Are No 'Mixed-Race' People: Why it's troublesome to believe otherwise; https://medium.com/an-injustice/there-are-no-mixed-race-people-655eb510fbc;Feburary 15,2021

namesake of his father Dominic Tapscott Senior.

It was Hening's Statutes At Large that sealed the fate of Natives and People of African descent. Following is some of the laws aimed at the intermixing of white and other people. It was the Christian Churches behind the making of these laws which tied them to the race and slave-based system in Colonial America.

The 1691 law made interracial marriage illegal and set up severe punishments for white women who gave birth to the children of black men without being married. The Virginia Assembly hoped this would put an end to white women giving birth to free interracial children, while also allowing them to get more years of free labor out of any white woman who broke the law. Interracial marriage remained a crime in Virginia until the Supreme Court decision of Loving vs. Virginia in 1967.

Henings Statutes At Large;

[As of December 1662, the child of an enslaved mother was also a slave for life. The statute was a dramatic departure from the English tradition in which a child received his or her status from his or her father. Members of the General Assembly also hoped that an increased fine would discourage white men and women from having sexual partners who were African or of African descent.]

WHEREAS some doubts have arisen whether children got by any Englishman upon a negro woman should be slave or free, Be it therefore enacted and declared by this present grand assembly, that all children borne in this country shalbe held bond or free only according to the condition of the mother, And that if any christian shall committ ffornication with a negro man or woman, hee or shee soe offending shall pay double the ffines imposed by the former act.[15]

---

[15] Hening, ed., The Statutes at Large, vol. 2, p. 170.

And for prevention of that abominable mixture and spurious issue which hereafter may increase in this dominion, as well by negroes, mulattoes, and Indians intermarrying with English, or other white women, as by their unlawful accompanying with one another;

Be it enacted by the authority aforesaid, and it is hereby enacted, that for the time to come, whatsoever English or other white man or woman being free shall intermarry with a negro, mulatto, or Indian man or woman bond or free shall within three months after such marriage be banished and removed from this dominion forever and that the justices of each respective county within this dominion make it their particular care, that this act be put in effectual execution;

and be it further enacted, That if any English woman being free shall have a bastard child by any negro or mulatto, she pay the sum of fifteen pounds sterling, within one month after such bastard child shall be born, to the Church wardens of the parish where she shall be delivered of such child, and in default of such payment she shall be taken into the possession of the Church warders and disposed of for five years;

and the said fine of fifteen pounds, or whatever the woman shall be disposed of for, shall be paid, one third part to their majesties for and towards the support of the government and the contingent charges thereof, and one other third part to the use of the parish where the offense is committed, and the other third part to the informer; and that such bastard child be bound out as a servant by the said Church wardens until he or she shall attain the age of thirty years;

and in case such English woman that shall have such bastard child be a servant, she shall be sold by the said church wardens, (after her time is expired that she ought by law to serve her master) for five years, and the money she shall be sold for divided as is before appointed, and the child to serve as

aforesaid.[16]
The Bowden's of Popes Creek

When Mary Bowden turned 7 years old in 1737 her Indenture was assigned to George Washington's brother Augustine Washington Junior at what was then Pope' Creek. Mary and her daughter Patty (Bowden-Jackson) made up at least 5 generations of Female Indentured Servants in Westmoreland County Virginia. Over four generations beginning with a white woman, Lydia Hillard, (born about 1690), who had a daughter Mary Hilliard, by a Negro man, (about 1710). Lydia received 15 lashes for breaking the law and having a child by a negro man. The child was then indentured to Reverend Shropshire of Westmoreland County. William Monroe Senior went to court and sued for the Indenture and won.

The Negro man was unnamed, but he would have been born around the same time as Lydia Hilliard somewhere in Westmoreland County. Lydia received 15 lashes from Rev. Shropshire of the Anglican Church in Westmoreland County. She was then a Servant to William Monroe Senior and her child Mary Hilliard was moved to the Monroe Plantation. William Monroe Senior, is the grandfather of President James Monroe.

In 1730 Mary Hilliard, entered a marriage with William Monroe Junior, a white man. She and William Jrs., daughter, Mary Bowden, was born February 20, 1730. Mary learned of the law later that year when she was indicted for Bastardy. As a Mulatto woman, she could not by law, marry a white man, therefore their child was illegitimate.

In a stunning move (for 1730), the Grand Jury threw out the indictment. Seven years would pass before the Westmoreland County Courts took control of the child. By that time her mother disappears from the record (not unusual) and her father left the area. Mary Bowden was first sent to live with a family related to

---

[16] Act XVI, Laws of Virginia, April 1691 (Hening's Statutes at Large, 3: 87).

William Monroe's Seniors wife with the surname of Chilton.

When she was seven, she was sentenced to a thirty-year Indenture, to George Washington's father, and brother Augustine Washington Junior and Senior. When Augustine Senior married Mary Ball they moved to Fredericksburg and Augustine Junior was left in charge of the Washington Plantation William Monroe Junior did not remarry and instead went to Chillicothe Ohio and remained there until his death.

DNA Cousin Momia Junanita

Momia Juanita, (Spanish for "Mummy Juanita"), also known as the Lady of Ampato, is the well-preserved frozen body of a girl from the Inca Empire who is believed to have died sometime between 1440 and 1480, when she was approximately 12–15 years old. Legend has it that she was chosen -- along with other young women in the region of Arequipa -- to be sacrificed to Pachamama or Mother Earth. It is hard to believe the legend when her body is intact and may have been mummified in the same way as Egyptian Mummies. She and I share the same DNA which may connect to our Native DNA found in Columbia South America. My DNA is also the same as Eva Longoria. [17]

---

[17] GRI Genetics; Famous Relatives; https://vault.crigenetics.com/dna/report/UI344623/famous-people

MINQUA UNAMI OKEHOCKING & THE DOWN RIVER NATIONS

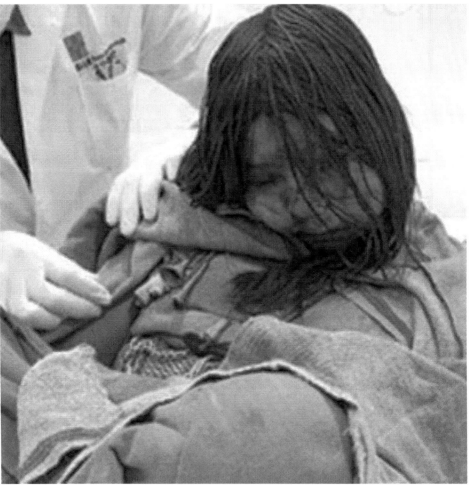

Momia Juanita (c. 1450) is one of our Turtle Island DNA Cousins.

Native (Sioux) Children entering Mission School – 1897 – Most were abused, and many were killed and never made it back home.

Vivian Martin-Baxter (mom) at 7 years old
Honey Brook (Chester County) Pennsylvania

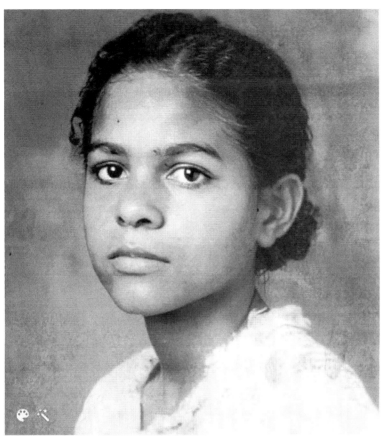
Mom Vivian Martin-Baxter age 13

Great-Great-Great Grandfather Charles Martin (seated) & Great-Great Grandfather Uriah Martin (served in the USCT out of Lancaster Pennsylvania) racially classified as Mulatto Coloured or Black.

Great-Great Grandfather Rev. Robert A. Pinn (1817-1886); father of Great Grandmother Maria Louisa Pinn-Ruth. He 1st married Elizabeth Jackson of Fredericksburg Virginia. He was a Baptist Minister like his grandfather Rawley Pinn; His son Walter Samuel Pinn served in the 54th Massachusetts USCT with Louis and Charles Douglass. He was the son of James and Jane Cooper-Powell-Pinn and his grandparents were Rawley and Sarah Redcross Evans-Pinn.

Great-Great-Great Grandparents Joseph and Hannah Underwood Davis Parents of Lydia Davis-Green.

Aunt Dot (Dorothea) Martin Passed January 27, 2022[18]

---

[18] Curtesy of Lorise Diamond

Welsh Mountain Green Cousin Nathaniel Awl. of Jacob (b. abt. 1825) and Nancy Green-Awl; The daughter of Charles and Harriet Dewitt- Green.

Certificate of Death for Amanda Green who was 82 years old (1873-1955) lived in Salisbury Twp. and owned her own home. She is buried at Pequea Presbyterian. She was the wife of Benjamin Green II a brother to Henry Green. As each Green descendant died their land was confiscated by Lancaster County.

Pinn Descendant -Grammy Leah Louisa Ruth-Martin (Maternal Grandmother)

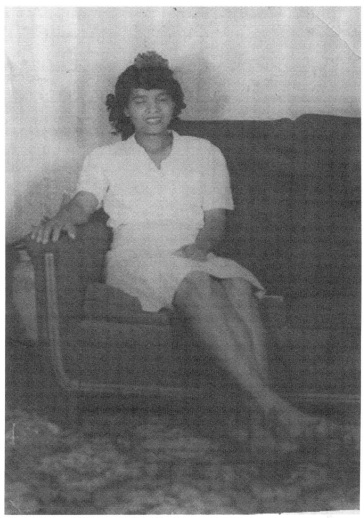

Mom Vivian Martin-Baxter

Native Pinn ancestors in Nova Scotia. During Colonization Natives fled from massacres and forced assimilation into Canada.[19]

---

[19] Curtesy of Cousin Lionel Pinn

Joseph and Hannah Davis

Joseph and Hannah Underwood Davis were my Maternal Great-Great-Great Grandparents through Lydia Davis-Green our Mothers' Paternal Grandmother. It is through our DelMarVa Davis lines that we are Manokin from Somerset Maryland. They resided throughout the Delaware Valley and were sometimes listed as Mulatto and other times assumed to be white. The Manokin are listed in the 1692 census for Somerset Maryland. The tribe members either became Christian or were redesignated Mulatto or left the area. My ancestors remained in the area as Mulatto or intermixed with the Quakers. Hannah Underwood the wife of Joseph Davis was mixed raced native/Quaker.

Great-Great-Great Grandparents Joseph and Hannah Underwood-Davis

The Manokin Indians were a sub-tribe or band of the Pocomoke Paramountcy and were in a Neck known as Arrococo by the native people and later called Revel's Neck. This area is best described as the lands on the south side of the Manokin River and the north side of a Creek known then and now as Back Creek. An Indian town was located in a fork, between the visiting Manokin River on the north and a branch on the south side of the river called Trading Branch (AKA Mumford's Branch and today King's Creek).

This area of Old Somerset Co. Maryland was well-documented trading post for early Europeans and the Indigenous people of the Eastern Shore. English settlers from the Colony of Virginia were this area long before the county of Somerset was formed, or the Colony of Maryland settled. The best evidence of this fact is recorded in Somerset County Judicial Records. [32]

The deposition of several residents and visitors to this area paint a picture of the trading on the Manokin River water shed. John Westlock states that he was trading with the natives in Manokin as early as 1620. In 1666 Westlock received a patent from the Calvert's called Brownstone, located on the north side of the Manokin River just to the north of Trading Branch Fork.

In a case of trespassing Randall Revell vs. Richard Ackworth, the provincial court at St Marie's ordered the Commissioners of Somerset Co. to summons a Jury of the twelve residents, to pick twelve local men to give deposition on the boundaries of land granted to Randall Revell called Double Purchase. German Gillett testified that in the year 1656 he was trading in the Manokan from the Rappahannock with one William Cooke his interpreter.

Gillett states that about two miles in the river he left me in the Sloope and proceeded on foot to the Indian town to obtain permission to come up to the Trading Branch. Two days later an Indian came to me and we went up to the Trading Branch, which was the second branch on the south side of the River.

Richard Burdick testified that the second branch on the south side of the Manokin River from the now Court House upward where a great stump is in the middle of the branch and a row of stakes where there had been an Indian bridge is the Trading Branch and the place where Mr. Cooke and several others traded with the Indians. Henry Hooper testified that in the year 1656 he had the fortune to meet with an Indian in the sound, coming to trade for corn with a vessel from the Rappahannock in Virginia.

We went in to the Manakin River up to the Indian Town and to the fork that is called the Trading Branch. Nicholas Fountaine testified that he went with Mr. Elzey and Col. Scarburgh to Rackcoone pointe, and with compass surveyed up the river to the Trading Branch and this was the northern boundary of Double Purchase. Christopher Nutter stated he had heard the Indians say that the point where Mr. Randall Revell lives on was formerly traded on. [33]

The Manokin Indians remained on the river for some time after the County of Somerset was formed. In 1706 Mr. George Phoebus gave deposition in Somerset Court in reference to the boundaries of land on Goose Creek belonging to Elzey and McClemmy. In his statement he claims that he remembers the Indian sweat houses and Indian Cabins on north side of Goose Creek near the first gut in from the river.

The records of Maryland and Somerset Co. fail to identify the native people living on the Great Manny River or Creek. The village is mentioned in the patent granted to Nehemiah Covington in 1665 for 300 Acres called Covington's Vineyard. The tract is described as a parcel of land with a Creek as its eastern boundary known as The Kings Branch running out of the Great Manny River. This Creek divides the land from the Manny Indian Town. Today this Creek is shown on modern maps as Harper Creek.[20]

Map of Eastern Woodlands Tribe

---

[20] Goldsborough, Philip Lee; Jonathan's Addition Genealogy & History, 199 Dennis Lane, Crisfield Maryland; https://www.pocomokeindiannation.org/Territories%20and%20Villages.htm; February 17, 2022

Baby Vivian Martin (mom) & Grandmother Leah Ruth-Martin Circa 1926. On the farm in Honey Brook Chester County PA

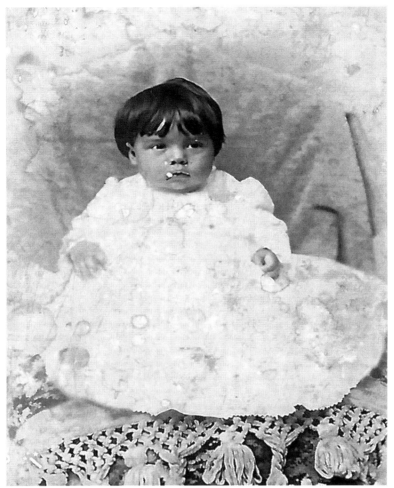

Great Aunt Blanche Martin – Great Grandfather William Penn Martin's sister. Daughter of Uriah & Tamzin Paige-Martin.[21]

---

[21] Courtesy of Blanche Martin-Robinson's Daughter Barbara Robinson-Black

Great Aunt Blanche Martin at (18 years); Daughter of Uriah &Tamzen Page-Martin[22]

---

[22] Courtesy of Barbara Robinson-Black

Aunt Vernelle and Uncle Chuck (Charles) Martin (now Deceased). Uncle Chuck was mom's brother and is said To favor Great Grandfather William P. Martin.

Map of Great Minquas Path

Credit: Wallace, Paul A.W., Indian Paths of Pennsylvania, Harrisburg: Pa., Historical and Museum Commission, 1971.
Great Minquas Path

    The Great Minqua Path (or The Great Trail) was a 17th-century trade route that ran through southeastern Pennsylvania from the Susquehanna River, near Conestoga (Lancaster County), to the Schuylkill River, opposite Philadelphia. The 80-mile (130 km) east-west trail was the primary route for fur trading with the Minqua (or Susquehannock) people. Dutch, Swedish, and English settlers fought one another for control of it.[2]

Great-Great Grandmother Tamzen Paige- Martin (1840-1899) wife of Uriah Martin. She was a midwife in Chester County and delivered many of the Quaker Children in the region.

Ancestor Catherine Martin (sister of Charles Martin)
And Daughter Nancy Martin-Miller.

CHAPTER THREE

THE DOWN RIVER NATIONS

> "They were sons and daughters of the Indigenous people whose ancestors were enslaved. Yet they are spoken of as Mulatto Colored or Negro to separate them from their Native Ancestors. They are Indigenous heroes Frederick Douglass Crispus Attucks and Tituba."
> Anita Wills

The Minqua had a village in Chinklacamoose., now called Clearfield, Pennsylvania. From the early first sighting up into the seventeenth century (when it was destroyed by Settlers), the Black Minqua village was along the Great Shamokin Path. Keep in mind it was Europeans who made a distinction between black and white Minqua.

The Path is an extension of the Great Minqua Path leading from Philadelphia into the Interior of Eastern Pennsylvania. The path starts at the old Indian village of Shamokin (Sunbury) and ran along the West Branch of the Susquehanna River west to the village of Kittanning. Today the trail west of Clearfield is U.S. Highway 322.

The Minqua were originally part of the Susquehannock. European settlers used the name of Minqua meaning "stealthy" or "treacherous." It is claimed that a distinction was made between White Minqua who lived above the falls of the Susquehannock and the Black Minqua who had villages below the falls. There were no racial distinctions within Tribes until the European came...,

Tribes below the falls had Villages in what is now Maryland Delaware and Pennsylvania. The truth is that the same tribes who lived above the falls in the Winter lived below them in the summer. They were more than likely darker in the summer then the winter hence the name "Black" Minqua. It was not as clear cut as Settlers make it out to be as the Minqua were one ethnic group.
Given the tendency of Europeans to classify folks by skin color

they called them as they saw them. John Smith claimed that Natives were born white and turned dark, but Natives did not identify themselves by dark or light skin. Smith also spoke of the Natives who lived below the falls and called them Susquehanna a river which traverses Pennsylvania.

It is rumored that Clearfield got its name from where the Minqua burned away the vegetation to create fertile farmland. They travelled along the Great Shamokin Path hunting game, fish, eels, and freshwater clams. They also travelled along the Great Minqua Path with markers now in Philadelphia Delaware and Lancaster County.

They also travelled on the West Branch of the Susquehanna using dugout canoes. The village of Chinklacamoose was surrounded by a circular mounded wall and pointed poles. Within the fence, twenty to forty people lived in shelters made from saplings and bark. There is no doubt but that the Erie, or Panther Nation spread over the region southward from Lake Erie to the Ohio. According to Herman's map of 1670, the "Black Minqua are placed in the region west of the Alleghany Mountains, and on the Ohio or Black Minqua River.

According to the Jesuit Relation, both of these peoples, the Wenro and the Minqua, traded with the people upon the upper Delaware, going back and forth by the trail to the waters of the West Branch, down to Shamokin (now Sunbury), then up to Wyoming (now Wilkes Barre) and across to the Delaware Water Gap, near the present city of Easton.

The legend on Herman's map reads, A very great river called the Black Minqua River — where formerly those Black Minqua came over the Susquehanna — as far as Delaware to trade, but the Susquehanna and the Sinnicus Indians went over and destroyed that very great Nation. How much of this was real or an attempt by Settlers to divide and conquer Natives has yet to be determined.

The Allegheny is the name given in the early years of the 18th Century to the entire region drained by the Ohio River and its various Tributaries West of the Mountains. On seeing this beautiful region and the people who maintained it for thousands of years Europeans plotted and planned to steal it. They plotted and planned to exploit the land in a way they had not exploited their European Homeland. We know what they plotted and planned because of the way the land has been exploited. Allegheny Indians were a popular designation of a geographical group of Indians, comprising the Delaware, Shawnee, Iroquois, and other tribes living within the region noted above. The term applied to

all the Indians living west of the waters of the Susquehanna, within the region drained by the Ohio. That the term did not refer simply to then Indians living on the Allegheny River is shown by its use in reference to those living on the Conemaugh, Allegheny, Ohio, Beaver, and other streams west of the mountains Beaver and other streams west of the mountains.[23]

That part of Maryland which lies east of the Chesapeake Bay has since the founding of the colony (1634), been known as the Eastern Shore; so, too, the Eastern Shore of Virginia. Most of it is a flat country of tidal rivers occupying "drowned valleys" into the heads of which flow sluggish freshwater streams. A low divide, or height of land, separates streams emptying into the Chesapeake from streams flowing into the sounds of the Atlantic Ocean, or into Delaware Bay.[24]

The Okehocking Land Grant

We are descendants of the Indigenous People whose villages were throughout the Delaware Valley and Pennsylvania for thousands of years. Our ancestors were labeled Minqua, Unami, Okehocking and Conestoga, tribes that were Tributary to the Susquehanna. In Virginia and North Carolina our Maternal Native Ancestors were the Wicomico, Nanzattico, Saponi, and Tuetelo.

The Manokin had a main Village that was at the Falls of the Susquehanna in what is now Somerset County Maryland. They were forced off their land and headed to the interior of Pennsylvania. Some went to the Ohio Valley and joined with the Iroquois. My mother stated to me that Grandpop Charles Martin often took the family to the Eastern Shore of Maryland. They spent summers fishing and crabbing while camped out along the river. The place they vacationed is where our Manokin Davis ancestor's village and hunting grounds were for thousands of years.

---

[23] Marye, W. (1938). The Wicomico Indians of Maryland. American Antiquity, 4(2), 146-152.

MINQUA UNAMI OKEHOCKING & THE DOWN RIVER NATIONS

The Davis, Johnson, Martin, Harris, Green and allied lines were in Delmarva (Delaware Maryland Virginia) and Eastern Pennsylvania for Thousands of years. In the Winter they traveled inland to what is now Bucks, Chester, Delaware, and Lancaster County. In 1702 William Penn set aside 500 acres of land for the Okehocking in Chester County some of which now sits in Delaware County.

The surnames of our Native Ancestors were assigned to them from various Christian Churches after they were Baptized. There was a period when Natives could not trade or do business unless they were Christened. There are grave markers at Saint John's Episcopal Church Compass Pa and several other churches in the area for our Martin ancestors. Some also intermarried with the Quakers in the region and are listed as members in the Philadelphia Quaker Meetings. Some of the Children from these unions were sent to Orphan Schools or Workhouses and the Adults were sent to Poor houses.

As a person of Afro/indigenous/European heritage genealogy and tracing our family history had numerous daunting challenges. I was told not to even attempt this feat since we have no history worth telling. That is exactly why I set out to document our family's history. The fact that anyone would tell an entire group they have no history is born of racism.

Trade and Wintering grounds sent many natives traveling thousands of miles outside of their "official" homelands. They often switched tribes, in one instance being a Mohican and another Mohawk. Tribal members were free to join any tribe they desired. The Mohawk considered themselves "Top Dogs" and often-sent Chiefs to rule in smaller villages in their name.

Their territory stretched as far west as the Mississippi, as far south as Kentucky and North to Canada. This is according to the Nanfan Treaty (of 1701), and map, which shows the territory of the Mohawk Nation. The Nanfan Treaty Map shows the Mohawk covered what is now Pennsylvania. It is helpful to remember that the boundaries of Native Tribes were changed by Europeans.

The Iroquois (Haudenosaunee) Confederacy were originally five independent nation states bound by a central constitution and a common set of laws. The five original nations unified under the Great

Tree of Peace and became the Iroquois Confederacy long before the arrival of Europeans. In 1722, the Tuscarora joined the Confederacy to form the Six Nations. Historically, the homeland of the Iroquois was in modern–day New York State and Pennsylvania, between the Hudson River Valley to the east and the Susquehanna River to the west.

The Conestoga Indians (Susquehanna) inhabited the Delaware Valley for thousands of years. The name Susquehanna translated means, "People of the Muddy River "(Susquehanna). They were also referred to as Black and/or white, Minqua, and eventually separated along racial lines. Another name given by Europeans was Conestoga (derived from Kanastoge), which the Conestoga Trail was named after. Conestoga was the name of the last Indian Village in Pennsylvania.

Their villages lined the Susquehanna River from Southern New York to Maryland. There were smaller tribes in the area like the Lenni Lenape, who are now referred to as the Delaware. These tribes did not have a concept of borders, or land ownership; they followed game, and moved from place to place freely. Warring tribes tended to stay away from each other and respected each other's sovereign rights. Eventually the Trail of Tears, disease, and attacks by settlers, caused the First Families of America (Natives), to decline in numbers.

Slaves escaping from Pennsylvania, and Southern States, ran to the mountains, with the assistance of Natives, then Europeans, and Free Blacks. Slavery was a foreign concept to Natives, who accepted conquered Tribes, as members of their Villages. To own another Human being, or even to own property was a foreign concept. The Whites who escaped into the mountains were usually Indentured Servants fleeing from abuse. This trio made up the Tri-Racial Isolates in the Welsh Mountain Region of Pennsylvania.

Although those on the Mountains had little education, were poor, and disenfranchised, they achieved racial harmony. They were a community in Pennsylvania made up of human beings whose contributions are yet to be recorded. The history is mostly oral and is often referred to as Myth and Folklore. One part of the history that is not folklore is that they owned that land, and that Henry Green my Great-Great Grandfather was in the Christiana Resistance and in the Civil War.

We know from the records of Thomas Green I (born about

1690), and his son Joseph Green (born about 1720), that they were in the region in the late 1600's. Land Warrants and Patents go back to the mid 1700's and show them as Landowners in Chester County. Benjamin Green, a Grandson of Thomas Green I, was granted Land for his participation in the War of 1812.

In 1820, there is a Ben Green living in Sudbury, Chester County PA wit; 1 free colored male under 14 (born 1806-1820); 1 free colored male 26-44(born 1776-1804); 2 free colored males over 45, (born before 1775) and 1 free colored female 14-25 (born 1795-1806).

Also, in 1820 there is a group of free blacks clustered together Jonathan Bosan, (Father of James Boson mulatto born 1815 in Lower Chanceford York PA 1850), Joseph Johnston, (1840 Norwegian Twp Schuylkill County PA), possible some went to Ontario), Jonathan Smith, James Shepard, and another Ben Green (b. abt. 1740). This Ben Green could be a brother to Thomas Green (I), or even a father to Ben Green II. He may be the Ben Green who fought in the Revolutionary War, out of Lancaster.

In the 1830 census for Salisbury Township, Lancaster County Pennsylvania, Benjamin Green II is listed as a "Free Colored Male", with three males under ten, five females, under ten, and one female, between twenty-four and thirty-five years old (also Free Colored). In the 1850 census, he is now sixty years old, and living in Colerain, with a wife named Sarah, who is identified as white and is forty-four years old, and a daughter named Effa Anne six years. She is my Great-Great-Great Grandmother who may have been a light skinned Native.

Benjamin is my Great-Great-Great Grandfather and the father of my Great-Great Grandfather Henry Davis Green. Henry is an important figure in history, as a participant in the Christiana Resistance and a Civil War Soldier. They are descendants of the Minqua Natives who inhabited the region for thousands of years. They did not just happen to be in the Mountains, although they mixed with others who were. There is a dearth of Quakers in my family who intermarried or intermixed into my Green, Davis, Johnson, and Martin lines.

In 1838, Benjamin Green was Baptized at St. Martin's Episcopal Church (at Marcus Hook Delaware County), along with a Harriet

Green and someone named Coombs, and all three were listed as, "Colored." This is the same Benjamin Green who was born in and resided in Salisbury Township Lancaster County. The Greens were listed as Mulatto (mixed raced), Colored, black, or Other Free. Yet, the oral tradition in our family is that they were Natives, who intermixed with Free Blacks and whites. In an article about Thomas (Tom) Green, written 1792, those on the Mountain are referred to as, "Negro/Indians".

The point of paper genocide was to disperse Natives and force them off the land. They were successful in that aspect and later the Covenant Conditions & Restrictions (CC&R's) kicked in. This is especially true when historians ignore the Oral Tradition. Some Genealogists and Historians are caught up in whether that person was identified as Native at the time of the census, when white census takers determined their race.

The records show some ancestors who start out as white, become, Mulatto, Colored, Negro, and then Black within their lifetime. We know that after the Lancaster City Massacre of 1763, no one was identified as Indian in the region. Some of my ancestors fled to Canada taking the same Underground Railroad as escaped slaves. They were not sedentary and had villages throughout the east including Ohio, New York, New Jersey, Delaware, Maryland, and Pennsylvania. If there was a River or Waterway Natives had a Village nearby.

Pequea Valley

The area now known as the Welsh Mountains are part of the Appalachian Chain. The Chain is a Mountain Range that stretches in a southwestern arc from the Newfoundland (Province of Canada) to Central Alabama. The Pequea Valley was originally in Chester County until the formation of Lancaster County. Paradise a town in Lancaster County runs through the Pequea Valley. The English translation of Pequea is, "Straight Arrow".

Shifting County Borders moved Native inhabitants from one county to the other. When York County was formed from Lancaster County, land owned by Joseph Green, became part of the Monmouth Settlement. Pequea Valley was a meeting place of the Great Valley for Natives until the land was taken from them. This from people who were themselves seeking freedom from poverty and persecution.

MINQUA UNAMI OKEHOCKING & THE DOWN RIVER NATIONS

Not one town or street is named after Chief Tanawa, the Last Indian Chief in the Region. He was one of Penn's Indians (under the protectorate of William Penn). One of the first statements mom made about our Pennsylvania Ancestors was that they were, "Penn's Indians."

At the time I had no idea what that meant but have since learned that they were granted land, and under the protectorate of William Penn. In fact, land granted to Thomas Green I, Joseph Green, and Samuel Green, was land patented and warranted, by Richard and Thomas Penn, sons of William Penn.

Boggs Township in York County was created in 1814 out of part of Spring Township, and was named for Andrew Boggs, the first white settler in what is now Centre County. The township was the location of two large early iron making operations: Milesburg Iron Works, built in 1795 by Samuel and Joseph Miles and Joseph Green; and the Eagle Iron Works, started as a forge in 1810 by Roland Curtin.[25]

Edgemont – Delaware County
- No 1. On a westerly branch of Ridley Creek, in Edgemont, a Sawmill, head and fall about 20 feet, owned, and occupied by
- George Green.

No 7. On the same branch (on an easterly branch of Chester Creek in Edgemont, a woolen factory, head and fall about 20 feet; owned by Robert Green, Esq. and occupied by Wm Owen and Co has 1 pair of stocks, 2 carding engines, 1 bill of 40 spindles, 2 jennies of 60 spindles each, and employs about 14 hands.
- George Green – Greens Run

In 1800 Great-Great-Great Grandfather George Green is listed in the Sussex County Delaware Census Records. In 1807 he is in Concord Delaware County running a Lumber Mill. In 1834 George Green signed a Bond to marry Lydia Davis, the daughter of Joseph and Hannah Underwood-Davis. The person who stood Bond for them had the last name McIlwaine. He was the Pastor of the Methodist Church in Sussex County , which is just across the river from Delaware

---

[25] Center County History, http://centrecountyhistory.org/history/newtour.html, November 12, 2021

County. It was not unusual for men to find wives within their own community in those days.

Census 1790 Bucks County Pennsylvania (Other Free)
- Green, Charles 5, Bucks County
- Green, Isaac 1, Bucks County
- Green, Marshall 4, Bucks County
- Green, George 1800 Sussex County Delaware Indian River Hundred
- Indian Slaves in Pennsylvania

Indian Slaves were lumped in with black slaves, and there is no way to count their numbers in Pennsylvania. African Slaves were working in the Delaware Valley as early as 1639. More slaves were transported to the region when Settlers contracted with the West Indian Company. Pennsylvania's reasoning was that the Colony needed cheap and free labor to work for Agriculture purposes.

The demand for slaves continued when the English assumed rule in 1664. The town magistrates of New Castle (in modern Delaware), then the major settlement of the region, petitioned, "that liberty of trade may have granted us with the neighboring Colony of Maryland for supplying us with Negroes, "Without which we cannot subsist."

The leading men of the colony owned them. Penn's own deputy, Governor William Markham, owned one, born in 1700, which, by the terms of Markham's Will, was to be freed at the age of twenty-five. In a bill of sale of the personal effects of Sir William Keith, dated May 26, 1726, an Indian woman and her son were mentioned among the seventeen slaves listed.

In 1780, a farmer of East Nottingham, Chester County, registered, at the county seat, the names of an Indian girl, aged twenty-five years, and a slave for life, and of an Indian man in slavery until he arrived at the age of thirty-one years. The action of the Friends' Yearly Meeting in 1719, also, shows that the members of that religious society owned Indian slaves, as well as Negro slaves.[26]

Once slavery ended in Pennsylvania, many of the formerly

---

[26] Columbia Spy: Feb 2,1884, pg. 3, Columbia: PA

enslaved Natives and Free blacks remained in the area. In census records, some are labelled as mulatto, colored, Negro, and/or black. The Indian and Negro Slaves worked together on Farms and Factories in the area. They intermixed and married creating the Negro/Indian mix in the Welsh Mountains. The Quakers also intermarried the Indians and Negroes who were formerly enslaved.

The Okehocking Tract

The Okehocking Tract is now located in Ridley Park, Williston, and the Westtown areas on the border of Delaware and Chester County. Growing up Mom told us about our grandfather Martins side of the family who referred to as Penn's Indians and had hunting and fishing rights throughout Pennsylvania. Our Great-Great Uncle and Great Grandfathers were even named William Penn Martin. She also said that our Native lines were connected to, "Indian" Hanna who was called the "Last" Indian in Pennsylvania.

This is what my mother told me about the "Last" Indian in Pennsylvania Indian Hannah Freeman. They gave her that name, but Hanna is a common name among Natives in my family even in Virginia where I have a Native ancestor, whose tribe was on the Rappahannock, and they called her Hanna. My mother said that Indian Hannah was Susquehanna and yet whites say she is Lenape. Her father and brothers left and never returned and may have been killed in Massacres. which tells me that they were probably killed.

In 1765 not that far from where Indian Hannah lived there was a massacre of Conestoga women children and elderly in Lancaster County. They too were tributary to the Susquehanna, and I wonder if Indian Hannah even knew about their murders. According to Marsh, the Indian Hannah story served the purpose of white conquest. First, it confirmed the property rights of those who took her land. Second, it flatters their descendants that William Penn's "Holy Experiment" was really better than what happened in other colonies.

Born in Chester County about 1730, Hannah had some other name as a child, but it doesn't seem to have been recorded. Freeman was a surname occasionally assumed by freed African slaves. Native Americans sometimes acquired English names when converting to Christianity or to commemorate a relationship, but neither applied to

Freeman.

The name Hannah, however, is more revealing. It was one of the most popular female names among local Quakers. In the Lenape language, it translates as "river." (Susquehanna, for instance, translates as muddy river). Hannah spent most of her life living along the Brandywine Creek. Freeman's mother was named Sarah, but they do not talk about what happened to her. There were also two younger brothers — both, like Hannah, born along Bennett's Run, a small tributary of the Brandywine that flows east from a point near Longwood Gardens.

Her Grandmother Jane, maternal aunts Betty and Nanny, and Freeman's father — whose name is unknown — rounded out the family. When Freeman was a young woman — say, about 1750 — life for the family took an abrupt turn. There is a suggestion that the other members of the village died, and Sarah was the only one left. By 1750 Natives in my family were being called Mulatto or Colored. So, did her mother and Aunts fade into the Mulatto *and* Colored Community?

The truth is that Hannah was not the last Indian in Pennsylvania we were and are still represented in Pennsylvania. So, no Indian Hannah was not the "Last" Indian in Pennsylvania. A stroke of a Pen and words on a document do not wipe out 20000 years of living on our ancestral lands. The state designated Natives as either Mulatto Colored Negro Black and/or White. In fact, our racial identity and rights to land were erased by the State of Pennsylvania. When the ancestors returned to their Homeland it was to work on the Farms of those who now occupied the stolen land.

The State did nothing to prevent Natives from being pushed off their land not only in Chester County but in Lancaster and Delaware County. There exist an 1800 Conestoga Land Grant that was set aside by William Penn that they were chased off or fled under the threat of violence. We had no control over the racial classification of Indian being removed from census records.

That was not our ancestors leaving the land it was their identity being erased by the Colonial Government. This was a common practice in the Thirteen Original Colonies and not unique to Pennsylvania. Long before the Revolutionary War and before the Colonies were States our ancestors were being dispersed and displaced from their land.

Our Green ancestors went into the Welsh Mountains where they owned the land but were still targeted by Sheriffs' and Law enforcement in the surrounding communities. The land was taken and some of them repurchased it and it was taken again. So, they worked on farms in the area along with slaves, free blacks and others who were disenfranchised.

George Green my Great-Great-Great Grandfather owned a Paper Mill in what is now Ridley Park. He travelled back and forth between Sussex County Delaware and Chester County. George Green married Lydia Davis, the daughter of Joseph and Hannah Underwood-Davis, in Sussex County Delaware in 1834. They are the parents of our direct ancestor Susannah Green-Brown who was raised in Delaware County.

However, the census records clearly show that they were moving back and forth on the Great Minqua Path. Just as Europeans have Summer Homes and Town Homes and so did Natives. Had it not been for mom passing the history orally we would have no knowledge of our history.

It is highly insulting for historians to continue to state that Natives abandoned their land because we have never left. Our mother and her father and his parents and their parents before them were near their Ancestral Homeland. I was raised there and most of the family continues to live in that region. Our indigenous ancestors were run off their land by Settlers who with the backing of the State terrorized and massacred the ones they could not assimilate. They stole the land and Natives were left with a Bible and Spirits in a Bottle (Whiskey).

The colony of Pennsylvania passed laws that gave no consideration for indigenous peoples not even allowing them to grow their staple crops like corn to feed themselves and their village. They were forcefully assimilated, Christened and made to accept Christian names some of which are: Green, Johnson, Davis, Paige and Martin.

Our Okehocking and Minqua ancestors lived on the land together and the "Great Minqua Trail" runs through the land ceded back to them in 1704. The Native People were the originators of those trails for thousands of years prior to the founding of the and were

Colonies. They moved freely between what is now Maryland, Delaware, and Virginia.

As borders changed or were created the tribes were squeezed further inward and off their tribal lands. The people never left and are today still living around the land ceded back to ancestors by William Penn in 1701. He stated that the land was to remain in their possession and use forever.

But whites' settlers using their guns took the land and no one came to rescue Natives. Colonization has left indigenous peoples land-less paying rent just to live in and on our own land. What is glaring is that much of the land they hold is empty, and it is almost like the land was taken just so Natives would be landless.

Our Green ancestors went into the Welsh Mountains where they owned land but were still targeted by Sheriffs and Law enforcement in the surrounding communities. They worked on farms in the area as did our Martin ancestors and our Great Grandfather William Penn Martin who was a Rancher who worked for King Ranch. He worked on the same land that was set aside by William Penn for the Okehocking. He also worked for the Quaker Darlington's for many years. His father and mother Uriah and Tamzine Paige Martin were married at Atglen and lived in Avondale which also sits on the Okehocking Land Grant.

Our Green and Davis Ancestors had a Paper Mill in what is now Ridley Park. George Green our fifth Great Grandfather and his forebearers traveled back and forth between Sussex County Delaware and Chester County. George Green married Lydia Davis, the daughter of Joseph and Hannah Collins-Davis, in Sussex County Delaware in 1834. They are the parents of our direct ancestor Susannah Green who was raised in Delaware County. What is difficult is making the connection when Indigenous names were changed.

Okehocking and Minqua ancestors lived on the land together and the "Great Minqua Trail" runs through the land ceded back to them in 1701. The Native People used that trail for thousands of years prior to the founding of the 13 colonies and were moving freely between what is now Maryland, Delaware, and Virginia.

The borders divided Native Villages further and they were pushed further from their tribal lands. Once the racial classifications changed it did not matter whether they stayed or left. Under reclassification our people never left and remained as Mulatto, Colored Negro, black and/or white. Descendants are today still living around the land ceded back to our ancestors by William Penn in 1701. He stated that the land was to remain in their possession and use for descendants forever. What is glaring is that the land is empty or owned by the State or a Corporation.

The Great Minqua Path begins on the Shores of the Delaware River, winds through Philadelphia and into the Interior of Lancaster County. It snakes through, Berks County, Bucks County, Delaware County, Chester County, and Lancaster County. It not only led to the interior but also connected to other paths and trails leading North to Canada and South through the Appalachian Mountains.

Many of the same trails were part of the Underground Railroad, a means of freedom for escaping slaves. The Minqua Path continues to exist, as Highways and Byways from Philadelphia into Lancaster County. In Chester County, it is now known as Lincoln Highway, but was formerly known as the Kings Highway and the Old Philadelphia Pike. Lincoln Highway has the distinction of being the first road across America. It is over 3000 miles long, stretching from coast-to-coast, from New York City to San Francisco.

It has taken quite a while to show where they were, but patterns have emerged, showing who was where and when. Documents including Census, Land Records and Wills show the Greens living all along the Great Minqua Path. There appears to be two sets of Green's who merged, with the marriage of our Great-Great Grandparents Henry and Susan Green. They were the parents of George Green II, Great Grandmother, Lydia Green-Martin, (direct ancestor), and Clara Green. Delaware Davis-Green Lines.

Prior to the 1800's the parents of Lydia Davis-Green, and her future husband, George Green resided in Indian River Hundred Sussex County Delaware. Lydia was born there in 1808, eight years after George Green was listed in the Sussex County Census. George and Lydia (Davis-Green), married in 1834, and by 1850, they were living (or working) in Concord Twp., Delaware County Pennsylvania. The parents of Lydia, Joseph and Hannah Underwood-Davis, left

Delaware sometime around 1850, and lived in Concord Township.

Besides owning a Lumber Mill Great-Great-Great Grandfather, George Green also owned businesses in the area with Abel Green and a Robert Green esquire. The Sussex County Green and Davis lines intermarried with the Chester and Lancaster County Green Line. The surname they carried was given to the Natives when they were "Christened" and may not mean there are close blood ties.

In Bucks County Isaac and Charles Green were listed as "Other Free" on the 1790 Census. Isaac Green and his family are living in Concord Delaware County in 1850 (according to the Census), and living with his family, was eleven-year-old Susanna Green. This same Susanna was the future wife of Henry Green (about 1860), and the daughter of George and Lydia Davis-Green.

She is also my Great-Great Grandmother and was the only person living in Isaac Green's Household, listed as being born in Delaware . She is listed as Susan Brown on her marriage certificate to Henry Green which may mean he was not her first husband. Henry was also married previously to a woman named Elizabeth and after Susan to Catherine Harris.

In 1800, George Green (Susanna Green's father), was listed as a resident in the Sussex County Delaware Census, and by 1834, he and Lydia Davis married. In 1854, he is listed as the owner of a Lumber Mill in Concord Delaware County, along what is now Ridley Creek. Also listed in the census are Lydia Davis-Greens' Parents, Joseph and Hannah Davis, whose child Lydia was born in Sussex County, Delaware in 1808.

A Settlement of Nanticoke, had a Village at Indian River Hundred, in Sussex County. Some of the surnames of the Nanticoke, are Davis, Harmon, Hall, Jackson, Johnson, Sammon, Harmon, Wright, Mosley, Thompson, Socum, Ridgeway, Prettyman, Morris, Street, Sterret, and Green.

In Maryland Census Records of the 1690's, there are Davis Surnames, listed as Manokin, in Somerset County. Native Americans first inhabited Delaware more than 14,000 years ago. They lived and hunted along the many tributaries and bays in the county. They travelled to the interior for the Winter Months staying near caves and water ways. The cycle could include a village for ever season as the followed fish and game.

Davis Ancestors Surnames with the notation of Manokin:
- DAVIS, Lydia   1692/10/07 IKL   b to Nathaniel & Lydia; Manokin
- DAVIS, Martha   1670/09/14 IKL   b to William & Anne; Manokin
- DAVIS, Mary   1674/03/16 IKL   b to James & Margaret; Manokin
- DAVIS, 1684/03/18 IKL   b to Nathaniel & Lydia; Manokin
- DAVIS, Rachel   1673/01/02 IKL   b to James & Margaret; Manokin

Green Connections – Delaware to Pennsylvania

Further up the road in Chester County were another, separate line of Green Ancestors, beginning with a Henry Green (I), in 1668. Land Records from the Chester County Archives, mention a Henry Green owning Land in 1668. He appears to be old enough to be the father of Thomas Green (I), who was born about 1680. He owned land which eventually was ceded to Chester and Delaware County. In 1705, Henry Green, the infant son of Thomas Green was baptized at St. Paul's Episcopal Church in Chester County PA.

"Infant, Henry, The Son of Thomas Green of Concord was Baptized the Twenty Fifth Day of November – 1705.[27]

The Church Wardens of St. Paul were William Pickle and Thomas Powell. Henry and Thomas were common names in that line of our Green Family, and this Henry may have been a son of Thomas Green I. There is no mention of Henry in the Will Thomas I left, which means Henry may have died before Thomas (who was deceased abt. 1737).

I did not find Benjamin Green, in The State of Delaware, but he was in Concord twp., at the same time as George and Isaac Green. Benjamin Green's son, Henry Green (Great-Great Grandfather), married the daughter of George and Lydia Davis-Green (Great-Great Grandmother). There is a discrepancy because her last name on her

---

[27] PA Church and Town Records, St. Paul's Episcopal Church Concord Twp., Chester County - 1705

death certificate was Brown. She was the daughter of George and Lydia Davis-Green.

Henry had another wife named Elizabeth with whom he had a daughter named Mary. His daughter Mary married a Brown who was quite a bit older and a Boarder in Henry and Elizabeth's home. He was 20 years old when the daughter was 12 and several years later, she was his wife. It is possible that Mary filled out Susan's death Certificate and listed her as a Brown. It may have been to cover up a relationship between Henry and Lydia who both had the same last name. Finding the Baptism of my Davis and Green lines gives some clue as to where they were along The Great Minqua Path. The surnames were given to Native People by Europeans and did not mean they were related.

The Shawnee at Pequea

In 1697, the Shawnee received permission from the Susquehanna Indians and William Penn to locate along the Pequea Creek in Lancaster County. The Chief of the Shawnee was Opessah and they remained at that location for Thirty-Five years. There was a Shawnee town in Sadsbury township, on the Octorara Creek, about two miles above the site of Christiana. Great-Great Grandfather William Penn Martin (named after his uncle), was born in Christiana in 1860. His parents were Uriah and Tamzin Page-Martin both of whom worked on farms in Lancaster County as did Uriah's father Charles Martin.

Although the numbers of Indians of the Lower Eastern Shore of Maryland dwindled dramatically during the late 16th through early 18th centuries due to diseases such as smallpox brought by the English, the wars with the English, and migrations out of the area, what finally destroyed the Indian culture as a whole was the encroachment of the English who were intent on building a plantation society.

The settlement of the English on large tracts of land left no room for the Indians who lived on the land for thousands of years. Court cases in Maryland between the English and Indians appear in increased frequency from the 1660s, and the final judgments and orders show a bias in favor of the English. By the end of the 17th century and into the early 18th century, for the Indians that survived, the obvious choice was to find a home elsewhere and migrate out of the area"[28]

In the early 18th Century, the Maryland Assembly set aside land for three reservations. Three thousand acres were set aside for the Nanticoke on Broad Creek along the river and creek areas. This helped at first, but it disrupted the seasonal hunting of the Nanticoke who needed to travel between their traditional winter hunting grounds and their spring and summer farming & fishing sites.

Remaining year round on the reservation severely restricted food and shelter. Traditionally, Indians moved away from the shores and went inland before the cold of winter came. Furthermore, Maryland authorities included a stipulation that the only way the Nanticoke could legally retain reservation lands was if they agreed not to leave.

Again, the Nanticoke leaders petitioned the authorities for temporary permission to leave during winter months to hunt. Finally, Maryland authorities agreed, but when the Nanticoke returned the following spring, they found homesteads on their land by squatters who assumed ownership by "right of occupancy."

Trespassers also destroyed reservation land by harvesting large amounts of timber. While visiting the reservations, traders brought liquor to exchange for furs. The Indians, who had never had alcoholic beverages, often awoke to find they had traded valuable furs for more liquor, instead of tools, clothing, and goods.[8]

There is a lot of folklore about the inhabitants on the Mountain and their marital status or lack thereof. In fact, there were miscegenation laws in Pennsylvania, which prohibited marriage between whites and Negroes. It was called, "An Act for the better Regulation of Negroes".

Early on there was intermixing between Natives and Whites. However, the children of those unions would have been considered white, or if dark enough Mulatto. The laws were like Virginia's Miscegenation Law which labelled Natives as Mulatto. Virginia's

---

[28] Richardson, Christine, Nabb Research Center General Resces - People & Cultures; Native Americans of the Delmarva peninsula; The Indians of the Lower Eastern Shore, http://nabbhistory.salisbury.edu/resces/profiles/shoreindians.html, November 3, 2012

ANITA L. WILLS

Negro Registries are available to researchers, in State and County Archives, not so with Pennsylvania. That is a valuable resource for those of us who are seeking answers.

The law set especially high penalties for free blacks who harboured runaway slaves or received property stolen from masters. The penalties in such cases were potentially much higher than those applied to whites, and if the considerable fines that might accrue could not be paid, the justices had the power to order a free black person put into servitude.

Under other provisions of the 1725-26 act, free negroes who married whites were to be sold into slavery for life; for mere fornication or adultery involving blacks and whites, the penalty for the black person was to be sold as a servant for seven years. Whites in such cases faced different or lighter punishment. The law effectively blocked marriage between the races in Pennsylvania, but fornication continued, as the state's burgeoning mulatto population attested.

Other colonial Pennsylvania laws forbade blacks from gathering in "tippling-houses," carrying arms, or assembling in companies. These, however, were loosely or unevenly enforced. But throughout PA colony, the children of free blacks, were bound out by the local justices of the peace until age 24 (if male) or 21 (if female). All in all, the "free" blacks of colonial PA led severely circumscribed lives; they had no control even over their own family arrangements, and they could be put back into servitude for "laziness" or petty crimes, at the mercy of the local authorities.

Those laws affected those who lived on the Mountain, whether they were free or slave. Those Mulattoes on the Mountain were considered born out of the law (illegitimate), and therefore subject to how little control our ancestors had over their lives. This is the law the People of the Mountains lived under the Colony of Pennsylvania, and why the Mountains were closed to outsiders. Yet through all the obstacles against them, the Green Lines have reaped the most colorful characters.

They were the Indian/Negroes who are documented as far back as the 1600's, in the Pequea Valley. The oldest of the male line is a Thomas Green (I), who was born sometime in the late or mid 1600's. He died in 1737 and left land and property to his wife and adult children. In 1658 there is mention of a Thomas Green owning land in Delaware County.

Also mentioned in Chester County records was Joseph Green, who was named in Thomas' (I), Will as an heir. Joseph was listed as a Landowner in Chester and Lancaster County in 1737, as was Samuel Green. Thomas Green's son, Thomas (II), was mentioned in his Will, along with Moses, Joseph, and Samuel. By 1792, Tom (II), was a grown man living in the Welsh Mountains.

Tom II was featured in an article, which ran in 1792, in the Philadelphia Gazette, a Newspaper founded by Benjamin Franklin. The article described Tom Green as a Big Burly Negro, and the Leader of Green's Banditti. This reporter came from Philadelphia and went into the Welsh Mountains to confront Tom Green. He celebrates the fact that Tom "Got His due" when he was killed by a Waggoner. Then folks wonder why they isolated themselves in the Mountains!

It appears that, Tom Green Junior, (born about 1730), was the father of Benjamin Green II, (born about 1792), and the grandfather of Henry Green. However, there was a Ben Green living in Sadsbury Twp., in the Mid 1700's, a man of Color, old enough to be Benjamin Green's father. Given that the brothers named children after their siblings that may not be the case. Joseph Green was more than likely the brother mentioned in Thomas I, 1747 Will. Thomas Green (II) was mentioned in an article published in the Philadelphia Gazette in 1792, when he was an adult. According to the reporter, Tom was killed by a Waggoner a few years after the article ran.

"In the Philadelphia Gazette, there was printed a notice which warned travelers' on the State Road near the Gap in Lancaster County that they were liable to be attacked by "Green's Banditti". Tom Green, a burly Negro, was the leader of this Band. A few years later, he received his death wound in a desperate encounter with a Waggoner whom he had attacked, but his wife and family survived him, and his name has been perpetrated to this day." [29]

The article puts Tom Green and his family, in the Welsh Mountains in the late 1700's. The land records for patents and

---

29 Pennsylvania Gazette, published at Philadelphia in 1792

warrants also name Tom and Joseph as landowners, and not, as some have inferred, squatters. The article ran in 1790, two years before Benjamin Green, his son, was born. Joseph Green is mentioned in records with Tom and in 1822, with Benjamin. There is no mention of who Thomas' (II), wife was, but the mention of family means there were children and other family members. Generations of family tended to live together on the Mountains.

The newspapers of the day referred to the residents on the Mountain as a mixture of Indian/Negro. All Freemen (Yeomen) who owned land were required to volunteer for the Militia. Joseph and Thomas Green were part of the Lancaster County Militia during the Revolutionary War for Mt. Joy Township. Joseph for 9th (Hanover Twp.), Battalion, 2nd Company, under Capt. Abraham Scott.

Thomas (Tom) Green was on the list for the 7th Battalion (Mt. Joy Twp.), 2nd Company, under Capt. Abraham Scott. The documents show that both were residing in Mt. Joy, the area where they owned land. Tom and Joseph Green remained on Inactive Militia Status.

The Warrants and Patents naming Thomas Green were signed by Richard, John, and Thomas Penn. Thomas Green is the oldest ancestor, and purchased Warranted Land in the Pequea Valley (Chester County), in the early 1700's. Once Lancaster County was formed, his land was ceded to the new County. He left a will in 1737 naming his wife Ann as executor and his heirs, including my direct ancestor, Thomas Green.

MINQUA UNAMI OKEHOCKING & THE DOWN RIVER NATIONS

By the Proprietaries.

Pennsylvania, ſſ.

AT the Request of *Thomas Green* of the County of *Lancaster* that We would grant *him* to take up *two hundred & fifty* Acres of Land lying on a Branch of *Pequea* in the said County of *Lancaster* for which *He* agrees to pay to our Use at the Rate of *Fifteen Pounds ten Shillings* current Money of this Province for One hundred Acres, and the yearly Quit-rent of *a halfpenny Sterling* for every Acre thereof; THESE are to authorize and require thee to survey or cause to be survey'd unto the said *Thomas Green* at the Place aforesaid, according to the Method of Townships appointed, the said Quantity of *250* Acres that hath not been already survey'd or appropriated, and make Return thereof into the Secretary's Office, in order for a further Confirmation; which Survey, in case the said *Thomas Green* shall fulfil the above Agreement within *Six* Months from the Date hereof, shall be valid, otherwise to be void. GIVEN under my Hand, and the lesser Seal of our Province, at *Philadelphia*, this *twenty first* Day of *January* Anno Dom. 1733.

To *Benjamin Eastburn*, Surveyor General.

Copy of Deed for Thomas Green in the County of Lancaster (Pa)

Mt. Holly School (Pa) for Coloured Children built on Land owned by our Ancestors

1850 Delaware County (Pa) Census Green, Isaac and Lydia (son and daughter of George and Lydia Davis-Green)
Marcus Hook Delaware County

Although they lived in Lancaster County, Benjamin Green and Joseph Green were Merchants who purchased goods in Philadelphia and sold them in Lancaster. In 1822 Benjamin and Joseph were cited for selling Goods in Lancaster City without a License. Benjamin was born about 1790 to Thomas Green, in Lancaster County. The pastor noted that Benjamin Green was Colored on his daybook. Following are excerpts about the history of Marcus Hook, Delaware County.

"The Leni Lenape (Delaware) Indians erected several semi-permanent villages in the area; occupancy was seasonal, tied to fishing or hunting cycles with some farming. The Sachem Naaman

A network of trails utilized the ridge lines to connect these villages and the main "Swedes' Path" (now U.S. Route 13) and "Minqua Path". The European settlers adapted these routes to be the first roads surveyed in the Township, and they still are the principal local highways. The "Old Chi Chester and Bethel" (now Larkin Road, "Old Concord Road" (now Chi Chester Avenue) and Poulson (now Blueball) Road were laid out in the first decade of English settlement.

The Marcus Hook area of the Delaware River Waterfront has attracted settlement since the movement of the Leni Lenape into this region. Reputedly, the town derives its name from a major Indian Settlement, which became a Swedish trading outpost and colonization site in the 1640s.

A report by the Swedish Commissary Huddie, dated 1645, speaks of two principal villages on the west bank of the Delaware: "Maarte" and "Wissenmenet." The word "Hook" meant a point of land and presumably refers to the natural harbor formed below Marcus Hook then Chi Chester Creek.

During colonial times Marcus Hook served as the first port of call for Philadelphia and rivaled Chester in size. It briefly became a notorious haven for pirates in the early 18 century, the most famous cutthroat being Edward Teach, "Blackbeard." The waterfront (now approximately 2 blocks inland) remained an infamous neighborhood because of the many taverns along Discord Lane (present Second Street). The ship-building industry here was started before 1750 and was well-known for coastal traders and herring sloops.

As a settlement, which spans the three hundred and fifty years of European settlement, Marcus Hook has welcomed many races and religions. Saint Martin's Church was founded in 1699 (and opened for worship in 1702) by a bequest of local resident Walter Martin to provide an alternative place of worship and burial for non- Quakers."[30]

Report of Delaware County PA Concord Twp.

"Although the land thus conveyed is in Chester township, being part of the Green and Carter farms lying along Chester Creek, the

---

[30] Record of Upland Ct, pp. 149 and 150. Chapter XXXV South Chester Borough, http://www.delcohistory.org/ashmead/ashmead_pg435.htm

record is interesting, as therein occurs, as before stated, the first reference to Lamokin, which is traditionally asserted to be an Indian word signifying "the Kiss of the Waters." The accuracy of this derivation we have no means of ascertaining.

The land lying between Chester and Marcus Hook was, early in the last century, very thinly settled, and the public duty of maintaining the King's Highway through that section pressed so heavily upon the people. At court held Aug. 28, 1707, was presented an "application of the overseers and Inhabitants of the West side of Chester Creek, that the road there are very burdensome and chargeable to them in regard to their small number, and requesting the Court would appoint the inhabitants on the East side of the said creek to aid and assist them in mending and repairing the Bottoms and low grounds in the Road to Chi Chester, so far as their township goes, promising them to maintain and hereafter to keep all the said road."[31]

In 1799 Cornelius Green and John Green were Mulattoes taxable in Edgemont. Cornelius served in the Revolutionary War out of Lancaster County. He and John (Possibly a brother) were Millwrights at Edgemont. Millwrights were the Engineers of their time. They handled the axe, hammer, and plane, with equal skill and precision.

They could calculate the velocities, strength, and power of machines. This was a labour-intensive occupation, which included constructing buildings, conduits, and water cases. A Millwright was a person capable of designing, assembling, and adjusting new machinery. A person who could make it work commercially without excessive breakdowns. Unschooled, apprenticed, and self-taught the millwright knew the architecture and the layout of different size and types of mills.

Cornelius Green a Mulatto worked at George Green's Mill after his Revolutionary War Service. His son Cornelius Junior was in the Civil War out of Chester County and is buried there.

Chester County Deeds – Green Surnames

---

[31] Report of the Committee of Delaware County, on the Subject of Manufactories, unimproved Mill Seats, & C. in said County, 1826

- Green Joseph East Caln et. al. Richard Downing West Nantmeal 1767 Mortgage P 85
- Green Robert East Fallowfield John Truman Fallowfield Deed K.2 151
- Green Robert Westtown 1795 Release M.2 524
- Green Robert Birmingham, Ann Nathaniel Hollingsworth Goshen 1796 Deed N.2 66
- Green Thomas Concord et. al. John Moore Concord 1707 Deed B 284
- Green Thomas East Caln William Branson East Caln 1752 Mortgage H 263
- Green Thomas East Caln Mary William Branford East Caln 1758 Deed O 243
- Green Thomas East Caln Joseph Green West Nantmeal 1767 Deed A.2 268
- Green Thomas East Caln William Green West Nantmeal 1767 Deed A.2 268
- Green Thomas Edgemont Catharine James Hunter Edgemont Mortgage S 62
- Green Thomas Middletown Catharine Nicholas Wollis Edgemont 1774 Deed B.2 448

Report of the Committee of Delaware County 1826 Upper Chi Chester

- No 1 On Green's Creek, a branch of the west branch of Chester Creek in Aston, a Grist mill and a Sawmill, embracing the waters of both branches, head and fall 17 or 18 feet; owned by Wm. Peters; grinds from 6 to 10,000 bushels of grain, and saws about 50,000 ft of lumber per annum.
- No 8 On Chester Creek, above the West Branch, in Middletown and Aston, a Mill seat, fall of water 9 or 10 feet, owned by William Martin and Joseph W. Smith
- No 9 On Chester Creek, in Aston, a Stone Cotton factory, 35 by 55 feet, 3 stories high, head and fall 16 feet; owned by William Martin and Joseph W. Smith and occupied by William Martin.

CONCORD (Delaware County Pa)

- No 1 on a southerly branch of the west branch of Chester Creek, in Concord, a Sawmill, head and fall about 12 feet; owned and occupied by John Myers
- No 3 On Green's Creek, in Concord, a Woolen factory, head and fall about 20 feet; owned by John Hannum and occupied by John Jones: has 1 pair of stocks, 2 carding engines, 1 bill of 36 spindles, 1 jenny of 50 spindles, employs from 3 – 5 hands, principally work for the neighbors.
- No 9 On the west branch of Chester Creek, in Concord, a Bark mill, head and fall 20 feet; owned and occupied by Thomas Marshall
- No 10 On the west branch of Chester Creek, in Concord, a Sawmill, head and fall about 10 feet; owned and occupied by Abraham Sharpless
- No 11 On the West Branch of Chester Creek, in Concord, a Stone Grist mill, head and fall 22 feet; owned and occupied by John Newlin; grinds from 10 – 15,000 bushels of grain per annum.

EDGMONT
- No 1 On a westerly branch of Ridley creek, in Edgemont, a Sawmill, head and fall about 20 feet, owned, and occupied by George Green.
- No 7. On the same branch (on an easterly branch of Chester Creek in Edgemont, a woolen factory, head and fall about 20 feet; owned by Robert Green, Esq. and occupied by Wm Owen and Co has 1 pair of stocks, 2 carding engines, 1 bill of 40 spindles, 2 jennies of 60 spindles each, and employs about 14 hands.
- No 8 On Chester Creek, above the West Branch, in Middletown and Aston, a Mill seat, fall of water 9 or 10 feet, owned by William Martin and Joseph W. Smith.
- No 10 On Chester Creek, in Middletown and Aston, a Mill seat, on lands of Abraham Pennell and Israel Taylor.
- No 11 On Chester Creek, in Middletown and Aston, a Mill seat

on lands of Abraham Pennell, fall of water about 9 feet.

> G | 32 | U.S.C.T.
>
> Henry Green.
> Appears with rank of Private on Muster and Descriptive Roll of a Detachment of U. S. Vols. forwarded for the 32 Reg't U. S. Col'd Infantry. Roll dated Lancaster Pa. Sept. 9, 1864.
> Where born Lancaster Co. Pa.
> Age 34 y'rs; occupation Laborer.
> When enlisted Sept. 1, 1864.
> Where enlisted Lancaster Pa.
> For what period enlisted 1 years.
> Eyes Black; hair Black
> Complexion Black; height 5 ft. 11 1/2 in.
> When mustered in Sept. 1, 1864.
> Where mustered in Lancaster Pa.
> Bounty paid $ 100; due $ 100 100
> Where credited East Earl Twp. 17° Sub. Dist Lan, Co. 9" Cong. Dist Pa.
> Company to which assigned
> Remarks: Anchor in blue on each forearm.
> Book mark:
>
> (340) Palmer, Copyist

Henry Green is described as Black here while on other documents he is described as Mulatto. His father Benjamin was described as Mulatto and his mother Sarah as White. If a Mulatto was light enough, they could and often did pass for white for economic reasons.

```
                                                        Inactive Duty
                                                            Militia
              GREEN, BENJAMIN
                                                    Rank
              BUCKS                                             2ND
Lieutenancy ................................................County. Battalion.........
              RICHLAND TWP.
Company .......................................................Class.........
Remarks: ..... FINED FOR LAST HALF 1780
         FINE BK.                       1780
Authority: Unit Muster Roll for the period ...................
                           N.D.                         56.5.0
[Certified .............. Dated ............... Muster Fines £ ........ ]

"Military Accounts: Militia," Records of the Comptroller General, at D. P. R.

          THE BASIC RECORD DOES NOT PROVE ACTIVE DUTY.
MA-8-10M.
```

Benjamin Green I was the grandfather of Henry Green and was called up for the Revolutionary War.

Chronological Genealogy – Green Davis Ancestors

Anita Baxter Wills (b. 1946), Coatesville Chester County PA; Daughter of, George (b. 1918, Orangeburg SC), and Vivian Martin Baxter (b. 1923, (Coatesville Chester County PA); Daughter of Charles (b. 1884, Chester County PA) and Leah Ruth Martin (b. 1884, Chester County PA); Son of William (b. 1862, Chester County PA), and Lydia Green-Martin, (b. 1862, Nine Points Lancaster County PA); Son of Uriah (b. abt. 1833, Chester County PA), and Tamyzine Paige Martin (b. abt. 1840, Bucks County PA); daughter of Henry, (b. 1828 Lancaster County Salisbury Twp., PA and), and Susanna Brown- Green, (b. abt. 1835, Indian River Hundred Sussex County); Daughter of George (b. abt. 1780, Indian River Hundred Sussex County DE), [parents unknown] and Lydia Davis-Green, (b. 1808, Indian River Hundred Sussex County DE) Daughter of Joseph (b. abt. 1770, Sussex County DE), and Hannah Underwood-Davis, (b. abt. 1780, Sussex County DE); Son of Benjamin (b. 1792, Lancaster County PA), and Sarah Garver-Green (b. 1805), Son of Thomas Green II (b. abt. 1740), Lancaster County PA, and Unknown Wife; Son of Thomas Green I (b. abt. 1680), and wife Anne (?), (b. abt. 1690, Chester County PA; Son of Henry Green (b. abt. 1640, and unknown wife), Chester County PA;

BUREAU OF INDIAN AFFAIRS
REQUEST FOR CERTIFICATE OF DEGREE OF INDIAN OR ALASKA NATIVE BLOOD

Requester's Name (list all names by which Requester is or has been known):		Requester's Address (including zip code):		Date Received by Bureau of Indian Affairs:
Requester's Date of Birth:	Father's name: Tribe: Roll No.: DOB: Deceased ☐ Yes ☐ No Year	Paternal Grandfather's Name: Tribe: Roll No: DOB: Deceased/Year	Paternal Great Grandfather's Name: Tribe: Roll No: DOB: Deceased/Year	
Requester's Place of Birth:			Paternal Great Grandmother's Name: Tribe: Roll No: DOB: Deceased/Year	
Is Requester Adopted? ☐ Yes ☐ No		Paternal Grandmother's Name: Tribe: Roll No: DOB: Deceased/Year	Paternal Great Grandfather's Name: Tribe: Roll No: DOB: Deceased/Year	
Are Requester's Parents Adopted? ☐ Yes ☐ No			Paternal Great Grandmother's Name: Tribe: Roll No: DOB: Deceased/Year	
If Yes, list natural (birth) parents: (If known)	Mother's Name: Tribe: Roll No.: DOB: Deceased ☐ Yes ☐ No Year	Maternal Grandfather's Name: Tribe: Roll No: DOB: Deceased/Year	Maternal Great Grandfather's Name: Tribe: Roll No: DOB: Deceased/Year	
Tribe(s) with which Requester is enrolled:			Maternal Great Grandmother's Name: Tribe: Roll No: DOB: Deceased/Year	
Roll Nos:		Maternal Grandmother's Name: Tribe: Roll No: DOB: Deceased/Year	Maternal Great Grandfather's Name: Tribe: Roll No: DOB: Deceased/Year	
			Maternal Great Grandmother's Name: Tribe: Roll No: DOB: Deceased/Year	

The BIA, no longer maintains current or historic records of all individuals who possess some degree of AI/AN blood. The BIA holds current rather than historic tribal membership enrollment lists, which do not hold the supporting documentation of the members listed.

Benjamin (Mulatto) and Sarah Garvey-Green (white) were Henry Green's Parents

George and Lydia Davis-Green 1834 Marriage Bond Indian River Hundred Sussex County Delaware

MINQUA UNAMI OKEHOCKING & THE DOWN RIVER NATIONS

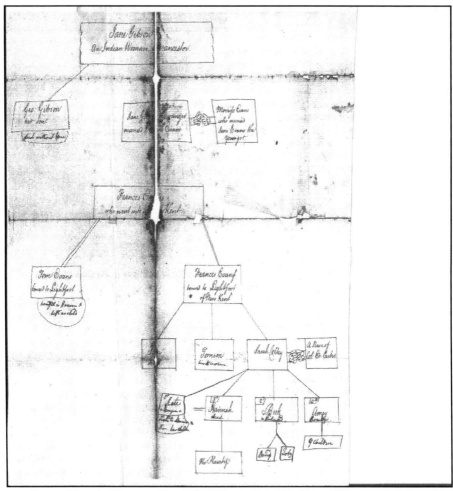

Jane (Bnu) Gipson Family Chart (an Indian Woman). The chart was introduced in court to prove that the Natives were not slaves. Janes children were enslaved by Gordon Lightfoot!

ANITA L. WILLS

Land Warrant and Patents

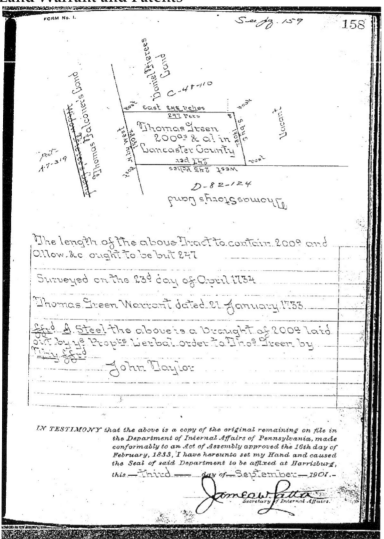

Thomas Green Warrant Land Survey-1733

FORM NO. 1   186

[survey diagram of rectangular tract]
- North side: South 84° West 184 p's
- labels around: William Harris; Samuel Green, 65 acres and Allowance, Situate in East Cain in Chester County; James Bains; North 84° East 184 p's; Vacant Land

The above described Tract of Land was Survey'd by warrant from the Honourable the Propr'ts. &c. dated the 17th day of August 1738. The 21st of the same Month. by Jno. Taylor.

IN TESTIMONY that the above is a copy of the original remaining on file in the Department of Internal Affairs of Pennsylvania, made conformably to an Act of Assembly approved the 16th day of February, 1833, I have hereunto set my Hand and caused the Seal of said Department to be affixed at Harrisburg, this _seventh_ day of _June_ 1911

Henry Houck
Secretary of Internal Affairs

Samuel Green Land Survey-1738

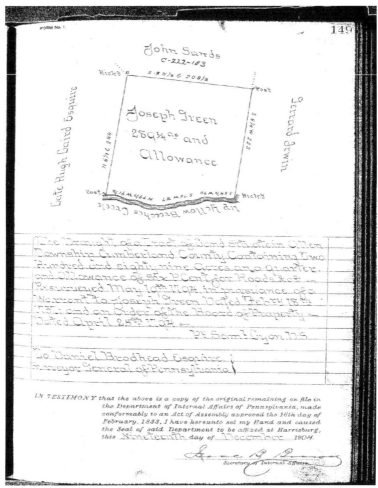

Joseph Green of Uncle of Benjamin Green received land grant in Cumberland County Pennsylvania.

Home of the Manokin Indians - 17th Century. Somerset County Hundreds Delmarva Peninsula [32]

---

[32] Map 17th Century Somerset County Hundreds; Delmarva History; http://nabbhistory.salisbury.edu/resces/geography/maps/mdsohds.jp g, November 19, 2012

CHAPTER FOUR

SEPERATING PEOPLE FROM THEIR LAND

"I do not think the measure of a civilization is how tall its buildings of concrete are, but rather how well its people have learned to relate to their environment and fellow man." – Sun Bear, Chippewa

By 1820 Ben Green II was listed as residing in Sadsbury Township near the border of Chester and Lancaster County. He may have been working in the area, because later he is back in Salisbury Township. Joseph (II) and Benjamin were sons of Thomas (Tom) Green (II), since they were still alive long after his death.

The Natives who were forced into Christianity lost their identity and ancestral lands. It was left up to descendants like me to unravel the mess created by land hungry settlers and the Colonial Government. The economic base that comes with having land was taken from Natives using their lifestyle and race as a reason. The cruel irony of creating a false narrative to justify the land grab was just icing on the cake. It is like a child caught with their hands in the Cookie Jar and saying that the Cookies "Made" me eat them.

Some Historians would have us believe the removal of Native Peoples from their Ancestral Homelands was voluntary. Still others point out that Natives had no knowledge of European's concept of Land Ownership. Native Villages were kinship communities where everyone had ownership in the land, and it was not for sale. There certainly was no concept of mortgaging land and housing for profit.

Some Historians would have us believe the removal of Native Peoples from their Ancestral Homelands was voluntary. Still others point out that Natives had no knowledge of European's concept of Land Ownership. Native Villages were kinship communities where everyone had ownership in the land, and it was not for sale. There certainly was no concept of mortgaging land and housing for profit.

Doctrine of Discovery

Some Historians would have us believe the removal of Native Peoples from their Ancestral Homelands was voluntary. Still others point out that Natives had no knowledge of European's concept of Land Ownership. Native Villages were kinship communities where everyone had ownership in the land, and it was not for sale. There certainly was no concept of mortgaging land and housing for profit.

"The Doctrine of Discovery established a spiritual, political, and legal justification for colonization and seizure of land not inhabited by Christians. Foundational elements of the Doctrine can be found in a series of papal bulls, or decrees, beginning in the 1100s, which included sanctions, enforcements, authorizations, expulsions, admonishments, excommunications, denunciations, and expressions of territorial sovereignty for Christian monarchs supported by the Catholic Church. [33]

Two papal bulls, in particular, stand out: (1) Pope Nicholas V issued "Romanus Pontifex" in 1455, granting the Portuguese a monopoly of trade with Africa and authorizing the enslavement of local people; (2) Pope Alexander VI issued the Papal Bull "Inter-Caetera" in 1493 to justify Christian European explorers' claims on land and waterways they allegedly discovered, and promote Christian domination and superiority, and has been applied in Africa, Asia, Australia, New Zealand, and the Americas.

European Historians in the America's would have us believe the removal of Native Peoples from their Ancestral Homelands was voluntary. They have their "experts" speak for Natives and block any narrative but their own from Social Discuss. The land was divided and given to Europeans who were not even in America.

---

[33] Native American History excerpted from Acres of Quakers, compiled by Nagy and Goulding, and available at Williston Township Administration, 688 Sugartown Road, Malvern, PA 19355.

During the period of Americus Vespucci and Columbus the Catholic Church created a Doctrine of Discovery. Indigenous People occupied the America's for at least 20000 years.

It took Europeans less than 100 years to wipe out a significant number of Natives. They used their Religion as an excuse to kill off enslave and/or remove Natives. We have heard that Jews are Gods chosen people, but it is Christians from Europe who believe they are Gods Chosen People. It is they who have rewritten the Bible to put them at the Center of Gods Universe.

Okehocking Preserve constitutes 155 acres of the 500-acre land grant from William Penn to the Okehocking band of the Leni Lenape Indians, the first Native American land grant in the American colonies. Because of the constant fear of being removed from their grounds, the Okehocking petitioned the Provincial Council for a secure tract of land where they would no longer be mistreated. They chose the Williston land because of a symbolic turtle-headed rock outcropping located within the Okehocking tract.

The Okehocking Clan belonged to the Unami (known as the Down River People), one of the three Leni Lenape tribes. The Unami Tribe's symbol was the tortoise, who they believed represented mother earth and was a symbolic "intermediary between the visible and invisible worlds around them." (Lindborg) The Unami Tribe was part of the Algonquin Nation, better known as the Leni Lenape, the "Original People."

Lenape was the Indian name for the Delaware River. The European settlers changed the river's name to Delaware; hence the Leni Lenape were labeled Delaware by the settlers. The scholarly consensus of the translation of Okehocking is "encircling land" - "okay" meaning encircled, "hocking" meaning land or earth.

In October 1702 the Okehocking Clan (or band) accepted the grant of 500 acres of mostly rugged and undulating ground. Unlike the tracts owned by the English Quaker farmers (Charles Whitaker, Francis Yarnall, Peter Thomas, and Thomas Massey) who lived nearby, this piece of land, except for the flood plain, was of little agricultural value.

MINQUA UNAMI OKEHOCKING & THE DOWN RIVER NATIONS

The land configured as a tilted square, located just north of present-day West Chester Pike, south of Goshen Road and bounded by Garrett Mill and Plumsock Roads. The orientation of this piece of land was unusual since all other tracts in Williston Township were of rectangular shapes whose boundaries followed either an east-west or north-south axis, and paralleled township lines. Instead of following property lines in the usual manner, the Delchester Road, laid out in 1710, ran directly through the center of the Okehocking lands, and divided the tract in half.

The Lenape are a matriarchal society, as are the Iroquois (and most of the Tribes) and to prevent inbreeding, men were never allowed to marry within their own clan. Instead, they "married" into the wife's clan and lived with her family. The increasing immigration of European settlers along the lower regions of the Crum, Ridley and Chester Creeks encroached upon the Leni Lenape lands, forcing the Indians to migrate inland and northward.

The Okehocking Clan, consisting of no more than two dozen men, women and children, relocated to the Williston land and used it for their summer encampment from 1696 to the mid 1730's. They wintered northward in their ancestral hunting grounds near the upper Schuylkill. By inhabiting two different locations yearly, they did not overuse any one area and thereby render it useless. In essence they created their own crop rotation system.

The floodplain along Ridley Creek provided limited fertile ground for the raising of crops. Burning of the fields to rid brush and undergrowth provided open ground for planting of crops, especially maize (multi-colored Indian corn), their main staple. Since the clan was migratory, their crop harvest was not abundant. In addition to crop growing, the women were the gatherers of fruit, seeds and nuts found in the nearby forests, and frogs and turtles from the streams while the men hunted and fished.

The Indians, who roamed through the Pennsylvania forests for centuries, did not understand the concept of land ownership or the creation of private property lines. Every living creature requires land or water to live on, were they also going to charge the wolves, bears, birds and fish? Their beliefs were in direct contrast with the posture of the nearby Quaker farmers, who purchased their land, established perimeter borders, and controlled the right of access.

As the Okehocking continued to pursue game beyond the confines of their land, the neighboring landowners became increasingly annoyed, and finally in 1718 the Indian families began the exodus from their summer home along the Ridley Creek. They removed initially to the Shamokin area (Swatara Creek), however they continued to return to their summer hunting grounds in Williston Township until 1735.

Many of the Lenape were forced to settle in Oklahoma, where by 1900 they had become farmers and merchants. Many of the Lenape returned to Pennsylvania and remain there to this day. In 1738 the Yarnall brothers, Amos, and Mordecai, received proprietary patents for the vacated land.[34]

As I mentioned several times my ancestors never left that land, and I was born on the land. We were racially redesignated as Mulatto and Colored just as our Native Ancestors throughout the colonies. Great-Great Grandfather Uriah Martin (b. 1838-d. 1909) was born in Atglen (Chester County) to Charles Martin (b. abt. 1808-d.1870) and Sarah Johnson Martin (b. abt. 1811 d. aft. 1840).

Sarah Johnson's parents Charles and Mary Slaughter Johnson are mixed raced Native white. The Martin's and Johnson are Iroquois through Native Mary Brant Johnson and her white husband William Johnson. We are direct descendants of Sir William and Mary Brant Johnson.

Although I have European Ancestors here in America, our racial designation is African American. So, when I criticize Europeans, they do not see it as constructive criticism and therein lies the rub. They imposed themselves on my ancestors. Our family History interferes with the romanticized version of the Colonization of the Americas. It is not enough that they occupy the land and set up a government of by and for the benefit of themselves. They (not all but some) also must control the historical

---

[34] Nagy and Goulding, Native American History excerpted from Acres of Quakers; available at Williston Township Administration, 688 Sugartown Road, Malvern, PA 19355.

narrative and create a scenario where they are the victims and not the aggressors.

The truth is far less flattering to those whose systems were built on stolen Native Lands and the labor of African Slaves. Natives were also enslaved exploited and, in many cases, shipped to the Caribbean or other locations. In Somerset County Maryland the Tribes were disbursed, and the land confiscated by European Settlers. There are entire lines of my Native ancestors who just disappeared and were never heard from again! Many were sent to Reservations in the Midwest, but many were unceremoniously slaughtered.

Settlers would move near or on Native Lands build a Church and force the Natives to either move or convert to Christianity. Instead of saying they died off or moved away it should be stated that they were massacred and/or forced off the land. When looked at in the historical context of the European settlement of the Delmarva, from the south to the north over time. It is clear the root issue was really over the settlement of the native lands by the Europeans.

As Europeans intruded further into the native lands, each negative response by the natives to this intrusion was met by Europeans as further justification for punitive expeditions, such as the one of 1677. We know about the militia of 1677 simply because the militiamen were paid by the Provincial Assembly for their efforts, and these payments were recorded, and these records survived in present day Archives.[35]

Somerset's first inhabitants were the native tribes of the lower Eastern Shore. Native American occupation of the region dates back thousands of years; its earliest inhabitants occupied a

---

[35] Frakes, Charles, Scotts Valley, CA (cefrakes@sbcglobal.net);15 Aug 2005; http://nativeamericansofdelawarestate.com/1600sDisputesDelmarvaNatives&Europeans.html, 23 Feb 2021

landscape far different than today with much lower sea levels. Spanning over fifteen to twenty thousand years, native American habitation matured from hunter-gathers to settled communities of tribes who resided along the region's numerous waterways, many of which still carry their names.

The Pocomoke, Manokin, Annemessex, Monie and Wicomico Waterways are named for these native tribes. Native American occupation is also represented by the thousands of artifacts that turn up in the soil, or through the written historical record as Anglo-American explorers, traders and ultimately settlers interacted with them across the peninsula.

One of the earliest explorers to leave a written record of his visit, describing the local inhabitants as well as their activities was Giovanni da Verrazano, who, during the 1520s, traveled along what later became Somerset County. Among his writings about the region's natives, he penned a description of how they moved about their watery world.

"They crafted Little boats made out of a single tree, twenty feet long and four wide, which are put together without stone, iron, or any kind of metal…[they] use the fourth element (fire) and burn the wood as much as necessary to hollow out the boat; they do the same for the stern and prow so when it sails it can plow through the waves of the sea Giovanni da Verrazano, 1524-28)"

The reference is to our Manokin ancestors who were in what is now Somerset County Maryland in 1692. They lived their lifestyle for thousands of years with no interference and Somerset was their Summer Village. During the Winter Months they moved further inland traveling the Great Minqua Path into Pennsylvania.

Manokin Davis Somerset Maryland

Our Somerset County Maryland Native Ancestors were Christened and given the surname of Davis beginning in the 1600's. Natives were Christened and given the surnames of Europeans who took over their land.

Nathaniel Davis

Name: Nathaniel Davis

Sex: Male

MINQUA UNAMI OKEHOCKING & THE DOWN RIVER NATIONS

Wife:	Lydia
Daughter:	Lydia Davis
Name:	Lydia Davis
Event Type:	Birth
Event Date:	7 Oct 1692
Event Place:	Somerset, Maryland, British Colonial America
Event Place (Original):	Manokin, Somerset, Maryland, United States
Sex:	Female
Father's Name:	Nathaniel Davis
Mother's Name:	Lydia

Manokin Lydia - mentioned in the record of Anne Davis

Name:	Lydia
Sex:	Female
Husband:	Nathanial Davis
Daughter:	Anne Davis

Other information in the record of Anne Davis from Maryland Births and Christenings, 1650-1995

Name:	Anne Davis
Event Type:	Birth
Event Date:	7 Apr 1688
Event Place:	Somerset, Maryland, British Colonial America
Event Place (Original):	Manokin, Somerset, Maryland, United States
Sex:	Female
Father's Name:	Nathaniel Davis

Mother's Name: Lydia

Queen Aliquippa Leader Of the Iroquois Federation

Queen Aliquippa was the leader of the Iroquois Federation in 1702. It is she who negotiated the settlement of the Okehocking Tract in a meeting with William Penn. She met with her were Natives who had been chased off their land and into the Ohio Valley. She told Penn that they did not wish to be chased around like dogs and he assured her the land was theirs. But that was not the case because as we see with the system that we live under now our Country is a White Male Patriotically Society.

No matter what laws are put in place if it is not to their benefit it is ignored. In the case of the Okehocking Tract as soon as William Penn returned to England Settlers showed up with guns. My ancestors did not leave they were forcibly removed from their land, and it was distributed to Settlers. I and my relatives and their people and the people before were born a stone's throw away. They wiped us out by listing us as "Colored" on our birth certificates.

You will not read about Queen Aliquippa in any history books because her deeds were wiped away. There is a depiction of her meeting with Washington but how many read the fine print. In fact she may be a relative since our Green ancestors were Seneca and so was Queen Aliquippa. She camped at Conestoga in 1702 when negotiating land for the Minqua Unami & Okehocking. The town of Aliquippa is named in her honor, yet she is not held up as a historical figure.

The tribes that made up the Iroquois were Matrilineal, and in fact women are more skilled (when given a chance) than men in leadership. Some of the Okehocking Tract is at the Crum Creek Watershed. The Crum Creek Watershed is at what is now Ridley Creek and rises in eastern Chester County in East Whiteland Township on the campus of Immaculata University, and then flows 24 miles southeast through Chester and Delaware Counties to its confluence with the Delaware River between Chester City and Eddystone Borough.

The Watershed is made up of the land ceded to the Okehocking by William Penn as land they were promised was

MINQUA UNAMI OKEHOCKING & THE DOWN RIVER NATIONS

redistributed to settlers. The story told is that descendants left the area and that is not true. Our ancestors were there and had been prior to when the land was ceded in 1704. Our mother her father his father and his father remained in the area. Or put it this way they were pushed off the land and still returned.

We the descendants were born and raised there and are still there. We were there with little or no protection by the laws from a newly formed Nation. We were there and not welcome on our ancestral land as it was disbursed to Land Hungry Europeans. The only people they do not want on our Ancestral Lands are the Indigenous People of the land. It has always been about land and resources from the moment Turtle Island was Colonized.

The first roads in Williston were Indian trails and the first Underground Railroad Agents were Native People who used the trails to guide escaped slaves to Canada. Several of the Black Settlements in Canada are near the Onondaga Reservation in Southern Ontario. The Great Minqua Path runs from Philadelphia through the Okehocking Tract and into the Interior of what is now Lancaster County.

When Penn met with Queen Aliquippa, they were in the Village of the Manokin in what Somerset County Maryland is now. As the leader of the Iroquois Queen Aliquippa was there on behalf of the Okehocking. Yet even with a Survey and Warrant the Okehocking were forced from the 500 acres now located in Ridley Park, Williston, and the Westtown area on the border of Delaware and Chester County.

Truth is the ancestors did not leave the area and were there in one form or another continuously. They were run off the land shortly after William Penn left for England and the Survey's and Warrants ignored. There was no law to protect against the encroaching white settlers because the laws were met to benefit settlers.

The roots of our Green, Davis, Martin, Johnson and allied lines are Manokin Seneca Mohawk and Susquehanna. Those lines are the Down River People whose village was at the Falls of the Susquehanna in what is now Somerset County Maryland.

They were displaced from the land and not welcome to walk on it. Our ancestors scattered as far away as Oklahoma and other points West, Virginia, North Carolina, the Ohio Valley, New York, and Canada after the 1764 Massacre of the Conestoga in Lancaster County. But thousands of years of connection to the land drew them back.

Instead, they were racially designated as Mulatto Colored Negro and eventually Black. I disagree that Natives would give up their land to become landless after thousands of years. In 1838 our Great-Great-Great Grandfather Benjamin Green joined St Martins Episcopalian Church in Concord. Thomas Green his father was a member of Saint John's Episcopal Church Compass Pa Church in Chester County. There is a Colored Graveyard at that Church and other Churches with the surnames of Green and Martin. There is a Graveyard at Octorara which has a "Colored Section as well.

Some of the descendants of the Native/Quaker unions did not fare as well and were relegated to workhouses or orphanages. The Amish Mennonites and Quakers all pacifists received land confiscated from Native People. They were beneficiaries of Native lands taken by gun point and laws to protect their interest. It is a reality in America that we as People of Color are not to point out who the beneficiaries are of racist and discriminatory laws.

Paper Genocide

Natives were left off the early census records until 1860 when enumerators counted only those American Indians who were considered assimilated (for example, those who settled in or near white communities). The Snyder Act of 1924 admitted Native Americans born in the U.S. to full U.S. citizenship. Though the Fifteenth Amendment, passed in 1870, granted all U.S. citizens the right to vote regardless of race, it was not until the Snyder Act that they could enjoy the rights granted by this amendment. People of Color continue the fight to this day for the right to vote without obstruction.

In some census, enumerators were told to categorize American Indians according to the amount of Indian or other blood they had, considered a marker of assimilation. In 1900, for example, census takers were told to record the proportion of white blood for each American Indian they enumerated. The 1930 census instructions for enumerators said that people who were white-Indian were to be counted as Indian "except where the percentage of Indian blood is very small, or where he is regarded as a white person by those in the community where he lives."

Any Native Person who had children or otherwise intermixed with the African Community lost their native identity. In the 1860 census, enumerators were told that people they counted who were both white and any other race should be categorized in the minority race. This is what we call divide and conquer and was another means of forced assimilation of Native People.

People of multiracial non-white backgrounds were categorized according to their father's race. There were some exceptions: If someone was both Indian and Negro (the preferred term at the time), census takers were told the person should be considered Negro unless "Indian blood very definitely predominated" and "the person was regarded in the community as an Indian."

Conestoga Manor

The Conestoga Wagon was used to transport goods and named for the region it came from In Lancaster County. I was reminded of that when our Ancestor Henry Green stated that he was a Teamster during the Civil War. Before they isolated themselves in the Welsh Mountain his father Benjamin Green and Uncle Joseph Green built wagons and drove from Lancaster to Philadelphia.

There they got divers goods from the Ships and returned to Lancaster to Sell them. In 1832 they were fined by the City of Lancaster for selling "divers" goods without a license. The Down River Nations wintered in the region for thousands of years. The Great Minqua Path led from the Delaware River into the Interior of what is now Lancaster County. It was the Natives who took Europeans like Joseph Cloud into the interior.

The Settlers created borders that cut the land Benjamin Green resided on in half. Both Lancaster County and Delaware County were created from Chester County. Joseph Green

Benjamin's brother owned land on the border of Lancaster County which was divided after York County was created in 1749.

The brothers who were listed as Yeoman (Landowners) were denied the right to sell their goods. In that region like in many others during that period of Colonization they were viewed as a threat in their own Homeland. Cities were built on the graves of murdered and massacred Native men women and children. A narrative was created that Natives left on their own or lost a war with the Iroquois.

In Cuba, the Arawak were shipped to Africa as slaves by Columbus. This was done throughout the America's as a method to gain access to the Land. It was always about the land and resources something Europe lacked. Later, the most prevalent way used by Europeans was to kill the Natives and take their lands. That included raiding villages shooting and killing men women and children. Once Natives were slaughtered the Villages were set on fire. Then there was the forced removal to Reservations in Oklahoma and other interior regions. As the Natives were herded out West European Settlers rushed to lay claim to their lands.

Another tactic used to free up land for European Settlers was the Power of the Pen. The Pen was mightier than the sword and was used in what has come to be known as Paper Genocide. With one swipe of the Pen those who were labeled "Indian" became Mulatto Colored Negro and then Black. With that designation all legal claims to the land were supposed to have ended.

One of our Native Ancestors "Indian" Charles Lewis (b. abt. 1700) was five years old when the adults from Nanzattico Village were sent as slaves to Antigua. The Nanzattico were the original Rappahannock Tribes and one of the oldest in Virginia. After the Adults were shipped to Antigua the children were indentured out to Plantation Owners. They were forbidden by law from returning to their ancestral lands and their racial identity was changed to Mulatto. This event happened 1704 under the Colonial Government which ruled by force against the Native People. [36]

Queen Aliquippa Leader Of the Iroquois Federation

Queen Aliquippa was the leader of the Iroquois Federation in 1702. It is she who negotiated the settlement of the Okehocking Tract in a meeting with William Penn. She met with her were Natives who had been chased off their land and into the Ohio Valley. She told Penn that they did not wish to be chased around like dogs and he assured her the land was theirs. But that was not the case because as we see with the system that we live under now our Country is a White Male Patriotically Society.

No matter what laws are put in place if it is not to their benefit it is ignored. In the case of the Okehocking Tract as soon as William Penn returned to England Settlers showed up with guns. My ancestors did not leave they were forcibly removed from their land, and it was distributed to Settlers. I and my relatives and their people and the people before were born a stone's throw away. They wiped us out by listing us as "Colored" on our birth certificates.

We were not allowed to claim Native which we were nor white which we were only colored! This is the truth that no one wants to speak here in a Nation that calls itself Christian. You will not read about Queen Aliquippa in any history books because her deeds were wiped away. There is a depiction of her meeting with Washington but how many read the fine print. In fact she may be a relative since our Green ancestors were Seneca and so was Queen Aliquippa. The town of Aliquippa is named in her honor, yet she is not held up as a historical figure.

The tribes that made up the Iroquois were Matrilineal, and in fact women are more skilled (when given a chance) than men in leadership. Some of the Okehocking Tract is at the Crum Creek Watershed. The Crum Creek Watershed is at what is now Ridley Creek and rises in eastern Chester County in East Whiteland

---

[36] Wills, Anita L. Along The Rappahannock: The Homeland of the Nanzattico (Nantaughtacund) Indian Nat Paperback – 28 August 2017

Township on the campus of Immaculata University, and then flows 24 miles southeast through Chester and Delaware Counties to its confluence with the Delaware River between Chester City and Eddystone Borough.

The Watershed is made up of the land ceded to the Okehocking by William Penn as land they were promised was redistributed to settlers. The story told is that descendants left the area and that is not true. Our ancestors were there and had been prior to when the land was ceded in 1704. Our mother her father his father and his father remained in the area. Or put it this way they were pushed off the land and still returned.

We the descendants were born and raised there and are still there. We were there with little or no protection by the laws from a newly formed Nation. We were there and not welcome on our ancestral land as it was disbursed to Land Hungry Europeans. The only people they do not want on our Ancestral Lands are the Indigenous People of the land. It has always been about land and resources from the moment Turtle Island was Colonized.

The first roads in Williston were Indian trails and the first Underground Railroad Agents were Native People who used the trails to guide escaped slaves to Canada. Several of the Black Settlements in Canada are near the Onondaga Reservation in Southern Ontario. The Great Minqua Path runs from Philadelphia through the Okehocking Tract and into the Interior of what is now Lancaster County.

When Penn met with Queen Aliquippa, they were in the Village of the Manokin in what Somerset County Maryland is now. As the leader of the Iroquois Queen Aliquippa was there on behalf of the Okehocking. Yet even with a Survey and Warrant the Okehocking were forced from the 500 acres now located in Ridley Park, Williston, and the Westtown area on the border of Delaware and Chester County.

Truth is the ancestors did not leave the area and were there in one form or another continuously. They were run off the land shortly after William Penn left for England and the Survey's and Warrants ignored. There was no law to protect against the encroaching white settlers because the laws were met to benefit settlers.

The roots of our Green, Davis, Martin, Johnson and allied lines are Manokin Seneca Mohawk and Susquehanna. Those lines are the Down River People whose village was at the Falls of the Susquehanna in what is now Somerset County Maryland.

They were displaced from the land and not welcome to walk on it. Our ancestors scattered as far away as Oklahoma and other points West, Virginia, North Carolina, the Ohio Valley, New York, and Canada after the 1764 Massacre of the Conestoga in Lancaster County. But thousands of years of connection to the land drew them back.

Instead, they were racially designated as Mulatto Colored Negro and eventually Black. I disagree that Natives would give up their land to become landless after thousands of years. In 1838 our Great-Great-Great Grandfather Benjamin Green joined St Martins Episcopalian Church in Concord. Thomas Green his father was a member of Saint John's Episcopal Church Compass Pa Church in Chester County. There is a Colored Graveyard at that Church and other Churches with the surnames of Green and Martin. There is a Graveyard at Octorara which has a "Colored Section as well.

Some of the descendants of the Native/Quaker unions did not fare as well and were relegated to workhouses or orphanages. The Amish Mennonites and Quakers all pacifists received land confiscated from Native People. They were beneficiaries of Native lands taken by gun point and laws to protect their interest. It is a reality in America that we as People of Color are not to point out who the beneficiaries are of racist and discriminatory laws.

Paper Genocide

Natives were left off the early census records until 1860 when enumerators counted only those American Indians who were considered assimilated (for example, those who settled in or near white communities). The Snyder Act of 1924 admitted Native Americans born in the U.S. to full U.S. citizenship. Though the Fifteenth Amendment, passed in 1870, granted all U.S. citizens the right to vote regardless of race, it was not until the Snyder Act that they could enjoy the rights granted by this amendment. People of Color continues the fight to this day for the right to vote without obstruction.

In some census, enumerators were told to categorize American Indians according to the amount of Indian or other blood they had, considered a marker of assimilation. In 1900, for example, census takers were told to record the proportion of white blood for each American Indian they enumerated. The 1930 census instructions for enumerators said that people who were white-Indian were to be counted as Indian "except where the percentage of Indian blood is negligible, or where he is regarded as a white person by those in the community where he lives."

Any Native Person who had children or otherwise intermixed with the African Community lost their native identity. In the 1860 census, enumerators were told that people they counted who were both white and any other race should be categorized in the minority race. This is what we call divide and conquer and was another means of forced assimilation of Native People.

People of multiracial non-white backgrounds were categorized according to their father's race. There were some exceptions: If someone was both Indian and Negro (the preferred term at the time), census takers were told the person should be considered Negro unless "Indian blood very definitely predominated" and "the person was regarded in the community as an Indian."

Conestoga Manor

The Conestoga Wagon was used to transport goods and named for the region it came from In Lancaster County. I was reminded of that when our Ancestor Henry Green stated that he was a Teamster during the Civil War. Before they isolated themselves in the Welsh Mountain his father Benjamin Green and Uncle Joseph Green built wagons and drove from Lancaster to Philadelphia.

There they got divers goods from the Ships and returned to Lancaster to Sell them. In 1832 they were fined by the City of Lancaster for selling "divers" goods without a license. The Down River Nations wintered in the region for thousands of years. The

MINQUA UNAMI OKEHOCKING & THE DOWN RIVER NATIONS

Great Minqua Path led from the Delaware River into the Interior of what is now Lancaster County. It was the Natives who took Europeans like Joseph Cloud into the interior.

The Settlers created borders that cut the land Benjamin Green resided on in half. Both Lancaster County and Delaware County were created from Chester County. Joseph Green Benjamin's brother owned land on the border of Lancaster County which was divided after York County was created in 1749.

The brothers who were listed as Yeoman (Landowners) were denied the right to sell their goods. In that region like in many others during that period of Colonization they were viewed as a threat in their own Homeland. Cities were built on the graves of murdered and massacred Native men women and children. A narrative was created that Natives left on their own or lost a war with the Iroquois.

In Cuba, the Arawak were shipped to Africa as slaves by Columbus. This was done throughout the America's as a method to gain access to the Land. It was always about the land and resources something Europe lacked. Later, the most prevalent way used by Europeans was to kill the Natives and take their lands. That included raiding villages shooting and killing men women and children. Once Natives were slaughtered the Villages were set on fire. Then there was the forced removal to Reservations in Oklahoma and other interior regions. As the Natives were herded out West European Settlers rushed to lay claim to their lands.

Another tactic used to free up land for European Settlers was the Power of the Pen. The Pen was mightier than the sword and was used in what has come to be known as Paper Genocide. With one swipe of the Pen those who were labeled "Indian" became Mulatto Colored Negro and then Black. With that designation all legal claims to the land were supposed to have ended.

One of our Native Ancestors "Indian" Charles Lewis (b. abt. 1700) was five years old when the adults from Nanzattico Village were sent as slaves to Antigua. The Nanzattico were the original Rappahannock Tribes and one of the oldest in Virginia. After the Adults were shipped to Antigua the children were indentured out to Plantation Owners.

They were forbidden by law from returning to their ancestral lands and their racial identity was changed to Mulatto. This event happened 1704 under the Colonial Government which ruled by force against the Native People. In other words, they came to a Country and with force took the land and set up their laws.[37] Natives racial identity was often used as a means of resolving the Indian problem. It was a way to block any claims to land or rights that existed prior to Colonization. They were required to convert to Christianity, attend Mission Schools, and accept the changing of their racial status to either White, Colored, Negro, or Mulatto.

Paper Genocide effectively wiped-out Native Identity and autonomy. By the time they understood the motives of Europeans, their rights, identity, and land had been stolen. Their Villages and Lands were taken over by squatters and their sacred sites turned into attractions for the Amusement of Europeans. They were surrounded by Armies there to protect the Interest of the Colonizers.

Samuel Green II, (b. abt. 1825) was the son of Samuel Green I, (b., abt 1786) and his wife Rachel, (b. abt 1796), the brother of Benjamin Green I. Rachel's birth name is still not known. Samuel Green II. (1825) married Jane A. Boots. Samuel Green II served in the 41st USCT. His enlistment date is September 1, 1864. He is buried in St Peter's Church Cemetery.

Their son Samuel Green III (1870) married Mary I. Boots. Mary was the daughter of John W. Boots and Catharine E. Mimms. John W. Boots was the son of Arthur Boots and Elizabeth S.

---

[37] Wills, Anita L. Along The Rappahannock: The Homeland of the Nanzattico (Nantaughtacund) Indian Nat Paperback – 28 August 2017

Marshall. Elmer Boots was John's brother, and Elmer Boots married Martha Green, the daughter of Samuel Green and Jane A Boots and sister of Samuel Green's (1870). There are many overlapping relationships between the Greens and Boots.

George Green was Samuel Greens (1786), son. George's son Samuel Green (1844), also known as E. Samuel or Ellsworth Samuel, fought in the Civil War in Company C of the 25th. This Samuel is buried in Morris Cemetery in Phoenixville in the Civil War section where he and his family lived. Another son George, Jr. (1845) fought in the 22 regiment of the United States Colored Infantry. He was 19 years old when he enlisted.[15]

"On August 17, 1754; there was surveyed to Thomas Green, of the County of Chester, Yeoman, a certain Tract of Land situated in East Caln Twp., in the said County of Chester…, The said Samuel Green by indenture, bearing date the thirteenth day of October 1730, did grant, bargain, sell, confirm the above described Tract and premises unto, Thomas Green (II), of the said County Yeoman, his heirs and assignees forever" Now at the insistence and request of the said Thomas Green that we would be pleased to grant him a confirmation of the same.

In fact, a Samuel Green granted Thomas Green, "The Manor of Springtown" in the County of Chester (in 1754), by that time Thomas Green I, was deceased. However, the deed mentions Thomas Green I, as purchasing the land as a Scrouges Treaty (land granted to natives), in 1730, Samuel was referring to the original purchase.

In 1786, Thomas Green (II), was the patentee on land in West Caln granted by Samuel Green. In a Warrant dated January 21, 1733, Thomas Green receives patented land granted by John, Thomas, and Richard Penn along the Pequea Branch in Lancaster County (550 acres).

It was in 1737 that Thomas Green I, (Thomas I), Yeomen, was granted 350 acres to make up the full quantity of 550 acres, which he had satisfied in Warranty payments. His widow, Ann sold 100 of the acres to Thomas Griffith after the death of her husband. The land patented to Thomas Griffith was in Lancaster County.

The names of the deceased (Thomas Green I) heirs were, Thomas Green Jr. (II), Joseph Green (I), Moses Green, Robert Dunlap husband of Martha (Green-Dunlap); Elizabeth Green, and Susannah Green (Spinsters). Land purchased by Thomas Green I, was located along Pequea Creek in Lancaster County. The signatures on the warrants were, John Penn, Thomas Penn, and Richard Penn Esquire. They were the sons of William Penn and fulfilling a promise he made to provide land to Penn's Indians.

Joseph Green (son of Thomas I) was also the owner of 250 acres of land in Cumberland County called Monmouth, which was given to a Jamie Laird in Trust. The document mentions mining rights, mineral rights, Ore, Gold and Silver. The document is signed by Joseph Green, but by a Thomas O' Dean on March 8, 1805. [38]

---

[38] PA State Archives, RG-17 Patent Book H-1, page 546, Joseph Green; RG-17 Patent Book p. 55, page 383; RG-17 Original Warrants, Lancaster County, G-34; RG-17 Original Warrants, Lancaster County, G-8

Mt. Holly School - Welsh Mountain School for Colored Children 1889. Green Boots Stewart Harris and other children from the Welsh Mountains attended this School.

This is Grandmother Leah Ruth-Martin Circa 1920 in front of her Tin Lizzie. Grandpop Martin was a mechanic and worked on vehicles at their farm. Grandmother Leah was one of the first women drivers in Chester County.

Grammy Leah Ruth-Martin holding 2-year-old Mom (Vivian Martin-Baxter) circa 1925 on the Martin family Farm in Honey Brook Chester County Pennsylvania.

Paternal ancestor Great-Great-Grandfather Charles Baxter – 1833-1968, He is 103 years old in this picture and was full blood Native from South Carolina. Through Brother Anthony Baxter's Paternal DNA which was 100% Native from the aboriginal people of Columbia South America. He is the grandson of Rev. Lewis James Crum as mentioned in one affidavit when he was applying for his pension for serving in the Confederate Army. He served alongside his slave master Rev. Lewis James Crum and his son Dr. Andrew Crum.

Paternal Grandfather Charles Wesley Baxter (1896-1954) was a descendant of slaves in Orangeburg SC. There was family talk of the Baxter's being Native which was proven to be true. When brother Anthony Baxter had a DNA test through African Ancestry it came back 100% Indigenous to Columbia South America for our paternal DNA.

Native American Sioux, Gros Ventre, Arikara, and Mandan following their arrival at Hampton Normal and Agricultural Institute, c 1879.[39]

---

[39] Photo Courtesy of Hampton University Archives

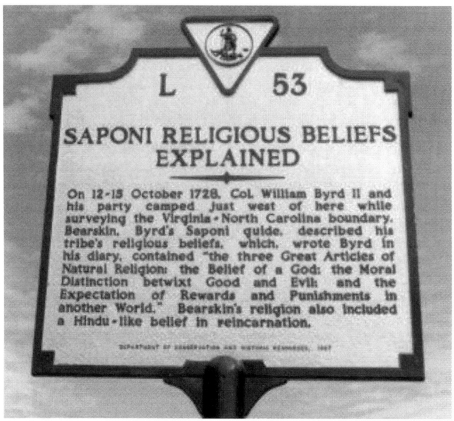

At the southern end of Danville Va, on the right-of-way of northbound U.S. 29 Business near where it enters Virginia from North Carolina, stands a marker erected during 1988 to honor the Saponi guide Ned Bearskin and his people. Bearskin along with numerous surveyors and woodsmen, camped nearby in October 1728. It was at a site in what is now Pittsylvania County that Bearskin related to Byrd many of the religious beliefs of the newly extinct Saponi tribe.[40]

---

[40] Mitchell, Henry H. (1989); Byrd and Bearskin Remembered; https://www.victorianvilla.com/sims-mitchell/local/byrd/we2/st01/; 1989

CHAPTER FIVE

THE NANZATTICO FIRST NATIONS PEOPLE OF THE RAPPAHANOCK

"They plow up the ground, pull down the trees killing everything..., They pay no attention. How can the spirit of the Earth like them? Everywhere the American has touched it, it is sore." Wintu Woman

The narrative of America must change to include the true history. The most glaring omission is the history oppression, killing, and attempts to assimilate Native Americans. This also means the truth about the enslavement, subjection, killings, and attempted assimilation of African Americans.

Native Americans are the Indigenous People of these lands a fact even European Archaeologist and Anthropologist admit. While digging up artifacts and marvelling at Longhouses the Natives themselves are ignored.

To deny Natives any rights to claim land, or indigenous rights, laws were passed to change their racial designation. The Natives who were not assimilated and/or accepted as white, were stripped of any rights with the racial classification of, Free Person of Color (FPC). This is Paper Genocide used to wipe out entire Enslaving the Nanzattico

In 1704 the entire adult population of Nanzattico Indians in Virginia were sent as slaves to Antiqua. They were one of the oldest residents of that region dating back thousands of years. One of the children "Indian" Charles is our direct Ancestor. His sons Ambrose and Charles Lewis were in the Revolutionary War out of Fredericksburg Virginia. It is through Charles Lewis my direct ancestor that I was accepted into the Daughters of the American Revolution (DAR). They were the original Rappahannock whose villages were in Caroline and King George County.

The Natives racial identity was also used as a means of resolving the Indian problem. It was a way to block any claims to land or rights that existed prior to Colonization. They were required to convert to Christianity, attend Mission Schools, and accept the changing of their racial status to either White, Colored, Negro, or Mulatto.

Paper Genocide effectively wiped-out Native Identity and autonomy. By the time they understood the motives of Europeans, their rights, identity, and land had been stolen. Their Villages and Lands were taken over by squatters and their sacred sites turned into attractions for the Amusement of Europeans. They were surrounded by Armies there to protect the Interest of the Colonizers.

With the swipe of a Pen Laws like Squatters Rights were passed to remove Natives from their land. There were laws passed against Natives growing Corn or Tobacco as a means of removing them from the land. It was not as simple as Natives signing treaties giving their lands away.

The missing part is the long-protracted war waged against Natives to remove them from their land. Much of the early land was sold to speculators in Europe who had never been to America. Europeans came to this country with more rights than the Natives who built and lived in it for thousands of years. They claimed God Given Rights to take possession of the land in the name of Christianity whose Deity Jesus Christ is a Beta Israel Jew from Ethiopia.

Pamahsawhu – The World and Everything In It

When the Jamestown Settlers arrived in Virginia in 1607, the region had been occupied by Natives for thousands of years. They were living on the land they called "Pamahsawuh" which meant "The world and everything in it." Forests covered most of the land and there were many different Indian tribes in the region.

There was no Virginia, Maryland, or North Carolina. It was all one area, and the tribal boundaries were set and respected. As Colonial Settlers came to the region they encroached on and took over traditional tribal land. The lands were divided into States, just as they were dividing Countries in Africa according to their (European) needs.

The Virginia tribes are classified as "Eastern Woodland Indians." Each tribe spoke a different dialect of one of three languages: Algonquian, Siouan, or Iroquoian. Each of these Indian language groups held different beliefs, traditions, and customs. The Algonquian Language was primarily spoken in the Tidewater (Coastal Plain). Some English words come from the Algonquian language including tomahawk, skunk, squash, wampum, and succotash.

The Algonquian Indians grew corn, beans, squash, and sunflower seeds. Many of these crops were dried or smoked and used for food during the winter months. They ate fresh vegetables in the summer and fall. They hunted deer, turkey, and other small animals year-round, but especially in the winter. In the spring, they ate fish, berries, nuts, wild plants and roots.

Because they farmed, tribes in the Algonquian Language Group settled villages. The Rappahannock Tribes including the Nanzattico lived by the Rappahannock River. They depended on rivers for drinking water, cooking, bathing, food, and transportation. The water was also necessary to nourish plant life, animals, trees, and vegetation.

Longhouses are Native homes used by the Iroquois Tribes and some of their Algonquian neighbors. They are built similarly to wigwams, with pole frames and elm bark covering. The main difference is that longhouses are much, much larger than Wigwams.

Longhouses could be 200 feet long, 20 feet wide, and 20 feet high. Inside the longhouse, raised platforms created a second story, which was used for sleeping space. Mats and wood screens divided the longhouse into separate rooms. Each longhouse housed an entire clan-- as many as 60 people.

One of the Tribal Lands of the Nanzattico (Nantaughtacund) was on the southern bank of the Rappahannock River east of the city of Port Royal in Caroline County, Virginia. There is an archaeological dig that contains about 30 archaeological sites associated with a large, dispersed 54-acre square.

The Multinational Indian community of Nanzattico, was in Caroline County, Virginia from 1650 to 1704. The remains of at least eight houses and other structures connected with the social life of Nanzattico Indians has been preserved in twenty plots located on a large field half a mile east of the Camden Estate.

The description of the Settlement of Nanzattico left by a Frenchman named Durand de Dauphine in 1686, noted that it consisted of "quite cozy houses, the walls and roofs of which were decorated with ornaments made of wood and so securely fastened with deer tendons, that neither rain nor wind causes them anxiety.

"Noting that the Indians wore clothes both from cloth and deerskin, he continues: "Indian townspeople make pots, vases and earthenware pipes ... Christians buying these pots or vases fill them with Indian corn, which is their cost "

Native American Slavery "is a piece of the history of slavery that has been glossed over. Between 1492 and 1880, between 2 and 5.5 million Native Americans were enslaved in the Americas in addition to 12.5 million African slaves."

"Between 1704 and 1706, English Virginians destroyed the Nanziattico nation. First, they used an oyer and terminer trial to hang several of its young men, and then they separated Nanziattico children from their parents and bound the children out as indentured servants. Finally, they sold the surviving Nanziattico adults in the English sugar island of Antigua. These events occurred at the brutal intersection of many colonial histories-- Native dispossession and land seizure,

Native enslavement, the Atlantic slave trade, and the creation of archives that minimized this colonial violence. In this way, the story of the Nanzattico is not merely a tale of the early eighteenth century; instead, it is rooted in the previous century of English colonialism in Virginia and in a long and dire history for Native people attempting to navigate the dangers of colonialism. The English removed the Nanzattico in the service of two desires — control of land and the erasure of Native claims to Virginian spaces--thus underscoring that Native enslavement was not always about labor.

Though historians present the trade in enslaved Native people in the Southeast either as the result of coordinated slave raids made by the English and their Native allies or as the result of diplomatic or trade encounters, in this case the English used their courts and the language of justice to dispossess and to enslave. In how they told (or did not tell) the story of the Nanzattico, the English quietly eliminated an entire nation, an event seen only with difficulty in the archive.

The trial transcripts, while long on the damage that Nanziattico men allegedly did to English bodies, are short on witness statements and the names of any Nanzattico who were not executed. Virginia's colonial government reported even less to the Board of Trade and Plantations in London, sending only a perfunctory account of the trial and its resolution (which the Lords of Trade approved with no questioning of colonial actions).

The English effectively banished the Nanziattico, first from Virginian land and then from the archive. The story of the Nanzattico exemplifies what Michel-Rolph Trouillot describes as a "silencing ... due to uneven power in the production of sources, archives, and narratives." The Nanzattico, saved those sources in an archive dedicated to bolstering English claims to land, authority, and domination, and created narratives of Native perfidy and vanishing that celebrated the English remaking of the landscape.

If these sources inscribed "the insignificance of the story," as Trouillot would have it, the historian's task must be to signify the Nanzattico--their lives and their deaths. As one historian of Native Virginians has put it, "there is very little record remaining on the Nansiatico, (Nanzattico)" an indicator of the difficulty of reading those sources that remain to correct a colonial record that was indifferent to the suffering of Native people." [iii]

While natives were forced into slavery and servitude as early as 1636, it was not until King Philip's War that they were enslaved in large numbers. The 1675 to 1676 war pitted Native American leader King Philip, also known as Metacom, and his allies against the English colonial settlers.

During the war, New England Colonies routinely shipped Native Americans as slaves to Barbados, Bermuda, Jamaica, the Azores, Spain, and Tangier in North Africa, Fisher said.
While Africans who were enslaved did not know where they would be taken, Native Americans understood that they could be sent to Caribbean plantations and face extremely harsh treatment far from their homes and communities, according to the study. Fear of this fate spurred some Native Americans to pledge to fight to the death, while others surrendered hoping to avoid being sent overseas, the study found.

By late in the seventeenth century, African slaves were overwhelming the colonial market, providing more abundant labor with less internal conflict than enslaved Indians. Indentured servants, which had served as a primary labor source, were even less available and more expensive than slaves.

Punishing the Nanzattico

The General Assembly still found a use for Indian enslavement however, when it punished the Nanzattico Indians in 1705 for a single murder by exporting the entire surviving Nanzattico Community to Antigua for sale as slaves.

This was the same year that the assembly passed a comprehensive slave code solidifying the shift of the colonial economy from one based on indentured servitude to a Slave Labor System remaining until the American Civil War (1861–1865): it declared all slaves, African or Indian, "real estate." Enslaved laborers became de-humanized under the law, ushering in the southern economic system that protected the rights of white planters and viewed enslaved laborers as property to be exploited.[41]

The enslavement of the Nanzattico is an example of Indians being sold into slavery in Virginia […] This is what happened to the

---

[41]Shefveland, K. Indian Enslavement in Virginia. (2016, April 7). In *Encyclopedia Virginia*. Retrieved from http://www.EncyclopediaVirginia.org/Indian_Enslavement_in_Virginia

Nanzattico people in 1704. They are the first entire tribe enslaved and one of the tribes that I am descended from through my ancestors, Indian Charles (or Charles Senior), and his son, Charles Lewis.

This is one instance that we have in which a tribe was eliminated because of a conflict here [...] A small party of [...] Nanzattico Indians were accused of the killing of an [English] family [...] as a result of a long-standing dispute. [...] The Nanzattico were impugned to give up the killers and they did that and the killers were convicted in English court and hanged, but the General Assembly also decided that the entire nation could be retaliated against because of what these men had done.

So, they passed a ruling to enslave the entire population of the Nanzattico except for children who were under twelve. The entire tribe was sold into slavery to Antigua in the West Indies [...]. The Nanzattico complained to the governor of Va. that "an English claimant to their land south of the river had broken down their fences and 'turned them off their land,' while the rest of their land on both sides of the river was claimed by the Lomax's; they wanted new land." The government considered the matter but did not act. Inaction may have prompted the Rowley homicides.[42]

Sold into Slavery

Virginia settlers began to come to the area in the middle decades of the 1600s and by the end of the century they had taken most of the lands of Nanzattico. On August 30, 1704, several men from the community were accused of killing a family of colonists who had encroached on their land.

In April 1704, the Nanzattico Indians filed an official complaint, claiming that Thomas Kendall of Essex County had broken down their fences and had run them off of their land. The Nanzattico also claimed that Dr. John Lomax (the grandson and heir of Thomas Lunsford, patentee of 3,423 acres at Portabago) had taken the rest of their property, a clear indication that he had seized their legally allocated land bordering Portabago Bay.

---

[42] McIlwaine (1925) 2: 359, 369; McIlwaine (1915) 4: 74; and McIlwaine (1918: 391)

When the Nanzattico filed a complaint against Kendall and Lomax, they asked to be assigned some new acreage, a matter that the Council agreed to consider. As it turned out, the Council failed to act in time. In September, a group of Natives attacked the Richmond County home of John Rowley and several English people were slain. A young girl who survived the attack described it to the authorities.

As the Nanzattico were known to have had disagreements with the Rowleys, they became prime suspects with the Piscataway also implicated. Several Nanzattico men were apprehended, questioned, and confessed to the killings.

Other members of the group (men, women, and children) were detained separately, reportedly on Colonel William Tayloe's plantation, so that they could not influence the testimony of the alleged assailants. When Richmond County's court convened, five of the accused Nanzattico men were convicted of murder and promptly hanged.

Two others, who had served as informants, were sentenced to death, and one Indian, a man named Frank, was acquitted. In mid-October 1704 and again on March 6, 1705, Mrs. Jane Cammell, "Interpreter from the Tryall of the Nanzattico Indians," presented a claim for compensation, requesting 1,000 pounds of tobacco for "my attendance on several 5 days & night." In December 1705, she was authorized to receive 800 pounds of tobacco in payment for her services.[43]

The justices decided that the 40 or so other Nanzattico who remained in custody should be brought to Williamsburg to stand trial in accord with the 1663 law that held all tribal members accountable for wrongful actions committed by others in their group.

Captain Nicholas Smith and his troop of horsemen, who were from Richmond County, conveyed the Nanzattico to the riverside opposite Hobbs Hole (Tappahannock). After the Indians crossed the Rappahannock River and arrived in Essex County,

---

[43] Richmond County Order Book 4 [1704-1708]: 40,100; Miscellaneous Records 1699-1724:33

Lieutenant Colonel Richard Covington and the Essex County militia escorted them as far as the border of King and Queen County.

At that point, King and Queen County Sheriff Robert Bird conducted the Indians to New Kent County, where New Kent sheriff John Moss took over. The Nanzattico were to be incarcerated at various county jails as they made their way to Williamsburg to be tried by the colony's highest court.

Williamsburg jailor John Redwood was to make a list of the Indians who entered his prison and to note any deaths that occurred during incarceration. He was to secure matchcoats for the Indians who lacked clothing and to furnish them with the type of provisions they were accustomed to, including a portion of meat once a week.

In May 1705, after the Nanzattico had spent the winter months in Williamsburg's jail, the House of Burgesses concluded that the entire group was implicated in the Rowley murders based on association and decided that those who were age 12 or older should be transported out of the colony and sold as servants.

Those under the age of 12 were to be bound out until age 24. Although the Council of State recommended that an elderly couple, Maddox Will and Betty, be spared deportation and that the group's women and girls be sold as servants for seven years on the Eastern Shore, the burgesses were adamant that they be removed from Virginia. It is likely that the burgesses – and some of the citizens they represented – were eager to be rid of the Nanzattico, for the governor and his council had agreed to uphold the Indians' claim to their Essex County preserve or find other acreage for them.

In 1704, John Lomax, Gawin (Gawen) Corbin, John Taliaferro, John Catlett, Ralph Wormeley II, and others who owned Indian land, were in positions of power in the House of Burgesses or were county justices.[44]

The same day the governor and his council decided the fate of the adult Nanzattico Indians, they had the group's children

---

[44] (Nugent 1934:III:149,151, 167, 202, 226)

brought before them to determine their age. Afterward, youngsters ranging in age from 9 months to 11 years were distributed among the governor and members of his council by means of drawing lots; then, indentures were prepared for each child.

All the officials receiving Nanzattico Indian children lived on the James-York peninsula or close by. Two weeks later, the adult Nanzattico, who were in prison in Williamsburg, petitioned the Council for the return of their skins, wampum Peake, and other chattels "lately taken from the Indian town," an indication that they were living in a clustered settlement at the time of their arrest.

Although the Council agreed that the Nanzattico's belongings would be returned to them before they were transported, that never happened. Colonel William Tayloe was ordered to sell the Indians' perishable goods and take custody of the rest. Later, the proceeds were used to cover the expenses involved in dealing with the Nanzattico.

On May 12, 1705, John Martin, a sea captain, posted a bond guaranteeing "the transportation of the Nanzattico Indians" to Antigua (McIlwaine 1918:425). Then, on May 23, 1706, he presented a certificate from Antigua's lieutenant governor, Daniel Parke, verifying that he had taken the Nanzattico there and sold them into seven years of servitude.[45]

No records have come to light that disclose how many of the Indians survived the ocean voyage or what happened to them after they arrived on an island with numerous sugar plantations.

The Rappahannock and Portobago Indians, who had seen the Nanzattico forcibly removed from their preserve on the lower side of Portobago Bay, no doubt felt in danger of further aggression from the English. That may have been the reason that they withdrew further inland, reoccupying the preserve that had been allocated to the Rappahannock in 1682.

Account of incident from the Colonial Government:

In April 1704, the Nanzattico complained to the House of Burgesses that English settlers were encroaching onto their

---

[45] McIlwaine 1925-1945:III:98

remaining enclave, on both sides of the river. These complaints were never acted upon by the Virginia Colony, and on August 30, a war party of ten Nanzattico men were accused of killing one of the encroaching settlers, John Rowley, and his family.

A colonial militia from Richmond County, Virginia hunted down and captured 49 Nanzattico and tried them for murder. While 5 men were hanged for the murder, and all the other Nanzattico over age 12 were sold into slavery in the West Indies under a 1665 law that held communities responsible for any murders of English settlers. Children were forced to work as servants for officials of the Virginia Colony.

To the Seventh Generation

It is particularly cruel to rewrite history with no mention of Natives unless they are called Savages or Heathens. The continuous Genocide against Natives as if that will change History belies that so-called lie that the Settlers are Gods Chosen People. We are still here and will continue to be here in one form or another.

In Native tradition we look, "Seven Generations" behind and, "Seven Generations" to the future. That is, we honor our ancestors who have passed and future generations yet to be born. This means we act in ways that benefit, not sacrifice, future generations, specifically the seventh generation after us. This is part of the culture that was interrupted due to Colonization and the disbursing of Natives from their Ancestral Lands.

The American Dream has drawn People from all over the world while many Native and Africans are living the American nightmare. There are Europeans who barely get off the plane and tell those of us who have been here to go back where we came from. Every door from Housing Education Employment and Health Care is open to them in the land of our ancestors.

They leave Europe where most of the Countries are Socialist and come to America to live the Capitalist Dream. The dirty secret about Capitalism is that those at the top are guaranteed money housing food health care and education and live as Socialist. While those at the bottom struggle to survive day to day under the foot of Capitalism. It is not a system we the people voted on or approved but one that was thrust upon us by those at the top.

MINQUA UNAMI OKEHOCKING & THE DOWN RIVER NATIONS

We are the Down River People deliberately left out of history and whose culture and beliefs were co-opted. When history mentions us, they Romanticize Colonization and gloss over our ancestor's contribution to the pristine land they Colonized. Native history goes back long before Christianity existed and is not meant for outsiders to understand.

I would not understand how Europeans lived thousands of years ago. How they survived in caves during the Winters and had little natural resources. I do not have that lived experience, but I would not knock them or try to destroy their culture. It is curious to watch as Europeans dig up bones in Africa Asia and the Americas. Who is going to Europe to dig up bones or see how they lived thousands of years ago? Who indeed!

Europeans came from Villages and forest themselves and claim to come from a Superior Society. Yet within years of arriving from their ancestral lands they become American or Australia or South African. It is peculiar to say the least that these people can ditch their own Country and give their children no history before Colonization.

In fact, the former President of the United States spoke of people who were thieves drug addicts and murderers coming over our southern border. Yet some Europeans sent here were criminals especially when America was first formed as a "Penal" Colony. Those who came as criminals had one advantage a White Skin.

Racial classifications were assigned to set up a class system which only benefitted White Males whose only achievement was setting up a class system based on race. Racial classifications changed according to how they interpreted us. Our Native Ancestors going back to the 1600's was listed as white Colored Mulatto Negro and Black. This happened within their individual lifetimes and similarly those racial classification was attributed to the children. Once the classifications changed from white to mulatto, it was seldom reversed.

Within our family there are White people and people of color just like in some other families. The thing about it is eventually the families are torn apart by those who pass and those who do not. That means there are Whites who have Colored People in their family. Many of those whites live in the South and have at least some African DNA.

Some of those same whites are more racist than other Whites. They show up as cousins on Ancestry DNA and some make contact while others do not. We are divided within our own family by race and do not call our white relatives out in public. Still there were just as many who were light enough to pass but did not.

We were surprised when Anthony (my brother) took an African Ancestry DNA test and it came back 100% Indigenous from Columbia South America. Somehow our paternal grandfathers' people wound up as slaves in South Carolina. This is another example of how Indigenous People of the America's were forced off their lands and into slavery.

I was no less surprised when my maternal line African Ancestry DNA test came back European from Spain. This was the same result I got from Family Tree DNA but not from Ancestry DNA which is an Autosomal Test. Our Paternal Grandmother Annie Bonaparte-Baxter's female lines came from the Fulani Tribe in Northern Nigeria. This was disclosed when one of our paternal Aunts took the African Ancestry DNA test.

We know where some of the Africans came from and who some of the Europeans were. The Europeans in our family came into the "New" World during Colonization and intermixed with Natives and Africans. Their progeny is listed in Virginia as FPC or Free Persons of Color. In America our oldest identifiable European Ancestor is Lydia Hilliard, born say 1685, and was the white servant of the Reverend St. John Shropshire. On April 25, 1705, when she was convicted by the Westmoreland County court of having a "mulatto" child by a "Negro man."

She was the servant of William Munro of Washington Parish on 8 March 1706 when he complained to the court that he had maintained her "Mulatto" child for two years and that the Reverend St. John Shropshire refused to release the child to him, and who was a Servant to William Monroe Senior grandfather of President

MINQUA UNAMI OKEHOCKING & THE DOWN RIVER NATIONS

James Monroe.[46]

According to the records about 1710 Lydia bore a child by an unnamed "Negro" man and the child (Mary) was also indentured to William Monroe senior. We do not know if the man was a Negro or Indian because by that time Virginia had redesignated Natives as Mulatto Colored or Negro. The child was Mary Hilliard-Monroe and she entered a marriage with William Monroe Junior in 1729 and bore a child by him named Mary Bowden on February 20,1730. That child, Mary Monroe and Lydia Hilliard are our direct ancestors on my mother's maternal side.

Mary Monroe was taken to court under a charge of bastardy (no charges were filed against William Jr.). The case was dismissed because of the support from the Monroe's' and Mary's ignorance of the law. Her children, Mary Bowden and four Generations of her descendants were Mulatto Indentured Servants to George Washington's brother Augustine Washington Junior.

Martha (Patty) Bowden, Mary's daughter was born at George Washington Birthplace about 1752 and was a personal servant to Elizabeth Washington-Spotswood. Patty and Mary Bowden left Westmoreland County and joined the Free Persons of Color Community in Fredericksburg Virginia.

First Contact with Europeans

Estimates of the depopulation of the native peoples of North America because of disease run as high as ninety percent in many regions. Infections carried by Spanish Explorers traveling along the Gulf Coast annihilated the tribes of the lower Mississippi River so that their cultural presence, visible in the form of their burial mounds, was largely unrecognized until the twentieth century.

The devastating impact of disease was not limited to just the years of initial contact. In 1804, Meriwether Lewis and William Clark, leaders of the Corps of Discovery, were given hospitality by the Mandans during their winter stay at Fort Mandan on the Missouri River. The tribe, which numbered about twenty thousand,

---

[46] Heinegg, Paul,; Orders 1698-1705, 257; 1705-21, 22, 27a; https://www.freeafricanamericans.com/Haws_Hurst.htm; March 19, 2022

dwindled to 150 after an epidemic of smallpox brought by fur traders in 1837.

On first sightings in Virginia, Natives thought of the Europeans as younger brothers, and saw that they were not operating from a place of wisdom. The Europeans were referred to by the places Natives met them, or what they were doing. Native people called them "uglusio", meaning "ones who look sick" because they really were physically sick.

"They arrived on boats after months on the ocean, ate their own feces, and their teeth were hanging from their faces. They smelled so badly that Natives of the eastern coast could smell them a mile away when they were in the woods."

They were physically sick and were it not for Natives would have died. It is no surprise than that many Africans captured by Europeans, did not survive the Middle Passage. Besides being hunted and captured, they were exposed to the diseases of uglusio (whites) and chained in the bowel of Slave Ships, like livestock.

As for Christopher Columbus, he thought he was in India, and called the Arawak's Indian. Even after realizing his mistake, he continued to call Natives, Indian. Natives who survived slavery and genocide were forced to convert to Catholic and later into the Anglican Church (Episcopalian). Then there were Blankets infected with Smallpox given to Tribes at the behest of Jeffrey Amherst.

I am a member of the Monacan Indian Nation which is located in Amherst County Virginia. When I connected to them, some African Americans told me not to join the tribe. I did not realize how effective Divide and Conquer was until then. It was all so interesting that we whose history was stolen from Native and African sides would buy into the white lie. I was surprised at the attitudes of African Americans some of whom themselves have Native Ancestors. Then it dawned on me that they too were ignorant of our actual history.

In many cases Natives who got Federal, or State Recognition were afraid of losing Recognition. Other Native Ancestors had similar fates to remove them from their land. The Nanzattico were enslaved because whites encroached on their land and a white family was found dead. There were no laws such as the "Castle" Doctrine or Stand Your Ground to protect the Natives from Encroachers.

Indigenous Peoples beliefs run contrary to that of Europeans who themselves were Christian Converts. The change came during the Inquisition when the Roman Catholic Church set out to convert all of Europe. They were especially brutal to the Jews and Moors in Spain whose beliefs preceded their own. Burning at the Stake Public Hanging, and Public Whippings was a practice brought from Europe to the America's as well as other forms of torture for those thought to be witches.

Tituba – Salem Witch Trial

A Native woman Tituba was the first to be accused of practicing witchcraft during the 1692 Salem Witch Trials. She was enslaved and owned by Samuel Parris of Danvers, Massachusetts. Although her origins are debated, research has suggested that she was a South American Native sailed from Barbados to New England with here owner Samuel Parris.

She became a pivotal figure in the Salem Witch Trials when she was tortured into a confession and implicated two other women and Sarah Osborne participated in said witchcraft. She was imprisoned and later released by Samuel Conklin.

Tituba's husband was John Indian, an Indigenous man whose origins are unknown, but he may have been from Central or South America. Tituba may have originally been from Barbados. Here is another case of an Indigenous Person whose identity was changed. Over the years as a means of deflecting she was referred to as an African who practiced voodoo. Instead of dealing with why there were "Witch" Trials they were focused on Tituba.

The often-unreliable records of the enslaved persons origins make this information difficult to verify. There are historians such as Samuel Drake who suggest that Tituba was African. Her husband went on to become one of the accusers in the Witch Trials. They appear documented together in Samuel Parris's church record book.

Indigenous People believe every living thing has value and

deserves reverence and respect. In Native, belief the welfare of the tribe is more important than the individual. The European concept is vastly different and are Patriarchal with women being submissive to men. Although it is changing with the women's movement it is a slow process.

Their concept of rugged Individualism was foreign to the Indigenous inhabitants of Turtle Island. The Rugged Individual sees themselves as the Center of the Universe or Gods Chosen People. That person for the most part would be considered a Sociopath by today's standards. Yet that was the mindset of the People who were set on taking Native Lands by Any Means Necessary.

"To most of the traders and settlers of Pennsylvania, Delaware, Virginia and Maryland, the Indian was an Indian. To the great majority of the settlers who swept over the mountain ridges at the commencement of the XVII (18th) Century an Indian was simply a member of one of the Heathen tribes which occupied the Promised Land, and as such it was the duty of the Elect to blot them from the face of the earth, as Joshua of Old Had blotted out the Hivites and the Jebusites. It was the same attitude they had as they swept over lands occupied by Africans.

Ancestor George H. M. Johnson descendant of Molly Brant Johnson, Konwatsi'tsiaienni. Mohawk leader.

CHAPTER SIX

DIGGING UP OUR ROOTS

"When we talk about land, land is part of who we are. It's a mixture of our blood, our past, our present, and our future. We carry our ancestors in us, and they're around us. As you all do."
Mary Lyons (Leech Lake Band of Ojibwe)

When I started our Family History search in 1978 we lived in Oakland and there were not a lot of places to go. There was however the Mormon Temple which towered over the City of Oakland. My mother and I made a pact to preserve our family's history after we moved from Reading Pennsylvania to Oakland California. She baby sat while I headed to The Mormon Temple where there was a Genealogical Library with records on microfiche and in books. I was the only Person of Color at that Library and got to know the librarian who often assisted me the search.

Mom received a response to a letter she wrote to the Baptist Historical Society. In the letter it mentioned our ancestor Reverend Robert A. Pinn who was a Baptist minister in Philadelphia. He was the grandfather of our maternal Grandmother Leah Ruth-Martin. The Pinn's are one of our oldest Native Lines from Virginia and were Indigenous to the Wicomico Indian Nation which at one time encompassed Lancaster and Wicomico County on the Eastern Shore of Virginia. Wicomico Tribal Lands were divided by Europeans to create the States of Maryland and Virginia.

The challenge we faced was to piece together the scattered history here in America. A history of the enslavement and removal of our Native and African Ancestors. To claim the lands of Indigenous People all over the world Europeans felt it necessary to strip them of their identity. To justify actions of racism a narrative was created about the people whose land they colonized further stripping them of their humanity. It is a Physical Spiritual Cultural and Paper Genocide that has lasted over 500 years.

Before the seventeenth century, Africans came to America as free men some of whom may have been mixed bloods called, Atlantic Creoles. The Creoles were the offspring of relations between Europeans and Africans in the towns that emerged surrounding the slave castles on the West African Coast. Europeans were engaged in the slave trade beginning as early as the 1460's when Prince Henry of Portugal was importing significant amounts of slaves.

Meanwhile Native Lands were co-opted for Church Parishes in Virginia and other parts of the Colony. The Church Parishes had the power to tax (tithe) everyone in its jurisdiction. The Churchwardens were under Authority of the Church, to police those within the parish boundaries. Instead of Constitutional Law, Church Law, or Ecclesiastical Law, governed the states including the Natives.

This is what is called proselytizing or converting others to your Religion, a widespread practice in most major Religions. Colonization and Religion were a deadly mix for the Indigenous people who welcomed the strangers on their shores. Not only in America but in Africa India and other parts of Asia except for China. They were able to outsmart the land hungry Europeans and not be subjected to Colonization.

Colonization was nothing new to Europeans which had for centuries been ruled by Monarchs. They had a large Peasant Class who were landless and at the mercy of the Royals. When the Anglo Saxon went into Britain, they encountered the Welsh who were the original inhabitants.

The Welsh had Kingdoms and a thriving culture prior to Colonization by the Anglo-Saxons. The Anglo-Saxons and the Scots gradually conquered the Welsh Kingdoms. However, the Welsh have retained their own language and culture. Between 1,000 AD and the Conquest of Wales by Edward I in the 1280's
The main kingdoms were Gwynedd, Powys and Deheubarth. Our maternal Virginia Lewis (Llewelyn) lines traced back to Breconshire and Monmouth shire Wales.

The race-based Laws passed by the Colonizer, had no input from Natives who were most affected by them. The laws were passed and codified by White Males doing the bidding of the European Monarchy and Rulers. They saw opportunities to gain wealth land and dominance through Colonization. What better way to do that then through the Church the voice of the Monarchy?

The Anglican, Episcopalian, and Catholic Churches taught that Indigenous people were heathen and savage, and Africans were cursed by God and inferior to them. This basic belief allowed them to travel all over the world and kill off or conquer the people using Christ and the Christian Bible as justification. It was also a justification to steal the mineral wealth of the "Conquered" Country and build Europe.

In Colonial Virginia, (or the Upper South) there was no separation of church and state, the church was a tool of Europe's ruling class. Churches such as the Episcopalian, Anglican, and Catholic Church set up parishes. The Catholic Missions were set up in the heart of Indigenous Countries in attempts to covert assimilate or Annihilate the Natives. That is why there is a Mission Street in every city in America.

Each parish tithed (taxed) the people within its borders according to their household size and income. The tithes were not necessarily money but crops especially from Natives. In 1733 our ancestor Robert Pinn I, was taken up by the Church Warden in Wicomico Parish Church. He was ordered to pay his fines in Hogsheads of Tobacco. The church had total control and power over parishioner's lives, including the power to confer whippings, Prison, or death.

Wicomico Indian Village was divided between Virginia and Maryland. It was originally on the Eastern Shore of Virginia and was tributary to the Powhatan. There is now a Wicomico Village in Maryland that was a part of the Original Settlement in Indiantown. The Wicomico Settlement in Lancaster and Northumberland County Virginia was barren when we went there in 2000. There are Pinn descendants of the Virginia Wicomico Tribe still living in Virginia and Maryland.

Genealogy of Wicomico Pinn Ancestors

Robert Pinn I (b. 1710 • d. abt. 1740) Wicomico Parish, Lancaster County, Virginia, USA, son for Father Thomas Pinn (b. 1695–d. 8 Jan 1793 • St. George's Parish, Spotsylvania Co, Virginia, United States); Robert Pinn I married Margaret Winas (b. 1720 Essex, Virginia, - d. abt. 1750 Indiantown Lancaster County Va); her father, John, was 47, and her mother, Remember, was 40 when she married Robert Pinn I in Lancaster County, Virginia.

They had four children during their marriage, Robert Pinn II, (b. 1740–d. aft 1778) Rawley Pinn (b. abt. 1742 – d. aft. 1801), Birth of Son John Pinn (b. 1750 d. bfr. 1775); and Sally Pinn (b. 1750 d. aft. 1776). Winas-Pinn died as a young mother in 1750 in Lancaster, Virginia, at the age of 30. Margaret's father John Winas (b. 1673-1734) passed away on November 5, 1734, in Essex, New Jersey, at the age of 61. Her mother Remember Baldwin-Winas passed away in 1745 at the age of 65 in Elizabeth Union, New Jersey.

Rawley Pinn, our direct ancestor was apprenticed as a Cooper in 1760 and later led a group into the interior. He settled in Amherst County and married Sarah Redcross-Evans. They owned land and property in Amherst County and were the parents of our ancestor James Pinn and his second wife Jane (Jinsey), Cooper-Powell.

Our Pinn lines were indigenous to the Wicomico Indian Nation in Lancaster County Virginia. Robert Pinn was the Great Man (Chief) of the Wicomico and was also a member Their Village was divided in half when Maryland and Virginia were created as Colonial Settlements.

Susquehannock

Captain John Smith met members of the Susquehannock Indian tribe near Port Deposit, Maryland and traveled upstream to its village. It is Smith who named the tribe "Susquehannock," a Delaware Indian term meaning "muddy river."

According to Smith the Susquehannock built stockaded villages and lived in multi-family longhouses, measuring 60 to 80 feet in length. The Susquehannock were a matriarchal society meaning these American Indians trace their descent through their mother, and married men lived with their wives' families.

"The Susquehannock were an alert, well-organized, military people and great traders," a historian wrote. Their lower Susquehanna home put them close to European traders on the Delaware and Chesapeake bays. John Smith explored the Chesapeake Bay and Lower Susquehanna River in 1608. He meets the Susquehannock's and described them as giants. He claims one warrior's calf measures twenty-seven inches around.

The Susquehannock's, were powerful tribe, and lived along the Susquehanna in Pennsylvania and Maryland. Smith was impressed with their skills with weaponry. They were in the area that eventually became York County according to Smith, but we now know they had Villages along the Susquehanna River. are among the later American Indian groups to live in the area that eventually becomes York County. These Indians leave behind arrowheads, carvings on rocks and other artifacts for us to study. And what about their size? Well, Susquehannock graves give no indication that they were the size of giants.[iv]

The English wore armor and carried muskets, but the Susquehannock wore the heads of bear and wolves for their jewelry, and already possessed metal hatchets and knives" The Susquehannocks came to us, such great and well-proportioned men are seldome seene, for they seemed like giants to the English, these are the strangest people of all those countries both in language and attire; for their language it may well be seeme their proportions, sounding from them as a voice in a vault. Their attire is the skinnes of beares and woolves, some have cassocks made of beares heades and skinnes .

The halfe sleeves coming to the elbows were the heades of beares and the arms through the open mouth . . . one had the heade of a woolf hanging from a chain for a jewell . . . with a club suitable to his greatness sufficient to beat out ones brains. Five of their chiefe wereowances came aboard us . . . (of) the greatest of them his hayre, the one side was long and the other shorn close with a ridge over his crowne like a cock's combe . . . The calfe of whose leg was a yard around and all the rest of his limbes so answerable to that proportion that he seemed the goodliest man we ever beheld!"[47]

The Conestoga took Penn at his word, and for many years, their town served as a center for trade and diplomacy between colonial Pennsylvanians and Indians of the Susquehanna Valley. Sadly, after Conestoga Indian Town's population had declined its residents still claimed to possess a special relationship with their colonial neighbors rooted in Penn's promise.

At daybreak on December 14, 1763, more than 50 Paxton Boys attacked Conestoga Indian Town. They dismounted their horses and fired their flintlocks at the Indian huts. They rushed inside and tomahawking survivors. They scalped everyone including the women and children. As news of the attack spread, officials in Lancaster and Philadelphia began to worry that the men who murdered and attacked the Conestoga might return.

Local deputies were ordered to move the Indians into a substantial brick workhouse that stood directly north of the county jail at King and Prince Street. The workhouse had just been constructed, so the Conestoga became some of the first inmates. After several days, word reached the Paxton Boys that 14 Conestoga Indians lived. It took little convincing to muster the men to return to Lancaster and finish the job.

On the morning of December 27th, between 50 and 100 Rangers once again headed south. They reached Lancaster's snow-covered Queen Street at 2 pm. They dismounted at the Sign of the White Swan, gathered their weapons, and walked down King Street. When the Paxton Boys reached the workhouse, they encountered Sheriff Hay and Coroner Slough. However, as the Rangers approached, the two men stepped aside without protest.

The Rangers broke down the workhouse door and pursued the fleeing Natives into the yard. There they slaughtered the Conestoga. Parents were hacked to death in front of their children. The children were hacked to death as well and others were

---

[47] From The Voyages of Captain John Smith; of Jamestown, Va.; during the Years 1607- 60

murdered with musket fire at point-blank range. The Paxton Boys cut the hands and feet from several Indians. They were all scalped including the women and children.

The massacre took place after Penn after 1701 when William Penn deeded 10000 acres of the Conestoga land back to them. This was around the same time when the 500 acres of land was deeded to the Okehocking on the border of what is now Chester and Delaware County. This ethnic cleansing would not have happened if the people of Pennsylvania had not broken the treaty and stolen the land from the Conestoga. Penn also declared that the English and Conestoga' "shall forever hereafter be as One Head and One Heart."

That treaty lasted only 16 years since Penn's sons wanted the land for themselves. Eventually only 400 acres remained of the land, but all through the land grabbing, the Indians remained peaceful, learned English and were loyal to the crown during the French and Indian War. This is the land that my Green Martin Page Johnson and allied ancestors lived on.

After the massacre Squatters from Paxton began laying claim to the 400 acres but were made to leave and Rev. Barton was given the land, which is interesting. Reverend Barton ministered to the Native Americans in Lancaster. He was a close friend of Sir William Johnson, who was the British superintendent of Indian affairs, who sent his part-Native American son to live with Rev. Barton to further his religious studies.

After the massacre Barton asked Sir William to grant the Conestoga land for establishment of an Indian school. Sir William turned him down but did grant Barton the use of the land five years later to farm to support his family.[48]

After the Massacre by the Paxton Boys, Pennsylvania declared that there were no more Indians. The census records dropped the designation of Indian and noted Natives as Colored, Negro, Mulatto, or Black. Our Welsh Mountain ancestors

---

[48]Sir William Johnson had several children with Molly Brant who is one of our maternal ancestors on our Martin/Johnson side.

intermixed with Whites and the Children were labeled as Mulatto or Colored.

Queen Aliquippa

There is little documentation about Queen Aliquippa's early life. She was born sometime around 1680. Her father was from the ancient Susquehannock Nation, now Iroquoian, who signed a treaty with William Penn. Aliquippa attended the treaty and oral history implies that she is in the painting.

Aliquippa lived at Conestoga, Pennsylvania and had at least one son, named Canachquasy. In 1701, they traveled to New Castle, Delaware to say farewell to William Penn who was returning to England. By 1731, the family began to move westward and eventually settled near the Forks of the Ohio, adjacent to where McKees Rocks, Pennsylvania is today.

Few know the story of this Iroquois matriarch and staunch English ally named Queen Aliquippa. Yet, the town of Aliquippa, Pennsylvania is still named for her. In the 18th century, other area sites were also named after her including Aliquippa Town, Aliquippa Creek, Aliquippa Island, and Aliquippa Cornfield.

Queen Aliquippa was a Iroquois Chief from the Seneca Nation. The Seneca are part of the Iroquois Confederacy, a powerful government made up of six nations: the Seneca, Mohawk, Onondaga, Oneida, Cayuga, and Tuscarora. In the 18th century, the Iroquois government had dominance over other Indian nations in the Ohio River Valley.

"The most esteemed of their women do sometimes speak in council. He told me she was an empress; and they gave much heed to what she said among them...," T. Chalkley, 1706, Conestoga, Pennsylvania.[49]

She died in Huntington on the warriors path a Native Trail used for travel from Pennsylvania through New York and into the Onondaga Reservation in Canada. Those same paths were used by Natives and Underground Railroad Conductors to help escaped slaves. Those ancient trails are now Highways and byways for modern society, but they are thousands of years old.

Kanostoge' (Conestoga)

---

[49] Penn's Treaty with the Indians by Benjamin West, 1771; Art print courtesy of the PA Academy of Fine Arts, Philadelphia gift of Mrs. Sarah Harrison (The Joseph Harrison Jr. Collection)

MINQUA UNAMI OKEHOCKING & THE DOWN RIVER NATIONS

Queen Aliquippa

Queen Aliquippa was the head of the Iroquois Federation and is believed to be Seneca. Between 1702 & 1704 she negotiated land for the Minqua and Okehocking in Conestoga (Lancaster County) and what is now Chester and Delaware County. The Land Negotiations took place around the same time as the Nanzattico in Virginia were being removed from their village.

Little is known about her early life. Her date of birth has been estimated anywhere from the early 1670s to the early 1700s, but historians have indicated that she was born in the 1680s, in upstate New York.

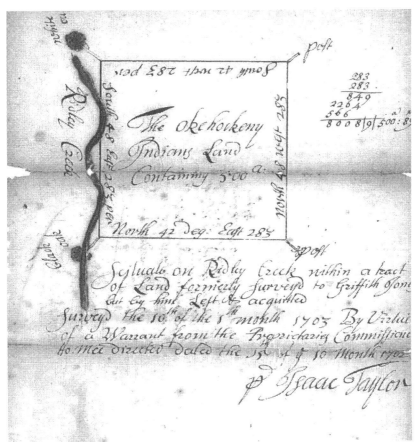

Okehocking Land Grant (1703) – Ceded by William Penn – Colonizers stole the land and ceded some of it back. The land located in Chester County (now parts of Delaware) was taken back by settlers after William Penn returned to England.

Sister Carolyn Baxter-Reams Wedding Picture (Circa 1968) Dad George Baxter Senior Brother -in-law Leroy Reams Sister Carolyn Baxter -Reams Mom Vivian Martin-Baxter

Martin sisters (now deceased)- right to Left; Aunt Dorothea Aunt Sara Aunt Lydia Aunt Ramona (Great Aunt Blanche Martin-Robinson) Aunt Ruth Vivian (Mom) Aunt Cora

MINQUA UNAMI OKEHOCKING & THE DOWN RIVER NATIONS

Daddy - Charles Franklin Martin

    Grandpop Martin attended Quaker School in Williston Chester County Pa and left in the 10th Grade. He was allowed to grow his hair out and This was one way to keep him from being sent To Mission School. His father worked for the Quakers and attended Quaker School as well.

CHAPTER SEVEN

THE EASTERN SHORE PINN CONNECTION

"If there is no struggle, there is no progress. Those who profess to favor freedom, and yet depreciate agitation, are men who want crops without plowing up the ground. They want rain without thunder and lightning. They want the ocean without the awful roar of its many waters." Frederick Douglass

The Native Pinn's are documented from about 1649 in Lancaster and Northumberland County. They lived in and around, Indiantown, which is in Lancaster County Virginia, and were identified as Mulatto and Free Persons of Color. The family roots are in the Eastern Shore of Virginia and Maryland, as part of the Chicawane and Yeocomico (Wicomico, Wiccocomoco) Indian tribes.

There is a Thomas Pinn, in Lancaster County in the mid 1600's, and appears to be the forbearers of our direct ancestor, Robert Pinn I (b. abt. 1710, d. bfr. 1760), who resided in Northumberland County Virginia with his wife Margaret. Robert had a son named Hezekiah, who was listed as Indian, and a brother named Indian David.

Wicomico Church Minutes (1669)

In Virginia Colonial Abstracts by Fleet, Vol. 19, a brief biography is found of Capt. John Rogers detailing that he was 45 years old in 1665. Four years later, 1669, he as 49, and 21 or 22 years before he built the first church when he was about 27 years old.

"It was a well-appointed church with red silk plush hangings on pulpit and altar. Three prominent families donated the church silver: in 1734 Major W. Lee gave a church bell. After a failed attempt at building a second church, the third church was erected on 9 May 1753. This would replace the second church which was contracted to be built and was not completed. The third church was completed by 1758.

It was to be an explicit copy of Christ Church, Irvington/Weems (Northumberland County), only five feet bigger. Serious delays and modifications set back the start of the third church until 1766, ten years before the American Revolution. Put into service in 1771, just five years before the American Revolution, it was the largest brick church in Virginia. Wicomico Parish Church continued functioning throughout the Revolution, and even ten years more after the War.

The Vestry minutes of 1703-1795 mention little if anything of the turmoil swirling around them. The Continental Congress passes an act in 1785 creating the separation of church and state. Just after that Act of 1785, the first Diocese of Virginia was established in convention at Philadelphia. The vestry continued until 1795, then the Minutes cease.

"This would appear to have been a mortal blow. Dispersed by the effects of wars, failing tobacco crops, and the disestablishment of the church, many left. Bishop Meade declared that there were no Episcopalians left in Wicomico Parish. He was mistaken, but barely, as the Parish was represented at the Diocesan Council in 1812 and 1813, then the records are silent."

Wicomico church parish was built on land formally inhabited by the Yeocomico (Wicomico) Indians, who lived in North-eastern Virginia and Southern Maryland. During Colonization, the Natives were enslaved, and their children converted to Christians. The other dynamic was that many white males intermixed with and intermarried Native women (at least until the laws forbade it).

Some of the children from the unions were accepted as white, with all the benefits implied. Those who were darker or This was the reality that the Pinn family lived with in the mid to late sixteen and seventeen hundred.

The Pinn's were Natives, some of whom were treated as whites for a period. Those who intermixed with Free Blacks was a matter of concern to those in power. They were a family who had never been slaves, and had rights afforded their status. Many of the men served in the Revolutionary War and were at Yorktown with George Washington and Marquis De Lafayette.

Rawley Pinn a son of Robert I (born about 1710 died before 1754), and his wife Margaret (born about 1720 died after 1753), his wife, followed a trail that led to Amherst County. About 1753, Rawley and his brother Robert II, were in Lancaster County, serving apprenticeships. Robert II remained in Lancaster County, married Ann Kesterman, and raised a family.

After serving his apprenticeship Rawley, began traveling, and eventually settled in Amherst County. That is where he was when the Revolutionary War broke out, and he enlisted. After the war, he became a preacher, purchased land, and farmed in Amherst County.

He also married, Sarah (Redcross) Evans), and began raising a family. His wife Sarah was the daughter of Charles Evans and carried the name of Redcross. She kept the surname of Redcross possibly from her mother's lines and Evans, which was not unusual for those times. Our Evans line are descendants of Jane the Elder (Bnu) Gibson an Indian Woman.

According to the Monacan Indian Rolls, the following marriages took place:
- William Evans------married 1700------Indian Woman
- Robert Johns--------1700----------------Mary Indian
- Robert Johns Jr-----1779---------------Elizabeth Lyons
- Will Johns-------------1790---------------Molly Evans
- Ned Branham--------1790----------------Nancy Evans
- Thomas Standhope Evans--1795-----Anna Pinn
- Robert Evans---------1795--------------Martha England
- Nancy Redcross----------1799---------------James Pinn
- John Redcross-------1807--------------Susan Thomas

According to the partial roll listed above the Evans, Pinn, Stanhope, and Redcross Families intermarried quite extensively.

Our Maternal Family Matriarch Jane (Bnu) Gibson (The Elder)

Jane the Elder Gibson (Bnu) is one of my oldest provable

Native lines. The Saura Indians, also known as the Cheraw, were one of several small Siouan tribes in the colonial backcountry (the modern-day Piedmont) of North Carolina. Jane was Cheraw and one of the original inhabitants of what is now North Carolina. Jane-Bnu Gibson is the Matriarch of our Evans line that traces back to Granville North Carolina.

Jane Bnu Gibson (the Elder) is a direct ancestor through Sarah Redcross Evans-Pinn the wife of Rawley Pinn. Rawley and Sarah are my direct ancestors through their son James Pinn and his second wife Jane (Jinsey) Cooper-Powell- Pinn. They were the parents of Great-Great Grandfather Reverend Robert A. Pinn IV. Rawley was Wicomico Indian from Lancaster County Virginia, the son of Robert Pinn I (1720 – 1750) the Great Man of Indiantown in Lancaster County Virginia.

Rawley and Sarah settled in Amherst County where he was a Revolutionary War Soldier and fought at The Siege of Yorktown. The unit marched from Amherst County and joined with General Marquis De Lafayette. Their son James and his second wife Jane Cooper-Powell-Pinn were the parents of My Great-Great Grandfather Robert A. Pinn, Christina Pinn, and George Washington Lafayette Pinn. James had an older daughter named Evelina with his first wife Nancy Redcross.

There was a Sally (Evans) Anderson the great-granddaughter of Jane Gibson the younger and the great-great granddaughter of Jane Gibson the elder. Both Jane Gibson's (mother and daughter) was noted for their doctoring skills. In the sworn deposition of Robert Wills in 1791. Jane Gibson the elder healed Robert "King" Carter of the Shirley Plantation.

Jane Gibson, (The Elder) Upper Congaree Shikora (Cheraw)

The Congaree were a Native tribe that existed in Richland and Lexington counties along the Congaree River. Not a large tribe, maybe a thousand or so spread across several villages. They were doing just fine until European colonists "discovered" the area and it pretty much went downhill from there. They brought war over land territory with the bonus of smallpox. This forced the Congaree to join forces with the Catawba tribe that lived north of the area known as Columbia, toward York County.

The Catawba (which means "River people" were fierce warriors and to be feared in battle. The other large tribe in the area, taking up the eastern half of the state were known as the Creeks. They had large battles, East vs West. It wasn't quite like Biggie and Tu Pac, but you get the idea. It didn't matter anyway, because the Euros invited themselves to the party and that's pretty much all she wrote.

As their numbers dwindled, so did many of the existing tribes, along with many of their traditions and languages. Thankfully, a few tribes survived and still live today on reservations given to them by the government. Those are the Catawba Indian Nation, The Ediso Natchez-Kusso, The Wassamasaw, The Santee, The Waccamaw, The Beaver Creek, The Pee Dee, Chicora, and the Cherokee. Of those state recognized tribes, only the Catawba have been federally recognized. [50]

The Conagaree is one of our ancestral Native Gibson/Evans tribes with villages along the Conagaree River in South Carolina. Our Gibson/Evans ancestors originated from this group of Natives and held Villages in what is now North Carolina and Virginia. The States Boundaries and borders were non incorporated until after the Revolutionary War.

- Richard EVANS: Great Uncle 7 generations removed (Great-Grandmother Maria Louisa Pinn-Ruth's Paternal lines)
Born 1737:
Birthplace: Brunswick, Virginia, United States
Residence: Pittsboro, Chatham, North Carolina, USA
Death date: Sep 9, 1815
Death place: Warren, North Carolina, United States
- Father: Charles M EVANS (Direct Ancestor):
Born in 1696 - York, Virginia, United States
Died in 1760 - Brunswick, Virginia, United States
- His Aunt: Elizabeth CUMBO (born Evans):

---

[50] King, Alex, Like A Local: A history of Native Americans in South Carolina; https://wach.com/news/local/like-a-local-a-history-of-native-americans-in-south-carolina; April 25, 2022

(Charles M. Evans Sister); (upper Congaree Skihori tribe)
Born in 1700 - British Colonial America
Died in 1750 - British Colonial America
- His Mother: Sarah Jane KRESSA (Direct Ancestor 8 Generations removed) Born in 1705 - Lunenburg, Lunenburg, Virginia, USA

Died in 1756 - Warren Co, North Carolina
- His Wife: Mary Mabery

Born in 1745 - Craven, South Carolina, United States
Died in 1804 - Carolina, Carolina, Puerto Rico, United States
- His Brother: Thomas Lee Evans Senior

Born in 1725 - Lunenburg, Luneburg Virginia, United States
Died in 1774 - Amherst, Amherst, Virginia, United States
- His Brother: Charles Evans (our direct ancestor)

Born in 1735 - Lunenburg, Virginia, United States
Died in 1810 - Mecklenburg, Virginia, United States
- His Brother: Morris Evans

Born in 1738 - Lunenburg, Virginia, USA
Died in 1834 - Wake County, North Carolina, USA
- His Brother: Arthur EVANS

Born in 1740 - Lunenburg County, Virginia
Died (?)
- His Brother: Erasmus EVANS

Born in 1745 - Lunenburg, Lunenburg, Virginia, United States
- His Sister: Sarah REDCROSS EVANS-PINN (Direct Ancestor 7 Generations removed)

Born in 1741 - Lunenburg County Virginia
Died in 1821 - Amherst County Virginia
- His Brother: Burwell EVANS

Born in 1750 - Lunenburg County, Virginia
Died in 1820 - Wake County, North Carolina, USA
- His Sister: Martha EVANS

Born in 1756 - Lunenburg, Lunenburg, Virginia, United States
Died - Virginia, United States
- His Sister: Joyce EVAN

Born in 1744 - Lunenburg, Lunenburg, Virginia, United States

Died (?)
- His Half-brother: Morris Evans

Born in 1738 - Lunenburg, Lunenburg, Virginia, United States
Died in 1835 - Hillsborough, Orange, North Carolina, USA
- His Daughter: Mary Wheatley (born Evans)

Born in 1730 - Hagerstown, Maryland
Died in 1803 - Kentucky

The court filings on behalf of descendants of Jane Gibson the Elder took several generations and was won by Morris Evans (1665-1739). His wife Jane Gibson (1660-1738) had a mother also named Jane Gibson. To distinguish between the two women, the mother is referred to as Jane Gibson the elder (born 1640-1722). The elder Jane Gibson was called "a free Indian woman" by a group of her descendants who were illegally enslaved. Though the Evans and Gibson families were free born, that did not prevent some white planters from illegally enslaving them.

Goodrich Lightfoot – Slaveholder

Some of the descendants of Morris Evans and Jane Gibson's daughter Frances Evans (1685-1771) were enslaved by a wealthy Slave owner named Goodrich Lightfoot. They were originally "bound out" to Lightfoot to be indentured servants but he instead enslaved them and after his death, they were subsequently sold to several slave owners. On 5 March 1804, the enslaved Evans through their attorney Edmund Randolph sued for their freedom and provided information that they descended from a free Indian woman – Jane Gibson the elder.

Petition of descendants of Jane Gibson The Elder

Evans, Milly Evans, Adam Evans, and Hannah Evans holden in slavery by Lewis Allen, of the County of Halifax humbly showeth; that your petitioners are descendants from Jane Gibson, a free Indian woman…,

That about seventy years ago he was well acquainted with Jane Gibson and George Gibson her brother who were dark mulattoes and lived in the County of Charles City, and were free people: That the said Jane Gibson had two children named Jane and George Gibson, that they were also free; That the said Jane Gibson the younger intermarried with a certain Evans of the said County, by whom she had several children, one named Frances Evans Grand Daughter of the said Jane Gibson above named, that the said Frances Evans removed to New Kent County, where she lived and had several children, two of whom, as the said Frances Evans informed this deponent were named Tom and Frances Evans, and were bound to one Goodrich Lightfoot of New Kent. This information was made to this Deponent by the said Frances Evans the elder when she was on a visit to her friends in this deponent County, who were neighbors to this deponent.

This; This deponent further saith, that after the said great Grandchildren Viz: Tom & Frances were bound to the said LIGHTFOOT he never heard anything more relative to them; That many of the descendants of the said GIBSONS and EVANS now in this deponents knowledge are alive, and are enjoying their freedom unmolested and have remained so since this deponents first acquaintance with the said Jane Gibson the elder;

That many of them are black, some nearly white and others dark mulattoes, which this deponent supposes proceeded from a promiscuous intercourse with different colors.

Questions by the defts agent.

Do you know anything of the descendants of the said Frances Evans, who was bound to LIGHTFOOT? No, I do not.

What became of Frances Evans and her brother after they were bound to LIGHTFOOT? I know nothing of them, but from the information of their mother aforesaid.

Do you know any free mulattoes or blacks who have descended from a branch of the name of EVANS, who are they and from whom did they spring?

I know several of them, to wit, in Charles City, the SCOTTs, BRADBYs, SMITHs, Recrosses alias EVANS, Morris's alias EVANS, and in Henrico the BOWMANs, all descendants from the original stock of the GIBSON to wit, Jane EVANS Daughter of Jane GIBSON.

Do you know or have you ever known of any other free persons by the name of EVANS of a different family? I do not except in

ANITA L. WILLS

Caroline.

How do you know that the children of Frances Evans were named Tom & Frances, and how old would they be were they now alive: I heard their mother say so; I cannot tell how old, but they would be many years old.

How old are you? I am in my eighty first year.

And further this deponent saith not.

The following month on 9 July 1791, Robert Wills was back in court providing additional testimony which clarified a few points.

A transcription can be found here:

Questions by the defendant. How old were you when you were firs acquainted with the elder Jane Gibson and George her brother?

Answer I believe I was ten or eleven years old or thereabouts.

Quest. How old do you suppose they were and how long did they live afterwards?

Answer. Jane Gibson the elder was very old, I apprehend she was eighty years of age, being past all labour– Mr. Carter our Master took her to live with him at Shirley Plantation where I then lived to brew a diet drink, he being afflicted with a dropsy – The old Jane Gibson I suppose might live two or three years. Her daughter Jane widow to an EVANS (whose Christian name I am not certain of but believe it was Morris), lived a considerable number of years after our first acquaintance with her– she bore the name of EVANS as did all her children.

Quest. About what time were you acquainted with Jane and George Gibson the children of Jane, and how old were they when you were first acquainted with them?

Answer. I knew Jane Evans the daughter some time before I knew the old woman, which I believe as I have deposed in our former deposition must be seventy years ago; she was an old woman when I became acquainted with her, she practiced midwifery and doctoring in families but was not above sixty I should suppose: George too was an old person, I believe – Jane was the older.

Quest. About what time did Jane and George Gibson the children of Jane Gibson die?

Answer I do not knowQuest. About what year did Jane Gibson the younger intermarry with ___ EVANS?
Answer That I cannot tell it must have been long before I was born.
Quest. About what year do you believe to the best of your recollection or judgment was Frances Evans the Granddaughter of old Jane Gibson born?
Answer She had children bound out when I first knew her, so that she must have been born long before I was, as I should suppose.
Quest. Then as you know so little about her how do you know she (Frances Evans) was the daughter of Jane Evans, and that Jane Evans was descended from Jane Gibson?
Answer. I know nothing but common reputation they called each other by the name of Mother and daughter.
Quest. About what year did the said Frances Evans remove to New Kent?
Answer. I never knew her until she came on a visit to her mother, she then lived there as she reported; when she came there to live, I knew nothing about it.
Quest. About what year did the said Frances Evans inform you she had bound two of her children Frances and Tom to Mr. Lightfoot of New Kent when she came on a visit to her friends in Charles City?
Ans'r. I cannot recollect that with any certainty, I suppose fifty-eight or fifty-nine years ago or somewhere thereabouts.
Quest. Did you understand from her how old they were at that time, if not how old do you suppose they were, and how long had they been bound before she informed you of it?
Answer. That I know nothing about.
Quest. If the said Frances Evans and her brother Tom who are said to have been bound to one LIGHTFOOT were now alive how old would they be to the best of your judgment?
Ans'r. I do not know that; they were probably as old as myself; I never saw either of them or asked any questions about their age.
Quests. by the plaintiff 1. Was not the mother of Sarah Recross (now living in Charles City) alias Sarah Evans named Frances Evans, and was she not related as by common reputation believed to Frances Evans that was bound to LIGHTFOOT.

Ans'r. About twenty-four or twenty-five years ago Frances Evans was about in Charles City County, and was claimed as a mother by Sarah Redcross, and Sarah Redcross said that her mother was the granddaughter of Jane Evans the daughter of Jane Gibson – she went away, and I know not what became of her, but have been informed (I suppose twenty years ago) that she was dead.
Quest. by deft. Why do you in this deposition call Mr. Carter your master?
Answer. Our father gave me to him when I was ten years of age, and he brought me up and had me taught our trade of a carpenter.
Quest. for how many years were you acquainted with that particular family of the GIBSONs and EVANS, which have been the object of your testimony in this suit meaning the three first generations and where did you live during that time?
Ans'r. I lived at Shirley (Plantation) where the said Jane Gibson died, and as Jane Evans lived within two miles of Shirley I was frequently in her family and she was very often at Shirley as was the rest of the family being employed there in different sorts of work, as for how long, I have already said about seventy years ago I first became acquainted with old Jane Gibson and Jane Evans, and knew them to their death, but cannot say exactly how long they did live from the time I first knew them.
Quest. Will you please to answer the second question in this deposition more fully, you have in your answer to that question said nothing about George Gibson the elder?
Ans: I never mentioned more than one George Gibson, the son of the elder Jane Gibson, brother to Jane Evans. If it be so expressed in our former deposition it was misconceived, I never did know any but one of that name. And further this deponent saith not."

     From both of his depositions, we learn that Robert Wills was an apprentice of Mr. Carter of the Shirley Plantation which is how he became familiar with the Evans/Gibson families. He personally knew both Mother Jane Gibson the elder and the daughter Jane Gibson the younger. Jane Gibson the elder lived at the Shirley Plantation and practiced doctoring as did her daughter Jane Gibson the younger who was also a midwife.

Robert Mills initially referred to Jane Gibson the elder and her brother George Gibson as dark mulattos but later clarified that it was Jane Gibson the younger who had a brother named George Gibson. So, he was instead referring to them as "dark mulattos."

The only information or testimony provided that spoke directly to the identity of Jane Gibson the elder was the information provided by her descendants via their attorney Edmund Randolph which called her a free Indian woman. Additional testimony about the Indian origins of the family comes from Ann Meriweather who was the wife of John Meriweather who provided testimony discussed above and whose father Col. William Meriweather illegally purchased Frances Evans' children as slaves from Goodrich Lightfoot.

Ann Meriweather testified in 1798 that "from the Complexion & strait black hair of Sarah Colley this deponent believes they were descended from Indians". Sarah Colley was the daughter of Frances Evans. Though judging phenotypes is not necessarily a correct way to assess one's ethnic heritage, it is still rather telling when put in context with the rest of the testimony and documentation about the Gibson/Evans family.

The other testimony from the Meriweather family and from Robert Wills most often describe Jane Gibson the elder's offspring and descendants as "mulattos". It should be noted in 1705, the Acts of Assembly of Virginia legally classified mulatto as: "the child of an Indian, the child, grandchild or great grandchild of a Negro."

The freedom lawsuits of Jane Gibson the elder's descendants have been cited in scholarship on the history of the slavery in the U.S. Historian Loren Schweninger, professor emeritus from the University of North Carolina, Greensboro, who created a digital library on American Slavery, published a book in 2018 called Appealing for Liberty: Freedom Suits in the South.

Charles Evans and others sued for their freedom based on their descent from Jane Gibson, "an Indian Woman, the ancestor." They submitted this genealogical chart as evidence in *Charles Evans et al. v. Lewis B. Allen,* filed in the Superior Court of Chancery for the Lynchburg District. Their attorney had a stroke and failed to appear in court, so the court dismissed the suit in 1821, and the plaintiffs all remained in slavery.

There is a Family Tree Chart which shows that Jane Gibson the elder had a son named George Gibson and a daughter named Jane Gibson who married Morris Evans (Morris and Jane are direct ancestors). He and his wife Jane Gibson (1660-1738), had a daughter also named Jane Gibson. To distinguish between the two women, the mother is referred to as Jane Gibson the elder (born 1640-1722).

The elder Jane Gibson was called "a free Indian woman" by a group of her descendants who were illegally enslaved. Though the Evans and Gibson families were free born, that did not prevent some white planters from illegally enslaving them. My ancestor Sarah Redcross Evans-Pinn who is mentioned in the deposition was the daughter of Charlie Evans.

As others of Jane's descendants had won their freedom in two separate Virginia Suits, in 1792 and 1795, Randolph included in his paper's depositions from the earlier trials, among them two given by eighty-one-year-old Robert Wills of Henrico County. As a young boy, at Shirley Plantation in Charles City County, Wills had attested, he had worked as an apprentice in the brewing of a diet drink for his master, Robert "King" Carter, who was afflicted with dropsy.

So it was that Wills became "Well acquainted with Jane Gibson and George Gibson her brother who were dark mulattoes' and free persons; he also knew Jane's two adult children, who bore the same names as the mother and brother and, like them were free.

At the time, Wills noted, Jane Gibson was extremely old, about eighty, and she died one or two years later. Based on testimony in the prior court cases and from his ten clients, Randolph drew up "A Genealogical of the Family of Slaves Claiming Freedom," the progenitor being "Jane Gibson and Indian Woman." The court accepted the depositions as well as the genealogical chart and decreed that the ten plaintiffs be granted their freedom."

Not atypically, the defendant in the Evanses' case took umbrage at being charged by his own human chattel with the illegal possession of slaves. In fact, Lewis B. Allen denied that he had ever heard of Indian slaves named Evans.

As the trial date approached, he kidnapped the lead complainant, Charles Evans: tied him up; and carried him to an undisclosed location. It was rumored that Allen planned to flee and take with him some of the Evans slaves, to remove them from the court's jurisdiction. When Randolph discovered the intended abdication, he promptly wrote a letter to the judge requesting that the court prevent such a removal.

The court took no action, however, and Charles Evans Was indeed spirited away. Nine years later, in Lynchburg City, he and several other Evans family members filed a second suit against Allen; the case dragged on for years. In 1820, it slid into limbo when the court appointed Attorney Henderson Clark suffered a stroke and failed to appear in Court with the plaintiffs. The case, long unresolved, was dismissed in 1821.

The outcome was not uncommon, although the actual number of cases that failed because slave owners managed to stay one step ahead of a subpoena by moving to another County or state is unknown.[51]

TRANSCRIPT
Freedom Suit Claiming Indian Descent of Enslaved Family, 1814

Jane Gibson, an Indian woman
 /
George Gibson, her son
 /
 Tom Evans bound to Lightfoot the ancestor
 | \
Jane Gibson, + Morris Evans

---

[51] Source: City of Lynchburg Court Records, Chancery Records, Charles Evans and others v. Lewis B. Allen, 1821-033. Local Government Records Collection, City of Lynchburg Court Records, Library of Virginia. 04-1407-01/03.

the younger who married
Morris **Evans Jane** Evans the younger |
Frances Evans who went
into New Kent
```
     /
```
Tom Frances Evans bound
to Lightfoot of New
Kent
```
    | \
```
Tomson   Sarah Coley   +   a slave
              of Col
```
 / |  \    Ed Carter
```
  Hannah Beck Amey
```
     |
```
The Plantiff

Transcript

To the honorable, the judge of the Richmond chancery-district-court; The petition of Charles Evans Amy Evans, Sukey Evans, Sinar Evans, Solomon Evans, Frankey Evans, Sally Evans, Milly Evans, Adam Evans, and Hannah Evans; holden in slavery by Lewis Allen, of the county of Halifax humbly sheweth: that your petitioners are descendants from Jane Gibson, a free Indian woman, who and most of whose posterity have obtained their freedom by judgments of different courts: that there is a great danger of their being removed out of the commonwealth by the said Allen; as some of the same blood have been sold by the said Allen in the state of North Carolina.

   I beg leave to certify it to be my opinion, that the above allegations are supported by documents in my possession, and that the petitioners are intitled to freedom and to sue in forma pauperum & c. March 5. 1804

   EDM: RANDOLF, a counsel in the said court.

Docketed:

Evans &c} Petition
   vs

Allen[52]
Solomon Cumbo descendant of Jane (The Elder) Gibson
Siblings: Stephen Cumbo, Virginia (born Cumbo), Aaron Cumbo, James Cumbo, Elisha Cumbo, Mary Cumbo, Matthew Cumbo
First name: Solomon
Last name: Cumbo, "Mollatoe"
Birth: Circa 1767
Place: Robeson Co, NC
Marriage: Date: Oct. 23, 1799
Place: Robeson County, North Carolina, United States
Spouse: Sarah Cumbo (born Broom)
Death: 1803
Place: Brunswick County North Carolina
Parents: Patriot Cannon Cumbo, Minqua Anny Cumbo (born Bryant-Chickasaw)
Wife: Sarah Cumbo (born Broom)
Children: Christian Oxendine (born Cumbo)
Parents: Cannon Cumbo, Sr., Anny Cumbo (born Bryant)
Wife: Sarah Cumbo (born Broom)
Children: Reuben Cumbee, Christina Oxendine (born Cumbo), Isom Needham Cumbo, Mary Polly Lowry (born Cumbo)
Siblings: Stephen Cumbo, Virgina (born Cumbo), Aaron Cumbo, James Cumbo, Elisha Cumbo, Mary Cumbo, Matthew Cumbo)[53]

    Above are our Evans Cumbo lines who were descendants of Jane Gibson an Indian woman from Granville North Carolina. Jane's children were Natives born free and sold as slaves. The descendants went to court to prove they were free. It took several generations and many moves, but they won and were granted freedom. Charles Evans my direct ancestor was removed after

---

[52] Citation: Genealogical chart and Petition, Lynchburg City (Va.) Chancery Causes, 1807–1945. Charles Evans and others vs. Lewis B. Allen. 1821-033 Local Government Records Collection, City of Lynchburg Court Records. Library of Virginia, Richmond, Virginia; Education and Outreach Division

[53] Wills, Anita Baxter; Baxter Family Tree; My Heritage; https://www.myheritage.com/site-family-tree-448802811/baxter; October 20, 2021

filing a complaint with the courts. That is how they arrived in Amherst County as slaves.

Their dark skin color was the reason given for why they were slaves and not Native. At one point my ancestor Sarah Redcross Evans-Pinn and her siblings were sold as slaves to Colonial William Merriweather. This is also where I found what may have been the family surname of Bnu. It appears that my direct ancestor Charles Evans married a Native named Sarah Bnu. Sarah Evans- Pinns' Ancestry

Sarah Evans was a descendant of a Free Indian Woman named Jane Gibson whose children were redesignated as Negro and enslaved. Thomas Evans spent years proving that they were indeed Native and had been illegally enslaved. [54]
Edm'd Randolph Esqr., Richmond
Charles City County, to wit.

The deposition of Robert Wills in the suit Thomas Gibson alias Mingo Jackson plt. against David Ross deft. taken in presence of the plt. & Mr. Vannerson agent for Mr. Ross by consent, at the house of the said Wills this 25th day of June 1791, who being first duly sworn deposed and saith, that about seventy years ago he was well acquainted with Jane Gibson and George Gibson her brother who were dark mulattoes and lived in the County of Charles City and were free people.

That the said Jane Gibson had two children named Jane and George Gibson, that they were also free; That the said Jane Gibson the younger intermarried with a certain _____ Evans of the said County, by whom she had several children, one named Frances Evans Grand Daughter of the said Jane Gibson above named, that the said Frances Evans removed to New Kent County, where she lived and had several children, two of whom, as the said Frances Evans informed this deponent were named Tom and Frances Evans, and were bound to one LIGHTFOOT of New Kent. This information was made to this Depon't by the said Frances

---

[54] Evans Family of Granville County – descendants of Jane."
https://www.pinterest.com/pin/544724517407035585/.

Evans the elder when she was on a visit to her friends in this County, who were neighbors to these deponents. This deponent:

This deponent further saith, that after the said great Grandchildren Viz: Tom & Frances were bound to the said LIGHTFOOT he never heard anything more relative to them. That many of the descendants of the said GIBSONS and EVANS now in this deponent's knowledge are alive and are enjoying their freedom unmolested and have remained so since this deponent first acquaintance with the said Jane Gibson the elder; That many of them are black, some nearly white and others dark mulattoes, which this deponent supposes proceeded from a promiscuous intercourse with different colours.

Questions by the defts agent. Do you know anything of the descendants of the said Frances Evans, who was bound to LIGHTFOOT? No, I do not.
What became of Frances Evans and her brother after they were bound to LIGHTFOOT? I know nothing of them, but from the information of their mother aforesaid.
Do you know any free mulattoes or blacks who have descended from a branch of the name of EVANS, who are they and from whom did they spring?
I know several them, to wit, in Charles City, the SCOTTs, BRADBYs, SMITHs, REDCROSS es alias EVANS, MORRISS es alias EVANS, and in Henrico the BOWMANs, all descendants from the original stock of the GIBSON to wit, Jane EVANS Daughter of Jane GIBSON. Do you know or have you ever known of any other free persons by the name of EVANS of a different family? I do not except in Caroline.

How do you know that the children of Frances Evans were named Tom & Frances, and how old would they be were they now alive: I heard their mother say so; I cannot tell how old, but they would be many years old.
How old are you? I am in my eighty first year.
And further this deponent saith not.
Rob't Wills
Taken before me a Justice of the peace for the County afores'd the

day above

Stith Hardyman

b. Thomas Evans, born about 1756, a wagoner living at the head of " C. Run" in the lower district of Lunenburg County in 1802 and 1803 when he was counted in the "List of free Negroes & Mulattoes" [LVA, Lunenburg County, Free Negro & Slave Records, 1802-1803]. He returned an inventory of the estate of Martha Epps to the Lunenburg County court on 14 September 1809 [WB 6:259]. Sally Epes was living in his household in 1814 when he was counted in the "List of free Negroes and Mulattoes" as a planter on Susanna Moore's land [Magazine of Virginia Genealogy 33:267].

He was a "Free man of Color" about sixty-three years of age on 23 December 1819 when he applied for a pension in Lunenburg County for his services in the Revolution. He stated that he enlisted in September 1777 while resident in Mecklenburg County and served until 1780 [23 December 1819 Lunenburg County Legislative Petition, LVA].

He stated that he had been living in Petersburg Town about 1795 but moved to Lunenburg County where the clerk of the court issued a paper certifying that Thomas Evans was a respectable and credible person [Mecklenburg County Legislative Petition of 19 January 1836, LVA].

? Charles Evans, born say 1760, underage on 12 September 1777 when Daniel Redcross called him his "brother" in his 10 June 1779 Lunenburg County will. He may have been the Charles Evans who was listed as a "yellow" complexioned soldier, born in Petersburg and living in Mecklenburg County when he enlisted in the Revolution [NSDAR, African American Patriots, 149].

Thomas Evans, born say 1710, was called "Thomas Evans" in Amherst County court on 2 September 1766 when the sheriff attached a fork of his for a debt, he owed Samuel Woods. He was added to Henry Bell's Road gang on 7 December 1767.

In December the court ordered his male laboring tithable to keep the road in repair from Buffalo River to Stovall's Road and ordered that Thomas be surveyor thereof [Orders 1766-9, 74, 233; 1773-82].

By his 28 June 1774 Amherst County will, proved 5 Sept. 1774, he left to his son Benjamin his land and a horse as well as cattle and hogs for the use of his daughters Mary and Hannah and grandson Thomas as long as they abided together and left a shilling each to sons Charles, Thomas, William and Stanup (Stanhope) and daughter Nelly [WB 1:264-5].
He was the father of:

 Charles Evans, born say 1751, called son & heir-at-law of Thomas Evans, deceased, when he was summoned by the Amherst County court on 5 September 1774 to contest the will of his father [Orders 1773-82, 107].

 Stanhope Evans born say 1740 granted 350 acres in Amherst County on both sides of Johns Branch, a north branch of Buffalo River, on 14 July 1780 [Grants A, 177980, 634].

 Benjamin Evans, born say 1749.

 Thomas Evans, born say 1723, was head of a household in Lunenburg County, taxable on his own tithe and Solomon Harris in 1748, taxable on his own tithe in 1749 and 1750, taxable on his own tithe and John Evans/ Epps in 1751 and 1752, and taxable on his own tithe in 1764 [Bell, Sunlight on the Southside, 68-9, 109, 166, 193, 250]. He was called "Thomas Evans (Negro)" on 14 May 1764 when he was sued in Lunenburg County court by Sterling Thornton and Company who attached his effects for tobacco on 11 March 1781 [DB 5:72; 6:123

 Charles1 Evans, born say 1696, was sued for debt in Brunswick County court by Littlebury Epes, in December 1735 [Orders 1732-37, 68]. He was called "Charles Evans a mulatto" in December 1746 in Lunenburg County when the court dismissed charges brought against him by Andrew Bressler [Orders 1746-48, 81]. He received a patent on 20 August 1747 for 120 acres on Stith's Creek in the part of Brunswick County which became Lunenburg County in 1748 and Mecklenburg County in 1765 [Patents 28:135].

 Charles was taxable in Lunenburg County in the list of Lewis Deloney in 1748, taxable in the list of Field Jefferson in 1751 with his son Tom [Bell, Sunlight on the Southside, 68, 166] and taxable with Thomas and Major Evans in 1752 [Tax List 1748-52, 1].

He petitioned the Lunenburg County court in May 1753 to be exempt from personal taxes but was rejected "for Reasons appearing to the Court" [Orders 1753-54, 113]. He was granted 38 acres in Lunenburg County in the fork of Miles Creek and Dockery's Creek on 23 July 1753 [Patents 31:337].

He left a 22 March 1760 Brunswick County, Virginia will (signing), proved 27 October 1760, leaving his "manor" plantation on the south side of Dockery's Creek to his son Major Evans, left an equal quantity to his son Charles Evans and left the residue of his land on the Southside of Dockery's Creek to son Dick Evans on condition they give twenty pounds or 100 acres of land to his youngest son Erasmus. He left a bed and furniture to his daughters Sarah and Joyce but left only a shilling to his "undutiful" son. Thomas [WB 3:375-6]. He died before June 1760 when a suit against him in Lunenburg County court abated by his death [Orders 1759-61, 136].

Sara Redcross Evans married Revolutionary Soldier, (Rawley Pinn). They were married and resided in Amherst County Virginia, in Lexington Parish. On 18 October 1764 Sarah and Richard Evans sold about 39 acres in the fork of Miles and Dockery's Creek in Mecklenburg County which was land they had been given by Charles Evans [DB 1:514].

Charles 2 Evans, born say 1737, was taxable in the Lunenburg County list of Edmund Taylor for St. James Parish in 1764, listed with 60 acres [Bell, Sunlight on the Southside, 248]. On 18 October 1764 he, Sarah Evans, and Major Evans (his brother) sold 120 acres on Stith's Creek in Lunenburg County adjoining Philip Morgan [DB 8:356].

On 9 April 1782, the Mecklenburg County, Virginia court allowed his claim for providing 275 pounds of beef for the use of the Continental Army [Orders 1779-84, 124]. He was head of a Mecklenburg County, Virginia household of six persons in 1782 [VA:34] and was taxable in Mecklenburg County from 1782 to 1794: taxable on slave named Ned, 9 cattle, and 4 horses in 1784 and taxable on slave Jack in 1786 [PPTL, 1782-1805, frames 2, 54, 107, 192, 291, 343, 401, 500]. He sent a note to the Mecklenburg County clerk approving the 20 December 1788 marriage bond of his daughter Nanny to Eaton Walden. His daughter was, Nanny, born about 1772, married Eaton Walden, 20 December 1788 Mecklenburg County bond.[55]

The Pinn-Evans Family left records telling of their accomplishments and providing a look into life in the 1700's. But more important was the oral history that was kept and passed down. I heard some of the Oral History from Pinn cousins like Victoria Ferguson and Dr. Horace Rice. Amherst County and Nelson County were built on and around Native Lands.

As previously mention our Evans are descendants of an Indian woman Jane Gibson (the Elder) and I am descended from the union of Rawley and Sara Evans-Pinn, through their son James Pinn and his second wife, Jane Cooper-Powell Pinn, who were the parents of Robert Pinn IV, who married Elizabeth Jackson (in Fredericksburg VA (1838) and they were the parents of Maria Louisa Pinn-Ruth my Great Grandmother and the mother of Leah Louisa Ruth-Martin, who was the mother of Vivian Martin-Baxter who was my mother.

DNA and Genealogy Research

In 2003, I took a DNA test through Family Tree DNA, which traced our Maternal Line. The test came back 87% European, 8% Native, and 5% African, with the Haplogroup of T2 (Tara). This female left Africa (Morocco) about 10,000 years ago and traveled over the Iberian Peninsula more than likely trwith a group into Spain.

In 2012 I updated the test, and it came back T2b4f. According to FTDNA, the mitochondrial haplogroup T is best characterized as a European lineage. With an origin in the Near East greater than 45,000 years ago, the major sub-lineages of haplogroup T entered Europe around the time of the Neolithic 10,000 years ago.

---

[55] "Evans Family: The Lost Creek Settlement." https://lost-creek.org/genealogy/histories/evans-family.php.

Once in Europe, these sub-lineages underwent a dramatic expansion associated with the arrival of agriculture in Europe. Haplogroup T2 is one of the older sub-lineages and may have been present in Europe as early as the Late Upper Paleolithic. This is my maternal line through, my mother's, mother's, mother's..., The surname I connect to in Virginia is Lewis (Llewelyn's), from Wales (or Britain). These are the lines that intermixed early on with Natives in Colonial Virginia.

They settled in what is now the Basque Region of Spain before traversing Europe and arriving in Britain (Wales). They are one of the oldest tribes in Wales, which mixed with the invading Anglos. They were the Llewelyn (Lewis), Clan, who left Monmouthshire Wales and settled in Virginia. The information gathered on our family lines was from the research I completed, and which the DNA Test confirmed.

In 2005, Anthony, our brother took a Y-DNA test, which came back 100% Native American for our paternal Baxter side of the family. The test connects our paternal line ancestors, to Columbia South America. It stated that our ancestors were Indigenous to the Americas. Yet they were slaves in South Carolina near Columbia South Carolina. during and after slavery.

In Pennsylvania and Virginia our ancestral lines connect to the many Nations that congregated there. We are Mohawk, Seneca, Conestoga, Okehocking, Nanzattico, Manokin, Wicomico, Tutelo, Saponi, and other mixes from North Carolina, South Carolina and throughout Virginia. Our ancestors were hunted and preyed upon here on Turtle Island. Many were killed and buried in unmarked graves throughout America. They live on through us and we learn from their lives and sacrifices.

Since Colonization began in the Americas entire Nations of Indigenous people have been slaughtered. That is even before many died from Disease due to exposure to the invading forces. The voices of innocent men women and children were silenced from Genocide, forced removal, forced assimilation and the redesignation of their racial identity.

It has left those of us who are of Native Heritage with a gap in our history and genealogy. Yet when we go back look and find what was ripped away often, we are told too much time has passed. But in the spirit world of our ancestors, it is just the right time. They did not leave us it was an attempt to remove any threat to the Colonizers whose history began with Columbus and Americus Vespucci.

Their greed and lust for power will not allow them to accept that this beautiful pristine land with fresh running water, forest, and foliage, plenty of game and fish belonged to Indigenous people. A Narrative was created in which Europeans were Gods Chosen People. Now God is to blame for the destruction visited up Indigenous Peoples lands all over the world.

The 13 American colonies' population grew from about 2,000 to 2.4 million between 1625 and 1775 while displacing Native Americans from throughout the Americas. After the colonies declared independence in 1776 from Great Britain and formed the US, the settlers started to move west, clashing with and eradicating the Apache, Cherokee, Cheyenne, Chinook, Navajo and Sioux tribes. Some of the names today are sadly used for American warfare helicopters and ubiquitous sport utility vehicles.

The national holiday, Thanksgiving, celebrated in November, is traced to the 1620s when European settlers invited Native Americans to a feast. The settlers later killed the population and gave thanks to God for allowing them to slaughter the "savages."

The surviving descendants of Native American tribes live in poverty on federally recognized Indian reservations across the United States. Almost 100 million indigenous people in the Western Hemisphere have been killed or died prematurely because of the Europeans and their descendants in five centuries, according to David E. Stannard in his book, American Holocaust: The Conquest of the New World.

Around 12 million indigenous people died within present US geographical boundaries between 1492 and 1900, according to Russell Thornton in American Indian Holocaust and Survival: A Population History since 1492.

Despite having unalienable rights -- life, liberty and the pursuit of happiness – as enshrined in the American Declaration of Independence, not all in the new colonies were considered equal. The colonies had a system of slavery, which European settlers carried as a practice into the Americas from the Old World, despite English Protestants praising themselves as Puritans. A conservative estimate of 35 million men, women and children were brought from Africa to the New World between the 16th and 19th centuries.

Around 12.5 million of those brought to North America were used as free labor in fields and worked under grueling conditions, according to the Trans-Atlantic Slave Trade Database. The systematic repression of Africans continues to the present day in the US government application of laws, health, and education.

A century before gaining civil rights and liberties, Blacks had to fight in the white man's wars in the US military. More than 200,000 Blacks joined Union forces in the American Civil War, while an unaccounted number of free and slave Blacks were used for manual labor in the Confederacy. The war that began in 1861 and lasted until 1865 left 750,000 soldiers dead with an undetermined number of civilians.

Despite overthrowing its colonial ruler, Great Britain, the US pursued colonial interests in Southeast Asia during the late 19th century. Around 20,000 Filipino combatants and as many as 200,000 civilians died from violence, famine, and disease during the Philippine–American War between 1899-1902, according to the State Department's Office of the Historian.

On the domestic front in early 20th century, the Tulsa race massacre in 1921 saw white residents attacking Black population and burning their businesses and homes. Almost 300 Black people were killed as a result, and more than 800 were injured in the massacre that left over 10,000 Black people homeless.

An example of reclassification in Virginia
"Dr. Ariela Gross contends that the "vanishing Indian" was a result in this time frame of the reclassification to mulatto and negro and follows several examples forward through time. The 1705 Virginia statue that declared that a Mulatto is "a child of an Indian" as well

as "the child, grandchild, or great-grandchild of a negro" was not modified until 1785 when a "colored person" was defined as all persons with "one fourth-or more negro blood":

and only those with "no negro blood" were allowed to be classified as Indians. It is more than a contention it is a proven fact in my family and other families. Henings' Statutes at large is a stack of Law Books written to codify the racist laws of Virginia which were also enforced by the Anglican Episcopalian and Catholic Churches as well as other Christian denominations. For a while it was only the Ana Baptist who stood up against slavery. Rawley Pinn became a part of the Ana Baptist Movement and built a Baptist Church in Amherst County Virginia.

In October 1705 in Virginia, the following act was passed:

"Be it enacted and declared, and it is hereby enacted and declared, That the child of an Indian and the child, grandchild, or great grandchild, of a negro shall be deemed, accounted, held and taken to be a mulatto."

Which was followed by:

"That all male persons, of the age of sixteen years, and upwards, and all negro, mulatto, and Indian women, of the age of sixteen years, and upwards, not being free, shall be, and are hereby declared to be tithable, or chargeable."

Let's look at what the various census instructions to enumerators and census forms said about Indians:

- 1790 – "Omitting Indians not taxed, distinguishing free persons, including those bound to service, from all others." Indians living "wild," generally meaning plains Indians in the west, or on reservations were not taxed, but those who were enumerated were recorded in the "all other free" column on the census form.
- 1800 – Indians living off reservations and not "wild" would have been recorded in the "all other free persons" column on the census form. Options were free white, slave and "all other free persons."
- 1810 – Indians living off of reservations would have been recorded in the "all others" column on the census form. Options were free white, slave and "all other."

- 1820 – Indians living off reservations would have been recorded in the "free colored persons" categories. Other options were free whites, slaves and "all others except Indians not taxed."
- 1830 – Indians living off reservations and not "wild" would have been recorded in the "free colored persons" category. Other options were free whites and slaves.
- 1840 – Essentially the same as 1830 with the exception that an additional column labeled "pensioners for revolutionary or military services" with a blank for the pensioner's name to be included and applies to all individuals.
- 1850 – 1850 is the first census in which every individual in the household was enumerated. In prior years, only the name of the head of household was recorded and other household members were recorded by age grouping by category. In 1850, the instructions say that Indians not taxed (meaning on reservations) were not to be enumerated and the categories for race were white, black, mulatto. if your ancestor looked "dark" and was an Indian, chances are they were recorded as M for mulatto. There was no "Indian" category until 1860.
- 1860 – Indians not taxed were not enumerated. However, the categories differed a bit this year. "The families of Indians who have renounced tribal rule, and who under State or Territorial laws exercise the rights of citizens, are to be enumerated. 56In all such cases write "Ind." opposite their names, in column 6, under heading 'Color. There is a census in Indian Territory, but Indians are not included."

Jacob and Nancy Green Awl had the following children:
- **Catherine Alice "Cassie" Awl** - 4 April 1888 - 6 August 1960 - married James Book
- **Bertha Ann Awl** - 1 October 1891 - 30 October 1946 - married George Washington Quarles

---

[56] Min. Cozmo El; I am Cherokee; The reclassification of Cherokee families as Free Persons of Color and the history of Nancy Anderson Stewart Allen

http://nativeheritageproject.com/2013/05/14/indians-and-the-census-1790-2010/

- **Margie Sylvester Awl** - ca. 1896 - 9 January 1901
- **John Henry Awl** - 1 July 1906 - 14 August 1906 - buried at St. Peters
- **Stephen Edward Awl** - 1 July 1906 - 8 August 1906 - buried at St. Peters
- **Margaret Maggie Awl** - 9 May 1908 - July 1977 -
- **Elizabeth Juliet Awl** - 28 April 1913 - 22 June 1913 - buried at Mt. Hope
- **Malin A. Awl** - 5 July 1916 - 16 May 1951 - buried at Mt Hope

Burials at the Friendship Missionary Baptist Cemetery (Mt. Hope) Salisbury Twp Lancaster County Pa- Organized in 1883

- **Elizabeth Juliet All (Awl?)** - Colored - Mount Hope - April 28, 1913 – June 22, 1913 - Parents Jacob All & Nancy Green
- **Mathew All (Awl?)** - Colored - Chapel Ceme. Mt. Airy? - Abt. 1844 - Oct. 24, 1912 - Married – wife's name is not listed - Parents Jacob All (Awl) & Emily Britain
- **Jacob Armstrong** - black - Mount Hope - March 15, 1851 – June 27, 1914 - Parents Jacob Armstrong & UNKNOWN - Wife – Rachel Armstrong
- **Rachel Armstrong** (Dec.25,1855-Dec.6,1935)- White - buried at Free Will Baptist Cemetery Wife of Jacob Armstrong.
- **Helen Awl** - Black - Mount Hope - Oct. 9, 1900 - June 17, 1935 - Wife of Nathaniel Awl - Parents Albert Rice & Jennie Lloyd
- **Jacob Awl** - 1845 - Nov. 1, 1912 - Could not find his death certificate.
- **Abraham Boots** - Black - Welsh Mountain Mission - Oct. 12, 1888 - Oct. 27, 1918 - Single - Parents Arthur Boots & Elizabeth Marshall
- **Albert Boots** - Colored - Mount Hope - Mar. 18, 1880 – June 10, 1934 - Single - Parents Arthur Boots & Elizabeth Marshall
- **Arthur Boots** - Feb. 1882 - Sept. 1935 Arthur Boots - colored - Mount Hope - Feb. 11, 1882 - Sept. 23, 1935 Single - Parents Arthur Boots & Elizabeth Marshall

- **Chas. Raymond Boots** - Colored - Mount hope - Sept. 26, 1911 - Jan. 7, 1916 Parents Elmer Boots & Martha Green
- **Edna Boots** - Negro - Mount Hope - June 25, 1915 - July 8, 1915 Parents Elmer Boots & Martha Green
- **Edna Catherine Boots** - Black - Mount Hope - Mar. 15, 1912 – July 29, 1912 Parents John Boots & Margery Stewart
- **George Boots** ? - Oct. 1890 PA Death Certificates Ancestry.com shows Sept. 1871 to Oct. 4, 1890 - murdered by Amos Bell Parents Arthur Boots & Elizabeth Marshall
- **John W. Boots (Boats)** - Colored - Mount Hope - May 26, 1858 - Dec. 15, 1933 Wife is Eliz. Mimm (white) - Parents Arthur Boots & Mary Book
- **Levi Boots** ? - Sept. 2, 1912 Could not locate.
- **Mary I. Boots** 1882 - Feb. 1915 - Boots was her maiden name
- Should be **Mary Ida Green** - Mulatto - Mount Hope - Feb. 18, 1882 - Feb. 22, 1915
  Married - Parents John W. Boots & Eliz. Mimm (white) Samuel Green signed the death certificate –husband?
- **William Boots** 1908 - Mar. 9, 1916 colored - Mount Hope - July 15, 1908 - Mar. 9, 1916
- Parents Elmer Boots & Martha Green
- **Abraham Dennis** - Black - Mount Hope - abt. 63 - July 29, 1930 Single - Parents Adam Dennis & Lucy Boots
- **Adrian Dennis** ? - Aug. 1930 Should this be Abraham Dennis?
- **Adam Stanton Dennis** - Colored - Mount Hope - age 45- Jan. 19, 1919 Married - Parents Adam Dennis & Loazan Boots
- **Charles Dennis** - Colored - Mount Hope - April 12, 1903 - July 14, 1925 Single - Parents Abram Stanton Dennis & Catherine Green Ancestry by mistake shows name as Dumis but record is correct.
  - **Milford Dennis** ? - Sept. 1935   Could this be M.D. in findagrave.com?

- **Milford Dennis** - Negro - Mount Hope - August 24, 1892 - Sept. 14, 1935 Married Amanda Moore Parents Adam Dennis and Lousana Boots
- **Catharine Elizabeth Dennis Ernest** - Black - Welsh Mountain Chapel – Feb. 1, 1919-Feb.16,1919 Parents Harry G. Ernest & Maggie Dennis
- **Margret Ellen Victoria Green** - Negro - Mount Hope May 31, 1904 - Nov. 5, 1918 Parents Abner Green & Mary Lynch
- **Paul Green**   1908 - Jan. 22, 1942 PA Death Certificate shows Paul Green was buried at the Free Will Baptist Church Cemetery in Salisbury Twp.
- **Paul Green** - colored - Free Will - May 4, 1907 - Jan. 15, 1942-Homicide by firearm. Parents Samuel Green & Mary Boots This could be a different Paul Green but the birth and death dates are similar - Shot by Milford Hagler in Green's Home[57]
- **Rachel Green**- Negro - Mount Hope - June 20, 1916 - June 26, 1916-Parents Abram Green & Beatrice Brown
- **Stillborn Green** - Negro - Mt. Chapel (Mount Hope?) - Jan. 10, 1915 - Jan. 10, 1915 Stillbirth - Parents Abner Green & Mary Lynch - Sister buried here - Mt. Hope Chapel?
- **Susannah Green** - Colored - Mount Hope - Aug. 9, 1877 - Mar. 19, 1932 Single - Parents Charles Green and Harriett DeWitt
- **Mary E. Henson**   ? - June 1931-Miss Mary Henson - Black - Mount Hope - Age 56 - June 8, 1931-Parents John Henson & unknown
- **Katie Eleora London** - Dark - Mount Hope - Mar. 18, 1897 - Feb. 28, 1917 - Married – husband's name not listed – signed by Israel Marshall Parents Davis London & Agnes Green
- **Catherine L. Stewart**   ? - Jan. 24, 1938

---

[57] Ancestry.com; New Holland Clarion dated January 23, 1942.

- **Catherine Alice Stewart** - Colored – Mount Hope about 68 - Jan. 24, 1928 (buried Jan. 27, 1928) - Widowed - Parents Charles Green & Harriet DeWitt
- **Chester L. Stewart** ? - Sept. 1932-Chester Lewis Stewart - black - Mount Hope - Sept. 10, 1906 - Sept. 11, 1932 - Single - Parents Isaac Stewart & Rachel Boots
- **Elizabeth Stewart** - Colored - Mount Hope - July 21, 1916 - Dec. 3, 1918-Parents - Isaac Stewart & unknown Boots
- **Margaret V. Stewart** 1835 - Mar. 1932 Was not born in 1835 - Margret Victoria Steward - colored - Mount Hope - 7 yrs. 5 mo. 18 days – Mar. 20, 1932 Parents Isaac Steward & Rachel E. Boots
- **Mary Stewart** - Negro - Mount Hope - August 24, 1900 - Nov. 26, 1944 - Single - Parents John Stewart & Rachael Grace Bosley
- **Catherine Elizabeth Boots** January 1, 1858 – September 5, 1939, white Husband – John W. Boots Parents - Isaac Mimm & Ann Larshey Free Will Ceme.
- **Elizabeth Boots** October 6, 1849 – May 15, 1938 Wife of Arthur Boots - Parents – William Marshall Nancy Green
- **Emma Bosley** January 20, 1920 – April 23, 1920-Parents William Wells & Rachel Bosley
- **Laura Butler** 1883 – September 23, 1928 divorced from James Watson Parents – Henry Butler & Sarah Batey **MD (Milford Dennis) A M(Aubrey Myers)**
- **Margaret Victoria Stewart** October 2, 1924 – March 20, 1932 Parents – Isaac Stewart & Rachel E. Boots
- **Mary Stewart** August 24, 1900 – November 26, 1944 – Parents – John Stewart & Rachel Grace Bosley
- **Raymond Tinsey** August 1, 1923 – October 7, 1923 Parents – Charles Tinsey & Georgie Woodburn
- **Anna Aul** – PDC File # 30456 Mt. Hope???? – March 28, 1936 age 29 Husband – Melvin AulParents – father unknown & mother Fannie Dixson

- **Mary Benton** - PDC File # 18269 colored – widowed - Mt. Hope   March 31, 1847 – February 13, 1935 - Husband – Stephen Benton Parents – George Washington & Emma Brinton
- **Percy S. Boots** (Ancestry.com shows Cercy S. Boots) – PDC File # 10988   Mt. Hope - November 12, 1928 – November 5, 1929 Parents – John Boots & Alice Boots
- **Arthur B. Bosley** – PDC File # 106584   Mt. Hope April 21, 1912 – November 9, 1930 Colored Single Parents
- **Frank Bosley** & Rachel Moore
- **Frank Bosley** – PDC File # 89212-Mt. Hope
- Doesn't know age – shows 46   ??? – August 14, 1918 Doesn't know parents' names.
- **Rachel Bosley** – PDC File # 4239 Mt. Hope
- February 12, 1882 – January 26, 1948 – Negro Widowed Husband – Frank Bosley (shows Frand Parents - Arthur Green & Martha Moore
- **Stillbirth (Bosley)** – PDC File # 891   Mt. Chapel Cemetery - January 10, 1915 – January 10, 1915 Parents – Frank Bosley & Rachel Moore - Father acting as undertaker.
- **Nancy Jay** – PDC File # 7887 March 30, 1867 – January 8, 1931 Mt. Hope Colored Husband – Oscar Jay Parents – Charles Greece (Green) & Harriet DeWitt
- **Benjamin London** – PDC File # 111815 Black - Mt. Hope Baptist   June 17, 1905 – December 17, 1942-Parents – John R. London and Agnes Marshall
- **Katie Eleora London** – PDC File # 14614 -Dark-Married no husband is listed – Israel Marshall was informant – relationship- March 18, 1897 – February 28, 1917 Mt. Hope – Parents – David London & Agnes Green
- **Kurtis London** – PDC File # 81160   Ancestry.com shows only as London- Black   June 2, 1917 – August 18, 1917 Mt. Hope-Parents – John R. London and Francis A. Marshall
- **Lillian Madeline London** - PDC File # 110783   Shows buried at Mt. Hope AME (?)-Negro   December 11, 1943 – December 15, 1943-Parents – Leroy States & Catherine London

- **Harry C. Marshall** – PDC File # 98358 - Mt. Hope-Negro- August 9, 1913 – October 9, 1913 - Israel H. Marshall & Harriet Ayers
- **Ruth Marshall** – PDC File # 51793 - Mt. Hope-August 7, 1925 – June 19, 1945n-Colored-Married - husband – George F. Marshall - Parents – Theodore Butler & Hazel Faulkner
- **William Henderson Marshall** – PDC File # 41167 - Free Will Baptist – Colored- since (wd. Was crossed out) - February 28, 1847 – April 4, 1936 - Parents – William Marshall & Nancy Green
- **Howard Moore**- PDC File # 4707 - Mt. Hope??? – January 3, 1925 – Black-Married- Signed Mrs. Howard Moore -Parents – Jacob Moore & Unknown
- **Martha Moore** – PDC File # 18255 - Welsh Mts. – Does not give name of Cemetery - Could be buried with her husband Howard Moore? - April 15, 1869 – February 24, 1935 - Parents – Arthur Green & Margaret Starr
- **Aubrey Myers** – PDC File # 80132 - Mt. Hope - September 30, 1905 – September 12, 1945 – Negro – Wife Alice E Boots - Parents – Jerry Myers & Mary Lucy Jefferson
- **Marian Myers** – PDC File # 14531 - Mt. Hope - October 11, 1945 – February 17, 1946 – Colored – Infant - Parents – Aubrey Myers & Alice Boots
- **Bertha A. Quarles** – PDC File # 86984 - Mt. Hope - October 1, 1891 – October 30, 1946 – Negro – Widowed-Husband –
- George Quarles - Parents – Jacob All (Awl?) & Nancy Martha Green
- **George Washington Quarles** – PDC File # 4012- Mt. Hope - March 26, 1891 – January 22, 1947, - Colored – Widowed Parents – Frank Quarles & Francis Samuels Stillborn (Stanton) – PDC File # 112809   Mt. Hope - November 7, 1916 – November 7, 1916- Parents – Adam Stanton & Anna Mary Steward
- **Amanda Stewart** – PDC file # 98672 - Welsh Mountain Chapel - November 18, 1927 – November 9, 1942 - Mulatto- Parents - John H. Stewart & Alice Millesock

- **Catherine Alice Stewart** – PDC File # 4353-Welsh Mountain Chapel - 68 years old – January 24, 1928 - colored – widowed - Husband – George Stewart Parents – Charles Green & Harriet DeWitt
- **Isaac Steward(t)** – PDC File # 88631 - Mt. Hope - January 17, 1884 – October 12, 1933 - Wife – Rachel Boots Stewart - parents – William Stewart & Sarah Book
- **John H. Stewart** – PDC File # 24154 - Mt. Hope- December 24, 1879 – March 8, 1946 – Negro -Parents – George Stewart & Catherine Green
- **Stillborn Stewart** – PDC File # 7295   - Mt. Hope - January 3, 1932 – January 3, 1932 – Colored - Parents – father unknown & Hazel Stewart
- **Anna Watson** – PDC File # 28858 - Mt. Hope- March 12, 1932 – March 12, 1935 – Black - Parents – William H. Watson & Estella Conley
- **David H. Watson** – PDC File # 62963 - Free Will Baptist December 25, 1866 – July 28, 1942 – negro – widowed Parents – William Watson & Lydia DeWitt
- **Unnamed or Stillborn Watson** – PDC File # 64164 - Chapel Cemetery in 1943? - July 30, 1943 – July 30, 1943 – Colored- Parents William Henry Watson & Estelle Comony (Conley???)
- **William Watson, Jr.** – PDC File # 16667 - Welsh Mountain Mission - February 27, 1927 – February 27, 1927 – Black Parents – William Watson & Stella Green
- **Margaret Woodburn** – PDC File # 100428 - Mt. Hope -???? – October 31, 1925 -Husband – George Woodburn - Parents –
- Harry (Henry) Green & Caroline Harris[58]

A Narrative of the Late Indian Massacres [30 January? 1764]

In the context of connecting to my Native Ancestors it is important to include instances like the Massacre at Conestoga. By

---

[58] Rineer, A, Hunter Jr; Churches and Cemeteries of Lancaster County Pennsylvania A Complete Guide; 1993; Lancaster County Historical Society – Lancaster Pa – P. 393

the time of the Massacres many of my Native Ancestors had been run off by white settlers seeking land. The laws that William Penn and even others had espoused were gone. This was especially true leading up to and after the Revolutionary War.

Our ancestors in what is now Lancaster County were the Conestoga who were remnants of the Susquehanna. In this recounting Sir William Johnson, a direct ancestor about 7 times removed makes an appearance in Lancaster County after the Massacre of the Conestoga. This took place and the issue was greed by Settlers who wanted land and were taking it by any means necessary. Even if they had to murder children, women and the elderly. In this recounting William Penn attempts to tak action against the murderers to no avail.

News of the massacre of six Indians at Conestoga Manor by men from Paxton and Donegal, two communities on the Susquehanna, on December 14, 1763, reached Governor Penn on the 16th. He laid the account before his Council three days later and informed the Assembly on the 21st.9 The House was in recess when word came to Penn on the evening of December 28 that "upwards of a hundred men" had ridden into Lancaster the afternoon before and slaughtered the fourteen Conestoga Indians placed in the workhouse for their own protection.

The governor informed the Council the next day and, on its advice, wrote General Gage to ask that British troops at Carlisle be placed under Penn's orders "to support the Civil Authority in the execution of the Laws in case of need, and to give a check to these daring attacks on Government." He also wrote Sir William Johnson begging him to "take the proper Est method" of telling the Six Nations the truth of the affair and of "removing any disadvantageous Impressions they may have received from an imperfect account of the matter."

After each of the attacks Penn issued a proclamation ordering all civil officers to use every possible means to identify the perpetrators. In the second proclamation he also offered a reward for the apprehension of the ringleaders.

By the time the Assembly convened again on January 2nd,

the main facts of the attack on the Lancaster workhouse and the killing of the Indians there were common knowledge in Philadelphia. Not surprisingly, however, many conflicting reports of the details began to circulate both within and without the city:

 The local officials in Lancaster, it was said, had done all they could to stop the attack; they had stood idly by other rumors suggested, and it was even alleged that some officers had secretly abetted the rioters. There were British troops in Lancaster at the time, but their commander had refused to provide protection to the Indians; or the troops were too scattered in billets around the town to be assembled in time to do anything before the rioters had galloped away; or there were no British soldiers nearer than Carlisle, and they would have had no authority to interfere in any case.

 The Indians had been shot down quickly…, the Indians had been hacked with knives and tomahawks and many of them scalped, and their bodies had been mutilated and then dragged into the street. For weeks after the affair at Lancaster these and other reports passed around, and many found their way into print in the pamphlets issued by sympathizers with the Paxton Boys or their opponents.

 Public opinion soon became sharply divided. For once all the proprietary officials, with the more substantial among their adherents, and the members of the "Quaker Party," with their supporters both within and outside the Assembly, stood together in shocked and vigorous denunciation of the massacres. The ruthless slaughter of defenseless men, women, and children was both an attack on government, as Penn had called it when writing to General Gage, and an offense against all principles of justice and humanity, as the Quakers and many others maintained.

 Reports that the Indians sheltered on Province Island were to be the objects of similar annihilation led the advocates of peace and order to form a common front against the lawless men who threatened to alleviate the Indian menace by exterminating every tribesman within their possible reach.

 On the other side stood many inhabitants of the western and

northern counties and substantial numbers of the less well-to-do, and hence unenfranchised, residents of Philadelphia. Sympathetic, though not always so outspoken, were some adherents of religious bodies, notably Presbyterians and Lutherans, partly because of their long-standing denominational antagonism to the Quakers and Moravians, who had been known for years as the chief friends of the Indians.

Throughout the month of January tensions continued to mount: more and more it became evident that if the men from Paxton and their allies should carry out their threats of coming to Philadelphia and, to use an expression of a later century, of "liquidating" the Indians sheltered there, they would find many sympathizers in the city, who certainly would do nothing to stop them and might even join them in their proposed attack.

In this situation Franklin came forward with an effort to influence public opinion against such violence as had already occurred and threatened to occur again. Just when his Narrative of the Late Massacres appeared from the press is not certain; it was not advertised in either of the Philadelphia newspapers. His reference, near the close, to General Gage's orders to Captain Robertson to stay with the Moravian Indians and guard them until he was relieved by other British regulars, makes certain that Franklin did not finish the writing until after January 16, when Governor Penn laid Gage's letter containing that information before the Council and Assembly.

A Narrative, &c. [January 30? 1764]

These Indians were the Remains of a Tribe of the Six Nations, settled at Conestoga, and thence called Conestoga Indians. On the first Arrival of the English in Pennsylvania, Messengers from this Tribe came to welcome them, with Presents of Venison, Corn, and Skins; and the whole Tribe entered into a Treaty of Friendship with the first Proprietor, William Penn, which was to last "as long as the Sun should shine, or the Waters run in the rivers."

This Treaty has been since frequently renewed, and the Chain brightened, as they express it, from time to time. It has never been violated, on their Part or ours, till now. As their Lands by Degrees were mostly purchased, and the Settlements of the White People began to surround them, the Proprietor assigned them Lands on the Manor of Conestoga, which they might not part with; there they have lived many Years in Friendship with their White Neighbours, who loved them for their peaceable inoffensive Behaviour.

It has always been observed that Indians, settled in the Neighborhood of White People do not increase, but diminish continually. This Tribe accordingly went on diminishing, till there remained in their Town on the Manor, but 20 Persons, viz. 7 Men, 5 Women, and 8 Children, Boys and Girls.

Of these, Shehade's was a very old Man, having assisted at the second Treaty held with them, by Mr. Penn, in 1701,5 and ever since continued a faithful and affectionate Friend to the English; he is said to have been an exceeding good Man, considering his Education, being naturally of a most kind benevolent Temper.

Peggy was Shehade's Daughter; she worked for her aged Father, continuing to live with him, though married, and attended him with filial Duty and Tenderness. John was another good old Man; his Son Harry helped to support him. George and Will Soc were two Brothers, both young Men. John Smith, a valuable young Man, of the Cayuga Nation, who became acquainted with Peggy, Shehade's Daughter, some few Years since, married her, and settled in that Family. They had one Child, about three Years old. Betty, a harmless old Woman; and her son Peter, a likely young Lad.

Sally, whose Indian Name was Wyanjoy, a Woman much esteemed by all that knew her, for her prudent and good Behavior in some very trying Situations of Life. She was a truly good and an amiable Woman, had no Children of her own, but a distant Relation dying, she had taken a Child of that Relation's, to bring up as her own, and performed towards it all the Duties of an affectionate Parent...,

On Wednesday, the 14th of December 1763, Fifty-seven Men, from some of our Frontier Townships, who had projected the Destruction of this little Commonwealth, came, all well-mounted, and armed with Firelocks, Hangers and Hatchets, having travelled through the Country in the Night, to Conestoga Manor. There they surrounded the small Village of Indian Huts, and just at Break of Day broke into them all at once.

Only three Men, two Women, and a young Boy, were found at home, the rest being out among the neighboring White People, some to sell the Baskets, Brooms, and Bowls they manufactured, and others on other Occasions. These poor defenseless Creatures were immediately fired upon, stabbed, and ratcheted to Death! The good Shehade's, among the rest, cut to Pieces in his Bed.

All of them were scalped, and otherwise horribly mangled. Then their Huts were set on Fire, and most of them burnt down. When the Troop, pleased with their own Conduct and Bravery, but enraged that any of the poor Indians had escaped the Massacre, rode off, and in small Parties, by different Roads, went home.

The universal Concern of the neighboring White People on hearing of this Event, and the Lamentations of the younger Indians, when they returned and saw the Desolation, and the butchered half-burnt Bodies of their murdered Parents, and other Relations, cannot well be expressed.

The Magistrates of Lancaster sent out to collect the remaining Indians, brought them into the Town for their better Security against any further Attempt, and it is said condoled with them on the Misfortune that had happened, took them by the Hand, comforted and promised them Protection. They were all put into the Workhouse, a strong Building, as the Place of greatest Safety.

When the shocking News arrived in Town, a Proclamation was issued by the Governor, in the following Terms, viz.

"Whereas I have received Information, That on Wednesday, the Fourteenth Day of this Month, a Number of People, armed, and mounted on Horseback, unlawfully assembled together, and went to the Indian Town in the Conestoga Manor, in Lancaster County, and without the least Reason or Provocation, in cool Blood, barbarously killed six of the Indians settled there, and burnt and destroyed all their Houses and Effects:

And whereas so cruel and inhuman an Act, committed in the Heart of this Province on the said Indians, who have lived peaceably and inoffensively among us, during all our late Troubles, and for many Years before, and were justly considered as under the Protection of this Government and its Laws, calls loudly for the vigorous Exertion of the civil Authority, to detect the Offenders, and bring them to condign Punishment.

I have therefore, by and with the Advice and Consent of the Council, thought fit to issue this Proclamation, and do hereby strictly charge and enjoin all Judges, Justices, Sheriffs, Constables, Officers Civil and Military, and all other His Majesty's liege Subjects within this Province, to make diligent Search and Enquiry after the Authors and Perpetrators of the said Crime, their Abettors and Accomplices, and to use all possible Means to apprehend and secure them in some of the publick Goals of this Province, that they may be brought to their Trials, and be proceeded against according to Law.

"And whereas a Number of other Indians, who lately lived on or near the Frontiers of this Province, being willing and desirous to preserve and continue the ancient Friendship which heretofore subsisted between them and the good People of this Province, have, at their own earnest Request, been removed from their Habitations, and brought into the County of Philadelphia, and seated, for the present, for their better Security, on the Province-Island, and in other Places in the Neighborhood of the City of Philadelphia, where Provision is made for them at the public Expense;

I do therefore hereby strictly forbid all Persons whatsoever, to molest or injure any of the said Indians, as they will answer the contrary at their Peril. "Given under my Hand, and the Great Seal of the said Province, at Philadelphia, the Twenty-second Day of December, Anno Domini One Thousand Seven Hundred and Sixty-three, and in the Fourth Year of His Majesty's Reign.
John Penn.
"By His Honor's Command, Joseph Shippen, jun. Secretary.
"God Save the King."

Notwithstanding this Proclamation, those cruel Men again

assembled themselves, and hearing that the remaining fourteen Indians were in the Workhouse at Lancaster, they suddenly appeared in that Town, on the 27th of December. Fifty of them, armed as before, dismounting, went directly to the Workhouse, and by Violence broke open the Door, and entered with the utmost Fury in their Countenances.

When the poor Wretches saw they had no Protection nigh, nor could possibly escape, and being without the least Weapon for Défense, they divided into their little Families, the Children clinging to the Parents; they fell on their Knees, protested their Innocence, declared their Love to the English, and that, in their whole Lives, they had never done them Injury; and in this Posture they all received the Hatchet! Men, Women, and little Children— were everyone inhumanly murdered! in cold Blood!

The barbarous Men who committed the atrocious Fact, in Defiance of Government, of all Laws human and divine, and to the eternal Disgrace of their Country and Color, then mounted their Horses, huzza'd in Triumph, as if they had gained a Victory, and rode off—unmolested!

The Bodies of the Murdered were then brought out and exposed in the Street, till a Hole could be made in the Earth, to receive and cover them. But the Wickedness cannot be covered, the Guilt will lie on the whole Land, till Justice is done on the Murderers. The Blood of the Innocent will cry to Heaven for Vengeance.

It is said that Shehade's, being before told, that it was to be feared some English might come from the Frontier into the Country, and murder him and his People; he replied, "It is impossible: There are Indians, indeed, in the Woods, who would kill me and mine, if they could get at us, for my Friendship to the English; but the English will wrap me in their Matchcoat, and secure me from all Danger." How unfortunately was he mistaken!

Another Proclamation has been issued, offering a great Reward for apprehending the Murderers, in the following Terms, viz. "Whereas on the Twenty-second Day of December last, I issued a Proclamation for the apprehending and bringing to Justice, a Number of Persons, who, in Violation of the Public Faith; and in Defiance of all Law, had inhumanly killed six of the Indians, who had lived in Conestoga Manor, for the Course of many Years, peaceably and inoffensively, under the Protection of this Government, on Lands assigned to them for their Habitation. notwithstanding which;

I have received Information, that on the Twenty-seventh of the same Month, a large Party of armed Men again assembled and met together in a riotous and tumultuous Manner, in the County of Lancaster, and proceeded to the Town of Lancaster, where they violently broke open the Work-house, and butchered and put to Death fourteen of the said Conestoga Indians, Men, Women and Children, who had been taken under the immediate Care and Protection of the Magistrates of the said County, and lodged for their better Security in the said Work-house, till they should be more effectually provided for by Order of the Government.

And whereas common Justice loudly demands, and the Laws of the Land (upon the Preservation of which not only the Liberty and Security of every Individual, but the Being of the Government itself depend) require that the above Offenders should be brought to condign Punishment; I have therefore, by and with the Advice of the Council, published this Proclamation, and do hereby strictly charge and command all Judges, Justices, Sheriffs, Constables, Officers Civil and Military, and all other His Majesty's faithful and liege Subjects within this Province, to make diligent Search and Enquiry after the Authors and Perpetrators of the said last mentioned Offence, their Abettors and Accomplices, and that they use all possible Means to apprehend and secure them in some of the public Goals of this Province, to be dealt with according to Law.

"And I do hereby further promise and engage, that any Person or Persons, who shall apprehend and secure, or cause to be apprehended and secured, any Three of the Ringleaders of the said Party, and prosecute them to Conviction, shall have and receive for each, the public Reward of Two Hundred Pounds; and any Accomplice, not concerned in the immediate shedding the Blood of the said Indians, who shall make Discovery of any or either of the said Ringleaders, and apprehend and prosecute them to Conviction, shall, over and above the said Reward, have all the Weight and Influence of the Government, for obtaining His Majesty's Pardon for his Offence.

"Given under my Hand, and the Great Seal of the said Province, at Philadelphia, the Second Day of January, in the Fourth Year of His Majesty's Reign, and in the Year of our Lord One Thousand Seven Hundred and Sixty-four. John Penn.[59]

We are America's Melting Pot

America's claim to be a Melting Pot is a meaningless phrase told to the world. Until the Indigenous People and the descendants of African People are free no one is free. The Borders from Mexico and South America only allow a few people in to work for little or nothing. They come with no rights and little chance to be citizens.

Those of us who are descendants of the Indigenous People are told we don't exist and if we do, we have no rights. We do not have rights to our ancestral homeland or rights to our Ceremonial and Spiritual Sights. If we are not free, then no one on this Continent is free. Racism is its own prison for those who stand guard to block the light of truth.

We are still here on the land of our ancestors the Chosen Ones of this land. We go back to the land we our journey here ends. In 1492, the First World War began with a possession ceremony by Christopher Columbus, and it was called ~ domination, called patriarchy… domination came to the Western Hemisphere. It is a foreign concept that did not exist then, and today it is not working for us as a people of consensus, as it is not working for the rest of the world.

---

[59] A Narrative of the Late Massacres, in Lancaster County, of several Indians, Friends of this Province, By Persons Unknown. With some Observations on the same. Printed in the Year m, dcc, lxiv. (Yale University Library); https://founders.archives.gov/documents/Franklin/01-11-02-0012

MINQUA UNAMI OKEHOCKING & THE DOWN RIVER NATIONS

Domination of the Americas came in the form of three ships with feminine names called Nina (the little girl), Pinta (the painted one), and Santa Maria (Mary the Saint). So "the little girl who is painted into a saint," the saint represents a religion based upon dominating the feminine - Mother Earth. The Spanish Inquisition in Europe lasted from killed most of its people of the earth, Muslims and Jews, witches, and warlocks – all 12 million in the name of this dominator god. The Inquisition was overseen by the Holy Roman Empire and lasted from 1478-1834.

The name in Italian is Cristoforo Colombo In Spanish, it is Cristóbal Colon, and in English – Christopher Columbus. The word "Colon" derives from "crooked, curved, bent; perverted" or colony in the sense "to make another place into a national dependency" and Colony means "people away from home."

Now you have the name of Christopher Columbus or "to colonize with Christ or the Christ bearing colonizer" He landed in the lands of the Arawak and claimed the land in the name of his god with a formal possession ceremony "with flags flying, and no one objecting". Of course, none of the Natives would object, especially when they did not know that they were there on a "Holy" Mission to steal kill and destroy. Domination does not fit in spiritual evolvement but seems snug in a religious-hierarchical transcendence. It cannot exist in relational thinking.

Doctrine of of Discovery – The Papal "Bull"

The Papal Bull "Inter Caetera," issued by Pope Alexander VI on May 4, 1493, played a central role in the Spanish conquest of the New World. The document supported Spain's strategy to ensure its exclusive right to the lands discovered by Columbus the previous year. It established a demarcation line one hundred leagues west of the Azores and Cape Verde Islands and assigned Spain the exclusive right to acquire territorial possessions and to trade in all lands west of that line. All others were forbidden to approach the lands west of the line without special license from the rulers of Spain. This effectively gave Spain a monopoly on the lands in the New World.

The Papal Bull stated that any land not inhabited by

Christians was available to be "discovered," claimed, and exploited by Christian rulers and declared that "the Catholic faith and the religion be exalted and be everywhere that barbarous nations be overthrown and brought to the faith itself." This "Doctrine of Discovery" became the basis of all European claims in the Americas as well as the foundation for the United States' western expansion. In the US Supreme Court in the 1823 case *Johnson v. McIntosh*,

Chief Justice John Marshall's opinion in the unanimous decision held "that the principle of discovery gave European nations an absolute right to New World lands." In essence, Indigenous people had only a right of occupancy, which could be abolished.

The Bull Inter Caetera made headlines again throughout the 1990s and in 2000, when many Catholics petitioned Pope John Paul II to formally revoke it and recognize the rights of indigenous "non-Christian peoples."

Excerpt

Wherefore, as becomes Catholic kings and princes, after earnest consideration of all matters, especially of the rise and spread of the Catholic faith, as was the fashion of your ancestors, kings of renowned memory, you have purposed with the favour of divine clemency to bring under your sway the said mainlands and islands with their residents and inhabitants and to bring them to the Catholic faith. Hence, heartily commending in the Lord this your holy and praiseworthy purpose, and desirous that it be duly accomplished, and that the name of our Saviour be carried into those regions, we exhort you very earnestly in the Lord and by your reception of holy baptism.

Whereby you are bound to our apostolic commands, and by the bowels of the mercy of our Lord Jesus Christ, enjoy, that Inasmuch as with eager zeal for the true faith you design to equip and dispatch this expedition, you purpose also, as is your duty, to lead the peoples dwelling in those islands and countries to embrace the Christian religion: nor at any time let dangers or hardships deter you therefrom, with the stout hope and trust in your hearts that Almighty God will further your undertakings.

And, in order that you may enter upon so great an undertaking with greater readiness and heartiness endowed with benefit of our apostolic favor, we, of our own accord, not at your instance nor the request of anyone else in your regard, but out of our own sole largess and certain knowledge and out of the fullness of our apostolic power;

by the authority of Almighty God conferred upon us in blessed Peter and of the vicarship of Jesus Christ, which we hold on earth, do by tenor of these presents, should any of said islands have been found by your envoys and captains, give, grant, and assign to you and your heirs and successors, kings of Castile and Leon, forever, together with all their dominions, cities, camps, places, and villages, and all rights, jurisdictions, and appurtenances;

all islands and main lands found and to be found, discovered and to be discovered towards the west and south, by drawing and establishing a line from the Arctic pole, namely the north, to the Antarctic pole, namely the south, no matter whether the said main lands and islands are found and to be found in the direction of India or towards any other quarter, the said line to be distant one hundred leagues towards the west and south from any of the islands commonly known as the Azores and Cape Verde...,

With this proviso however that none of the islands and mainlands, found and to be found, discovered and to be discovered, beyond that said line towards the west and south, be in the actual possession of any Christian king or prince up to the birthday of our Lord Jesus Christ just past from which the present year one thousand four hundred ninety-three begins.

And we make, appoint, and depute you and your said heirs and successors lords of them with full and free power, authority, and jurisdiction of every kind; with this proviso however, that by this our gift, grant, and assignment no right acquired by any Christian prince, who may be in actual possession of said islands and main land's prior to the said birthday of our Lord Jesus Christ, is hereby to be understood to be withdrawn or taking away. Moreover, we command you in virtue of holy obedience that, employing all due diligence in the premises, as you also promise —

nor do we doubt your compliance therein;

in accordance with your loyalty and royal greatness of spirit—you should appoint to the aforesaid mainlands and islands worthy, God-fearing, learned, skilled, and experienced men, to instruct the aforesaid inhabitants and residents in the Catholic faith and train them in good morals.

Furthermore, under penalty of excommunication "late sententious" to be incurred "ipso facto," should anyone thus contravene, we forbid all persons of whatsoever rank, even imperial and royal, or of whatsoever estate, Degree, order, or condition, to dare without your special permit or that of your aforesaid heirs and successors.

To go for the purpose of trade or any other reason to the islands or main lands, found and to be found, discovered and to be discovered, towards the west and south, by drawing and establishing a line from the Arctic pole to the Antarctic pole, no matter whether the main lands and islands, found and to be found, lie in the direction of India or toward any other quarter whatsoever, the said line to be distant one hundred leagues towards the west and south;

as is aforesaid, from any of the islands commonly known as the Azores and Cape Verde; apostolic constitutions and ordinances and other decrees whatsoever to the contrary notwithstanding.[60]

---

[60] The Doctrine of Discovery, 1493; A Spotlight on a Primary Source by Pope Alexander VI; Pope Alexander VI's Demarcation Bull, May 4, 1493. (Gilder Lehrman Collection); https://www.gilderlehrman.org/history-resources/spotlight-h

INDEX

"Castle" Doctrine, 176
"Great Minqua Trail", 106
"Holy" Roman Empire, 10
"Indian" Charles Lewis
   Nanzattico, 145, 151
"Indian" Hanna
   Chester County Pennsylvania, 104
"New" World
   Europeans and, 173
"Penal" Colony, 172
2nd Virginia Calvary, 20
41st United States Colored Troops, 37
54th Massachusetts
   United States Colored Troops, 36
   Walter Samuel Pinn, 25
Africa, 48
African American, 65, 179
   Churches, 65
African American Churches, 66
African Ancestry DNA, 173
African Ancestry DNA, 173
African DNA, 173
African People, 48
African Women, 22
Africans, 61
Africans and Natives
   mixing, 61

Alaska, 49
Algonquian Indians
   Virginia, 163
Algonquian Language. *See* Tidewater (Coastal Plain)
Algonquian Language Group
   Virginia, 163
Algonquian, Siouan, or Iroquoian
   Tribal Languages, 163
Aliquippa Cornfield, 186
Aliquippa Creek, 186
Aliquippa Island, 186
Aliquippa Town, 186
Allegheny Indians, 97
Allen, Lewis, 207
Allen, Lewis B.
   Slave owner, 206
America, 48
American
   Europeans and, 172
American Civil War, 38, *See* Slave Labor System
American Dream, 171
American Revolutionary War, 58
Americus Vespucci, 9, 11
Amherst County, 19
   Virginia, 18
   Virginia, 20

Amherst County Virginia, 18, 24, 28, 29, 196, See Monacan Indian Nation

  Tax Record, 19

Amherst County.

  Virginia, 195

Amish, 143, 148
Ana Baptist Movement, 20
Ancestral Homeland, 32
Ancestral Homelands, 133, 134
Ancestral Lands, 16

  Natives and, 171

Ancestry, 65
Ancestry DNA, 173, See Autosomal DNA Test
Anderson, Sally Evans. *See* Gibson, Jane the Younger
Anglican, 181
Anglican Church, 48, 65
Anglican Churches, 47
Anglo Saxon, 180
Anglo-American explorers

  Somerset County Md, 139

Anglo-Saxons, 180
Annemessex

  Somerset County MD, 139

Anthony

  Baxter, 173

Anthropologist

  Native Americans and, 161

Antigua

  Indians enslaved, 145, 151

Nanzattico Indians, 22
West Indies. *See* Nanzattico Indians
Antigua West Indies

  Nanzattico Indian Tribe and, 167, 170

Any Means Necessary, 47
Appalachian Mountain Range, 64
Appalachian Mountains, 108
Arawak, 47, 48, 145, 150
Arawak's

  Indigenous Tribe, 175

Argentina, 11
Atglen

  Chester County PA, 107
  Chester County Pennsylvania, 38

Atlantic Coast, 45
Atlantic Creoles, 180
Australia, 48, 64

  Europeans and, 172

Autosomal DNA Test, 173
Azores

  Native American Slaves and, 166

Barbados, 176

  Native American Slaves and, 166

Basque Region

  Spain, 215

Baxter, Charles – 1833-1968

Native Catabwa or Creek, 157
Baxter, George Senior, 34
Baxter, Vivian Martin, 10
Berks County, 108
Bermuda
   Native American Slaves and, 166
Beta Israel Jew
   Ethiopian Jews, 48
Black, 66
Black Church, 65
Black Minqua
   Sasquahanna, 96
Black Minqua River, 96
Bnu, Sarah, 209
Boots
   Welsh Mountains, 62
Bowden, 18
Bowden, Mary, 174
Bowden, Mary Monroe, 174
Brandywine Creek
   Indian Hannah and, 105
Brant, Jacob. See Joseph Brant
Brant, Joseph, 12
Breconshire
   Wales, 180
Britain, 180
British Colony, 56
Bucks County, 39, 98, 108
Burning at the Stake, 176
Camanchaca
   Turtle Island, 10

Camden Estate, 164
Camp William Penn. See United States Colored Troops
Canachquasy
   Son of Queen Aliquippa, 186
Canada, 11, 56, See Inuit
Capitalism, 171
Capitalism, Socialism, Communism
   "Ism" Systems, 17
Capitalist Dream, 171
Caribbean, 32, 47
Caribbean and Florida, 49
Caribbean Plantations
   Native Americans and, 166
Caroline and King George County
   Virginia, 162
Caroline County
   Virginia. See Nanzattico Indians
Carter, Robert "King".
Catholic, 65, 175
Catholic Church, 46
Cecil County, Maryland, 38
census records, 143, 148
Charles and Louis
   Douglass, 24
Cheraw, 18
   Siouan Indians, 196
Chesapeake Bay
   Manokin, 97

Chester and Bucks County
  Pennsylvania, 39
Chester City, 141, 147
Chester County, 16, 98, 108
  Pennsylvania, 39, 98
  Pennsylvania, 144
  Pennsylvania, 150
Chief of the Shawnee
  Opessah, 111
Chile
  Southern Tip of Turtle Island, 22
Chillicothe Ohio. See Monroe, William Junior
Chinklacamoose
  Black Minqua, 95, 96
Christian Bible, 48
Christian Church, 66
Christiana Resistance, 52
  Henry Green and, 100
Christianity, 48
Christopher Columbus, 175
Church Law, 180
Church Wardens. See Catholic Church
  Laws and, 47
Churchwardens, 180
Civil War, 52
  Lancaster County PA, 37
Civil War Soldier. See Green, Henry
Clark, Henderson

Evans Attorney, 206
Clark, William, 174
Clearfield, Pennsylvania
  Black Minqua, 95
Cloud, Joseph, 144, 150
Coatesville Pennsylvania, 35
Colley, Sarah
  Daughter of Frances Evans, 204
Colonial Government, 146, 151
Colonial Governor, 15
Colonial Settlers. See, See Virginia
Colonization, 61, 151, 162, 215
Colonization and Religion, 180
Colored, 61, 66
  racial status, 151, 162
Coloreds, 61
Columbia (Pennsylvania), 24, See Pinn, Robert IV
Columbia Pennsylvania. See Pinn, Robert IV, See Pinn, Robert IV
Columbia South America, 173
  DNA Connection, 215
Columbia South Carolina, 215
Columbia, Pennsylvania. See Pinn, Walter Samuel
Columbus, 9, 145, 150
  Voyage, 47
Concord
  Delaware County Pa, 102

Concord Delaware County, 109
Concord Township
  Delaware County Pennsylvania, 109
Conestoga. See Susquehanna
  Pennsylvania, 186
Conestoga Dam, 12
Conestoga Indian Town
  population, 184
Conestoga Indians
  Lancaster County Pennsylvania, 52
Conestoga Land Grant
  Lancaster County Pennsylvania, 105
Conestoga Tract, 51
Conestoga Tribal Village. See Conestoga Indian Nation
Conestoga Wagon, 144, 149
Conklin, Samuel, 176
Conquered Country, 181
Constitutional Law, 180
Corps of Discovery. See Meriwether Lewis and William Clark
Creoles, 180
Critical Race Theory (CRT), 17, 31, 32
Crum Creek Watershed, 141, 146
Cuba, 48, See Arawak, See Arawak

Darlington, Maurice. See Martin, William Penn
Darrell "Dusty" Crawford
  DNA, 17
Daughters of the American Revolution (DAR), 161
Davis, 98, 142, 148
  Somerset County Maryland, 12
  Welsh Mountains, 62
Davis, Hannah Underwood, 85, See Davis, Joseph
Davis, Harmon, Hall, Jackson, Johnson, Sammon, Harmon, Wright, Mosley, Thompson, Socum, Ridgeway, Prettyman, Morris, Street, Sterret, and Green
  Nanticoke Surnames, 109
Davis, Joseph, 85
Davis, Joseph and Hannah Underwood, 38
  Great-Great-Great-Great Grandparents, 108
Davis, William, 38
Davis/Greens
  Green, Henry. See
Deheubarth. See Wales
Delaware, 11, 96, 97, 105, 106, 107, 108, 109, 110, 118, 119, 120, 121, 135
Delaware and Chester County. See Westtown, See Westtown

Williston, 104
Delaware County, 98, 108
- Pennsylvania, 98
- Pennsylvania, 144
- Pennsylvania, 150

Delaware County Pa, 103
Delaware Davis-Green
- Lines, 108

Delaware River, 108, 144, 150
Delaware Valley, 97
- Native Nations and, 103
- Native Nations and, 99
- Natives and, 45

Delmarva
- Delaware Maryland and Virginia, 98

DelMarVa
- Delaware Maryland Virginia, 85

Doctrine of Discovery, 134
- Catholic Church, 46

Dorchester Road, 14
Douglass, Frederick, 24
Down River Nations. See Green, Henry, See Minqua Unami Okehocking, See Minqua Unami Okehocking
- Somerset County Maryland, 62

Down River People, 16
- Manokin, 142, 148
- Minqua Unami and Okehocking, 172

Dragon Ship
- Revolutionary War and, 23

Drake, Samuel. See Tituba
Durand de Dauphine
- Nanzattico and. *See* Nanzattico

East Nottingham
- Chester County Pennsylvania, 103

East Whiteland Township, 141, 147
Eastern Shore of Maryland, 24
Eastern Shore of Virginia, 97, 193
Eastern Woodland Indians. See Powhatan, Rappahannock, Matapuni, Pamunkey
Ecclesiastical Law, 180
Eddystone Borough, 141, 147
Eminent Domain
- Native Lands and, 51

England. See Penn, William
English colonial settlers
- Natives and. See King Philip

English Quaker farmers, 14
Episcopalian, 181
- Churches, 47

Episcopalian Church, 48
Essex County preserve
- Nanzattico Indian Prisoners, 169

Ethiopia

Jesus Christ and, 48
European, 23
European alleles
  racial mixing and, 49
European Ancestor
  Hilliard, Lydia, 173
European Archaeologist. *See* Indigenous People
European Colonization, 55
European Colonizers, 22
European DNA, 49
European Homeland, 96
European Monarchy and Rulers, 181
European Settlers, 145, 150
Europeans, 61, 151, 162, 175
Evans, 18
Evans, Adam, 207
Evans, Amy, 207
Evans, Charles, 195, 206, 207, 209
Evans, Frances
  Daughter of Jane Gibson, 199
Evans, Frankey, 207
Evans, Hannah, 207
Evans, Milly, 207
Evans, Morris, 199
Evans, Sally, 207
Evans, Sarah Redcross (Pinn), 19
Evans, Sinar, 207
Evans, Solomon, 207
Evans, Sukey, 207
Evans/Gibson families. See

Fairmount Baptist Church
  Rawley Pinn and, 20
Falls of the Susquehanna, 97
Family History, 179
Family tree DNA
  DNA Cousins, 65
Federal Recognition
  Monacan Indian Nation, 18
Fifteenth Amendment
  Right to Vote, 143, 148
First People, 45
Five Civilized Tribes. *See* Cherokee
Forks of the Ohio
  Queen Aliquippa, 186
Former Soviet Union Countries, 32
Fort Mandan
  Missouri River, 174
FPC
  Free Persons of Color, 173
France. *See* Treaty of Paris
Fredericksburg
  Virginia, 47, 61
Fredericksburg Virginia, 18, 161, 174, *See* Pinn, Robert A Reverend
Free Blacks and Mulattoes, 18
Free Blacks,, 61
free colored, 19
Free Person of Color (FPC)

Native racial reclassification. *See* Free Persons of Color. *See* Fredericksburg Virginia

Virginia, 47, 173

Free Persons of Color (FPC), 18, 47

French Colonization of the Americas, 56

Friends' Yearly Meeting 1719

Indian and Negro Slaves, 103

Fulani Tribe

Northern Nigeria, 173

Gaines, Daniel Colonial. *See* Pinn, Rawley

Garrett, Thomas

Abolitionist, 37

Genealogical Library. See Mormon Temple

General Assembly. See Nanzattico Indians

General Sherman's March to the Sea, 36

Gibson Jane (the Elder), 196

Gibson, George. See Jane Gibson the Elder

Gibson, Jane, 199, 200, 201, 202, 203, 204, 205, 207, 208, 209

The elder, 203

The Younger, 203

Gibson, Jane (the Younger), 19, 196, 199, 200, 204, 209, 210, 214

Gibson, Jane Bnu, 19

Gibson, Jane Bnu (the elder), 196

Gibson, Jane the elder, 199

GIBSONS and EVANS, 200

Giovanni da Verrazano

Explorer, 139

Gipson, Jane. See Evans, Sarah

Gipson, Jane (Bnu). *See* Cheraw Indian Woman, *See* Cheraw Indian Woman

Gipson, Jane Bnu, 29

God's Chosen People

Jews, 48

Grand Army of the Republic. *See* Pinn, Robert A. Sergeant

Granville North Carolina

Jane Bnu-Gipson, 196

Great Man of Indiantown

Lancaster County Virginia. *See* Pinn, Robert I, *See* Pinn, Robert I

Great Minqua Path, 95, 96, 108, 139, 142, 147, 150

Delaware River Valley, 144

Great Minqua Trail

Natives and, 52

Great Shamokin Path, 95

Minqua, 96

Green, 98, 106, 107, 108, 109, 110, 118, 119, 120, 121, 122, 124, 129, 130

Welsh Mountains, 62

Green, Benjamin, 37, 144, 149
  Great-Great-Great Grandfather, 143, 148
Green, Charles, 109
Green, George. See Davis, Lydia
  Great-Great-Great, 102
  Great-Great-Great Grandfather, 108
Green, Harriet. See Green, Henry
Green, Henry, 144, 149, See Green, Lydia
  Christiana Resistance and. See Stephenson, Thaddeus
  Great-Great Grandfather, 37
Green, Henry and Susanna, 51
Green, Isaac, 109
Green, Joseph, 144, 149
Green, Joseph
  brother of Benjamin, 144
Green, Joseph
  brother of Benjamin, 150
Green, Lydia. See Martin, Lydia Green, See Green, Susanna
Green, Lydia Davis, 38
Green, Susanna, 53
Green, Susannah Brown
  Great-Great Grandmother, 107
Greenland, 11, 22
Gulf Coast
  Mississippi River Tribes and, 174
Guyana and Trinidad. See Taino
Hah-nu-nah
  Turtle, 61
ha-no-wa
  every day turtle, 61
Harris
  Welsh Mountains, 62
Haudenosaunee
  Iroqouis, 11
Henning's Statutes at Large
  Laws Governing Race, 61
Henry Green, 51, 52, 54, 81, 99, 109, 110, 114, 123, 124, 126, 263
Henson, 62
Hieroglyphs, 50
Hiliard, Lydia. See Monroe, Mary Hilliard
Hilliard, Lydia, 70, 173, 174
Holy Roman Empire, 47
Honeybrook, 35
Iberian Peninsula
  DNA Test and, 214
Indentured Servitude. *See* Slave Labor System
India. See Christopher Columbus
Indian blood
  Negroes and, 144, 149
Indian Hannah story, 104

Indian Town
  Wicomico. *See* Manokin Rive
Indian/Negroes
  Pequea Valley, 113
Indigenous Ancestors, 21
Indigenous Nations, 46
Indigenous People, 11, 22, 32, 45, 46, 97, 135, 142, 147, 173, 176, 179, 235
  Native Americans, 161
Indigenous Peoples, 176
Indigenous Person, 176
Indigenous Population, 49
Inquisition, 48
Interior of Eastern Pennsylvania, 95
Inuit, 49
  Alaska and, 49
Iroquois, 18, 21
Iroquois Chief. See Queen Aliquippa
Iroquois Confederacy
  Six Nations, 12
Iroquois Tribes
  Algonguian Neighbors, 163
J. Edgar Hoover. *See* Baxter, George Senior
J.C.Erlichman
  Exterminating Company Reading Pa. See Baxter, George Senior
Jackson, 18

Jackson, Martha (Patty) Bowden, 174
Jackson, Samuel and Maria Lewis, 28
Jackson, William Rev., 31
Jamestown Settlers. *See* Virginia
Jamica:, 166
Jefferson, Thomas, 67
Jesus Christ, 48
  Beta Israel Jew, 162
John "Smoke" Johnson, 57
John Indian
  Husband of Tituba, 176
Johnson, 98, 142
Johnson, Mary Brant Mohawk, 137
Johnson, William and Mary Brant, 137
Jones, Ida Ruth, 11
Jones, Owen, 11
Keith, Sir William
  Indian Slaves, 103
King and Caroline County Virginia
  Nanzattico Indian Village, 22
King George County
  Virginia. *See* Lewis, Charles and Ambrose
King Philip
  Metacom Native American Leader, 166
King Philip's War, 165

[250]

King Ranch, 107
King's Ranch. See Martin, William Penn
Lancaster County, 39, 98, 108, 109, 111, 118, 124, 144, 145, 150

   Great Minqua Path, 96
   Great Minqua Path, 142
   Great Minqua Path, 147
   Pennsylvania, 37, See Welsh Mountain Region

Lancaster County Pa, 104
Land Hungry Europeans, 142, 147
Land Ownership, 133, 134
Leni Lenape

   Original People, 14

Leni Lenape lands, 15
Lewis (Llewelyn)

   Wales, 180

Lewis, Charles, 161
Lewis, Charles and Ambrose, 23
Lightfoot, Goodrich, 199, *See* Evans Family, See Gibson and Evans

   Evans Slave Owner, 204

Lightfoot, Sherwood, 19
Lincoln Highway

   Chester County Pa, 108

Llewelyn (Lewis)

   Wales, 215

Longhouses

   Algonquian and Iroquois Houses, 163
   Native Villages, 45

Longwood Gardens

   Chester County Pennsylvania, 105

Lower Eastern Shore

   Maryland, 111

Lukens Steel Mill

   Coatesville Pa, 33

Lynchburg City. See Evans, Charles
Major William Cabell Junior, 20
Mandans, 174
Manifest Destiny

   European Creed, 49
   Europeans and, 32

Manokin, 12, 18, 21, 40, 85, 86, 87, 97, 109, 110, 132, 139, 140, 142, 147, 148, 215

   Somerset County MD, 139
   Somerset Md, 85

Manokin River

   Somerset Maryland, 86

Markham, William Governor

   Governor of Pennsylvania, 103

Marquis De Lafayette. *See* Pinn, Rawley
Martin, 98, 106, 107, 108, 119, 121, 122, 124, 142, 148
Martin Ancestors

Welsh Mountains and, 62
Martin, Charles
   Grandfather, 66, 172
   Maternal Grandfather, 51
Martin, Charles and Leah Ruth
   Maternal Grandparents, 35
Martin, Charles and Sarah Johnson
   Great Great-Great Grandparents, 38
Martin, Charles Frederick, 35
Martin, Great Grandfather William, 35
Martin, John
   Sea Captain. See Nanzattico Indians
Martin, Lydia Green
   Great Grandmother, 35
Martin, Tamzin Paige, 11
Martin, Uriah, 38, 137
   Great-Great Grandfather, 37
Martin, Uriah and Tamzin Page, 111
Martin, William and Lydia. See Martin, Charles
Martin, William Penn, 35, 104, 107
Martin, William Penn II, 37, 111
Maryland, 12, 37, 107
Massacre by the Paxton Boys
   Indian Massacre, 52, 185

Massacre of the Conestoga
   Lancaster County, 143, 148
Matoaka, 23
McKees Rocks
   Pennsylvania, 186
Melungeon Communities, 65
Mennonites, 13, 143, 148
Meriweather, Ann
   Wife of John Meriweather, 204
Meriweather, John, 204
Meriweather, William
   Colonel, 204
Meriwether Lewis, 174
Merriweather, William
   Colonial, 209
mestizo
   Mixed Ancestry, 49
Metacom
   Native American Leader. See King Philip
Mexico, 32
Mills, Robert. See Gibson, Jane
Minqua, 96, 97, 106
Minqua Path, 108
miscegenation, 22
Mission Schools, 22, 61
   Christianity and, 151, 162
Mission Street, 181
Mississippi, 66
Mississippi River, 174, See Gulf Coast
Missouri River, 174
mixed ancestry people, 49

Mohawk, 45, 142, 215
Momia Juanita
  Mummy Junita, 71
Monacan, 18
Monacan Indian Nation. See Amherst County Virginia
  Amherst County Virginia, 21
Monmouth shire Wales, 215
Monmouthshire Wales, 180
Monroe, James President, 67, 174
Monroe, Mary, 174
Monroe, Mary Hilliard, 67, 174
Monroe, William Junior. See Monroe, Mary Hilliard, See
Monroe, Mary Hilliard, See Monroe, Mary Hilliard
Monroe, William Senior, 70, 173, 174, See Monroe, Mary Hilliard
Montross Virginia. See Monroe, Mary
Moors and Jews
  Inquisition and, 48
Mormon Temple, 179
  Oakland CA, 179
Mulatto, 61, 66
  racial status, 151, 162
Mulatto Indentured Servants. See Monroe, Mary Hilliard
Mulattos, 61

Multinational Indian community
  Nanzattico. See Nanzattico
Nanticoke
  Sussex County Delaware, 109
Nanzattico, 18, 22, 23, 167, 170
  Indian Tribe, 163, 167, 171, See
  Indian Tribe, 167
  Indian Tribe, 167
  Indian Tribe, 167
  Indian Tribe, 167
  Indian Tribe, 168
  Indian Tribe, 168
  Indian Tribe, 168
  Indian Tribe, 168
  Indian Tribe, 168
  Indian Tribe, 168
  Indian Tribe, 168
  Indian Tribe, 169
  Indian Tribe, 169
  Indian Tribe, 169
  Indian Tribe, 169
  Indian Tribe, 170
  Indian Tribe, 170
  Indian Tribe, 170
  Indian Tribe, 170
  Indian Tribe, 170
  Indian Tribe, 170
  Indian Tribe, 170
  Rappahannock Indian Nation, 145, 151
Nanzattico (Nantaughtacund), 163

Nanzattico Indians, 22, 161, 167, 168, 169, See Camden Estate

   Slavery and. See Antigua

Nation of Islam, 66
Native American, 215
Native American Slavery, 164
Native Americans, 143, 148

   Slavery, 161, 164, 166
   Slavery, 161

Native and Mulatto Soldiers

   Dragon Ship and, 23

Native Heritage, 215
Native Identity, 61, 151, 162
Native Men, 22
Native Nations, 45
Native People, 143, 148
Native Villages, 133, 134
Native/African/White. See Martin, Grandpop
Natives

   racial identify and, 151, 162

Negro, 61, 66

   racial status, 151, 162

Ness, Elliott

   FBI, 36

New Castle

   Delaware, 186

New England Colonies

   Slavery and, 166

New Jersey, 11
New World, 49
New York, 11

New York City, 108
North American Possessions

   United Kingdom and, 56

North Carolina

   Melungeon, 64

Northumberland and Lancaster County, 24
Northumberland County. See Wicomico Parish Church
Northumberland County Virginia, 193
Oakland California, 179
Octorara Creek, 111
Octorara Presbyterian Church, 53
Ohio River, 96
Ohio River Valley, 188
Ohio Valley, 11
Okehocking, 13, 14, 15, 16, 97, 98, 106, 107, 135, 136, 142, 147, 215

   Atglen & Avondale Pa, 107

Okehocking Tract, 12, 14, 51, 104, 141, 142, 146, 147
Old Philadelphia Pike, 108
Onondaga Reservation

   Canada, 187
   Ontario Canada, 142, 147

Osborne, Sarah. See Salem Witch Trials
Pachamama

   Mother Earth, 71

Page Galley, 22
Paleo-Indians, 55

Pamahsawuh. See Virginia

   The World and Everything in it. See Native Americans

Pamunkey Indian reservation, 19

Pamunkey River, 19

Paper Genocide, 145, 150, 180

   Native Americans and, 61, 151, 162

Paper Mill. See Green, George

Parris, Samuel, 176

Patriarchal

   European, 177

Patty (Bowden-Jackson). See Bowden, Mary

Peasant Class, 180

Pencader Hundred

   Delaware, 38

Pencader Hundreds Delaware

   Sussex County, 38

Penn, Richard and Thomas. See Penn, William

Penn, William, 12, 38, 39, 98, 104, 105, 107, 108, 111, 135, 142, 147, See Queen Aliquippa

   Holy Experiment and, 104

Pennington, Perry, 33

Pennsylvania, 66

People of Color, 143, 148

Pequea Creek

   Lancaster County, 111

Philadelphia, 95, 96, See Pinn, Robert A., See Great Minqua Path, See Great Minqua Path

Philadelphia County, 39

   Pennsylvania, 39

Philadelphia Quaker Meetings, 98

Pieces of the Quilt The Mosaic of an African American Family, 37

Pinn, 18

Pinn Descendants, 28

Pinn, Sarah Redcross Evans-Pinn

   Wife of Rawley Pinn, 28

Pinn, Margaret Winas

   Mother of Rawley Pinn, 29

Pinn, Nancy Redcross. See Pinn, James

Pinn, Rawley, 18, 28, See Amherst County Virginia Tax Record, See Revolutionary War

Pinn, Rawley and Sara Evans

   Amherst County, 214

Pinn, Reverend, Robert A., 21

Pinn, Robert A.. See Pinn, Elizabeth Jackson

Pinn, Robert A. Reverend, 25

Pinn, Robert A., Sgt, 27

Pinn, Robert I, 196

Pinn, Robert IV, 25

Pinn, Sarah Redcross Evans, 19, 196, 209

Pinn, Thomas

[255]

Father of Robert Pinn I, 193
Pinn, Walter Samuel, 25
Pinn, Walter Samuel, Corp, 24
Pinn, William II. *See* Pinn, Robert Sgt
Pinn-Evans Family, 214
Pocomoke
  Somerset County MD, 139
Poor Houses
  Quakers and, 16
Port Royal
  Caroline County Virginia, 163
Portobago, 170
Power of the Pen, 145, 150
Powhatan, 23
Powys
  Wales, 180
Prince Henry of Portugal, 180
Prison System, 49
proselytizing, 180
Province of Canada, 56
Public Hanging, 176
Public Whipping, 176
Quaker School, 35, *See* Martin, Grandpop
  Williston, 35
Quakers
  Pacifist, 143, 148
Queen Aliquippa, 142, 147, 186
race-based laws, 181
racial classification, 31

Natives in Pennsylvania, 161
racial classifications, 172
racial designation
  Native Americans and, 161
racial re-classification, 31
racial reclassifications, 47
racial status
  Natives and, 151, 162
Randolf, Edm
  Counsel, 207
Randolph, Edmonds
  Attorney descendant Jane Gibson the Elder, 204
Randolph, Edmund
  Evans Gibson Attorney, 199
Rappahannock, 22, 168, 170, *See* Nanzattico
Rappahannock River, 163, *See* Nanzattico Indian Tribe
Rappahannock Tribes. *See* Rappahannock River
Reading Pennsylvania, 179
Redcross. See Evans, Sarah
Remember
  Mother of Margarette Winas, 182
Reservations in Oklahoma, 145, 150
Revolutionary War, 18, 19, 20, 22, 23, 25, 29, 30, 52, 55, 100, 105, 115, 120, 124, 195, 196, 227, *See* Lewis, Charles

Revolutionary War Service,, 21
Richmond County
   Virginia. *See* Nanzattico
Rockets Landing, 47
Ridley Creek, 15, 141, 146
Ridley Park
   Delaware County, 104
   Delaware County Pa, 142, 147
Robert "King" Carter
   Plantation owner.
Roman Catholic Church, 48, 176
   Americus Vespucci and, 11
Romanticize Colonization, 172
Rowley, John
   Nanzattico Indians and. *See* Nanzattico Indians
rugged Individualism
   European's and, 177
Russia, 32
Rustin, Bayard. See Martin, Charles (Grandpop)
Ruth, Maria Louisa Pinn, 60
Ruth, Samuel
   Great Grandfather, 36
Sachem Naaman, 119
Saint Martin's Church
   Concord Delaware County, 53
Salem Witch Trials, 176, See Tituba

Samuel Parris. See Witch Trials
San Francisco, 108
Saponi, 18, 215
Saura Indian. *See* Cheraw
Schweninger, Loren
   Professor Emeritus, 204
Sears Catalog, 34
   Mom and, 34
See Charles Lewis.
See Lewis, Charles.
Seneca, 142, 215
Seneca language, 61
Seneca Nation. See Queen Aliquippa, See Queen Aliquippa
Seneca, Mohawk, Onondaga, Oneida, Cayuga, and Tuscarora. See Iroquois Confederacy
Settlement of Nanzattico. *See* Durand De Dauphine, *See* Durand De Dauphine
Settler Colonialism. *See* Turtle Island
Shamokin area
   Swatara Creek, 16
Shaw, Robert Colonial
   54th Massachusetts USCT, 25
Shawnee lands
   Susquehanna River, 12
Shirley Plantation. *See* Carter, Robert King, See

Evans/Gibson Families, See Wills, Robert
Sinnicus Indians, 96
Skraeling
    Native People, 49
slave castles, 180
Slave Labor, 48
Slave Labor System. *See* Indentured Servitude
Slave Ships, 175
Snyder Act, 143, 148
Snyder Act of 1924
    Gave Natives Right to Vote, 148
    Natives Right to Vote, 143
Somerset County
    Maryland, 38
Somerset County Maryland, 62, See, See Down River People, See, See Down River People
    Indian Tribes, 138
    Manokin, 139
    Manokin Indians and, 97
Somerset Maryland. *See* DelMarVa
South African
    Europeans and, 172
South America, 32
South American lands. See Guyana and Trinidad
South Carolina, 66, 173
Southern New York State, 12
Southern Ontario

    Canada, 142, 147
Spain, 48
    Jews and Moors, 176
    Native American Slaves and, 166
Spanish Explorers, 174
Spirits in a Bottle
    Whiskey, 106
Spiritual Practices, 48
Spotswood, Elizabeth Washington. See Bowden, Patty
Squatters Rights Laws, 162
St Martins Episcopalian Church
    Concord, 143, 148
St. Martin's Episcopal Church
    Marcus Hook Delaware County, 100
Stand YourGround
    Natives and, 176
State of Pennsylvania
    Native Lands and, 51
    racial classifications and, 105
Stewart
    Welsh Mountains, 62
Superior Society
    Europeans Claim of, 172
Susquehanna, 11, 18, 21, 45, 96, 97
Susquehanna and Delaware Rivers, 45

Susquehanna Indians
  Shawnee and, 111
Susquehanna River, 12
Susquehanna Valley, 184
Susquehannock Nation
  Conestoga Indian Nation, 12
Susquehannock town
  Pennsylvania, 13
Susquehannock-Conestoga, 13
Sussex County
  Delaware, 52, 102, 109
  Delaware, 50
Sussex County Delaware, 106
  Green/Davis lines. See Green, Lydia Davis
Taino
  Arawak's and, 49
Taino women, 49
Tanawa, Chief, 102
Tangier
  Native American Slaves and. See Tangiers North Africa
Tennessee
  Melungeon, 64
the Delaware River, 141, 147
The Siege of Yorktown. *See* Pinn, Rawley
Thomas Garrett
  Abolitionist, 38
Thule, 49

Tituba, 176, See Salem Witch Trials
  Salem Witch Trials, 176
tomahawk, skunk, squash, wampum, and succotash
  Algonquian Language, 163
Trail of Tears, 18
Tri-Racial Isolates, 64
Tri-Racial Isolates:, 47
Tri-Racial-Isolate, 64
Turtle Island, 11, 22, 31, 61, 62, 215
  Camanchaca, 10
  Colonization and, 142, 147
  Settler Colonialism and, 10
Tutelo, 18
Twin Towers
  9/11 New York City, 51
uglusio
  Europeans, 175
Unami, 97
Unami Tribe
  Algonquin Nation, 14
Underground Railroad, 108, See Garrett, Thomas
United States, 172
United States Colored Troops
  Civil War. See Green, Henry
Virginia, 47, 107, 173
  Melungeon, 64
Virginia and Maryland
  Wicomico Village and, 181

[259]

Virginia Lewis Ancestors, 22
Virginia, Maryland, or North Carolina, 162
Virginia's Free Colored Population, 25
voodoo. See Tituba
Wales, 215
Washington DC, 23
Washington, Augustine Junior. See Bowden, Mary, See Bowden, Mary, See Bowden, Mary
Washington, George
   Siege of Yorktown, 195
Welsh Kingdoms, 180
Welsh Mountain
   Ancestors, 185
Welsh Mountain Region
   Lancaster County PA, 51
Welsh Mountain Tract, 12
Welsh Mountains, 62, See Grandpop Martin
   Lancaster County Pennsylvania, 47
   Pennsylvania, 35
Wenro, 96
West African Coast, 180
West Chester Pike
   Chester County Pa, 14
West Indian Company
   Pennsylvania and, 103
West Marlboro Township, 35
Westmoreland County, 174
Westmoreland County Courts. See Monroe, Mary Hilliard
Westtown
   Chester County, 142, 147
White American Person, 48
White DNA Cousins, 37
White Male Privilege, 61
White Nationalist, 50
White Settlers, 67
   Native Territory and, 24
Wicomico, 18, 181
   Lancaster County Virginia, 18
Wicomico Indian. See Pinn, Rawley
Wicomico Parish Church, 28, See Northumberland County Virginia
Wicomico Tribal Lands, 179
Wicomico Waterways
   Somerset County MD, 139
Wigwams
   Native House. See Longhouse
William Penn, 107
   Okehocking, 141, 147
Williams, Ida Jones
   Cousin, 33
Willis, William, 38
Williston
   Chester County Pa, 35
Williston land

Chester County Pa, 14
Williston Land, 15
Williston Township, 14
   Summer Hunting Grounds, 16
Winas, John
   Husband of Remember Baldwin, 182
Winas, Remember Baldwin
   Mother of Margarette Winas-Pinn, 182
Workhouses
   Quakers and, 16
Wyoming (now Wilkes Barre)
   Minqua, 96
Xanthia Pennington, 33
Y-DNA Test, 215
York County, 39
   Pennsylvania, 145, 150
Yorktown Battle
   Rawley Pinn. *See* Revolutionary War

Anita Wills Author's Page

Anita Wills was born and raised in Pennsylvania and currently resides in the San Francisco Bay Area. She is a writer and Author of six books: Notes and Documents of Free Persons of Color (including Revised Edition), Pieces of the Quilt: The Mosaic of An African American Family, Black Minqua: The Life and Times of Henry Green, A Nation of Flaws: JustUs in the Homeland, Along the Rappahannock Homeland of the Nanzattico Indian Nation. She turned her maternal families Oral History into books that are valuable research tools. She is also a Human Rights Activist in the Bay Area.

Ms. Wills is a member of the DAR and the Monacan Indian Nation. Ms. Wills began writing and speaking about her findings in 2004 at the Central Rappahannock Library in Fredericksburg Virginia.

[i] Wills, A. (2013, January 08); Robert Alexander Pinn (1943-1911) BlackPast.org; https://www.blackpast.org/african-american

[ii] *Gale Research Company; Detroit, Michigan; Accession Number: 2962873, Biography & Genealogy Master Index (BGMI); Ancestry.com; Ancestry.com Operations, Inc.; 2009, Provo Utah USA; Ancestry.com; http://www.Ancestry.com*

[iii] Goetz, Rebecca Anne. "The Nanziatticos and the Violence of the Archive: Land and Native Enslavement in Colonial Virginia." Journal of Southern History, vol. 85, no. 1, Feb. 2019, pp. 33+. Gale Academic OneFile, link.gale.com/apps/doc/A575902159/AONE?u=anon~72bdf8f3&sid=googleScholar&xid=c96b68cd. Accessed 5 Sept. 2022

[iv] McClure, John York Daily Record; John Smith gave Susquehannocks their name; https://www.ydr.com/story/news/history/blogs/york-town-square/2007/09/21/leibhart-1/31607601/; September 21, 2007; October 14, 2021

Made in the USA
Middletown, DE
14 April 2023

28811111R00148